BLACK CITY

CINEMA

D0188073

In the series

Culture and the Moving Image

edited by Robert Sklar

BLACK CITY
CINEMA

AFRICAN AMERICAN

URBAN EXPERIENCES

IN FILM

Paula J. Massood

Temple University Press

PHILADELPHIA

Temple University Press, Philadelphia 19122
Copyright © 2003 by Temple University
All rights reserved
Published 2003
Printed in the United States of America

⊗The paper used in this publication meets the requirements of the American National Standard for Information Sciences—Permanence of Paper for Printed Library Materials, ANSI Z39.48-1984
Library of Congress Cataloging-in-Publication Data

Massood, Paula J., 1965–
    Black city cinema : African American urban experiences in film / Paula J. Massood.
        p.   cm. — (Culture and the moving image)
    Includes bibliographical references and index.
    ISBN 1-59213-002-X (cloth : alk. paper) — ISBN 1-59213-003-8 (pbk. : alk. paper)
    1. African Americans in motion pictures.   2. City and town life in motion pictures.
    3. Motion pictures—United States.   I. Title.   II. Series.
    PN19959.N4 M33 2003
    791.43'6520396073—dc21   2002020421

ISBN 13: 978-1-59213-003-0 (paper : alk. paper)

081308P

to matthew boyd goldie,
with love

If, after years of travel, the city on a hill appears no closer, should we ask whether or not it's a mirage?

—Charles Scruggs (1993)

Contents

Acknowledgments   ix

Introduction: Migrations, Movies, and African American
Cities on the Screen   1

1   The Antebellum Idyll and Hollywood's Black-Cast
Musicals   11

2   Harlem is Heaven: City Motifs in Race Films from
the Early Sound Era   45

3   Cotton in the City: The Black Ghetto,
Blaxploitation, and Beyond   79

4   Welcome to Crooklyn: Spike Lee and the Rearticulation
of the Black Urbanscape   117

5   Out of the Ghetto, into the Hood: Changes in the
Construction of Black City Cinema   145

6   Taking the A-Train: The City, the Train, and Migration
in Spike Lee's Clockers   175

Epilogue: New Millennium Minstrel Shows?
African American Cinema in the Late 1990s   207

Notes   227

Index   257

Acknowledgments

Expressing my gratitude to the individuals and institutions who supported me is both the most daunting and the most pleasurable part of this whole process. It's daunting because it has made me realize the unlimited generosity of the many colleagues, friends, and family members who helped made this book possible. It's pleasurable because it is a reminder that writing a book is never really an individual act and that the author is surrounded by supporters even when writing seems so terribly solitary. The thanks that I've listed here can only begin to convey my gratitude to all who helped along the way. I hope that everyone involved realizes the true extent of my appreciation for everything they've done toward the completion of this study.

I would like to thank the Cinema Studies Department at New York University, where the seeds of this book were first sown. Robert Stam has been a principal influence since the very beginning of this project, offering his insights into many of the texts discussed. His seminal work on Mikhail Bakhtin and his unceasing encouragement have shaped this study every step of the way. Ed Guerrero's scholarship has also been an influence on my work and began even before he came to NYU. For that, and all his comments, suggestions, questions, and friendship, I'm eternally grateful. Chris Straayer has been unflagging in her enthusiasm and support, no matter how many pages I asked her to read. She is a model scholar and teacher. Many thanks also to Toby Miller and Manthia Diawara; Toby, for offering support and guidance

ix

on this and many other projects, and Manthia, for his comments and his important contributions to the scholarship on African American cinema. Additionally, I would like to thank Bill Simon, Ann Harris, and Ken Sweeney for their encouragement from the very beginning.

Over the years I've had the opportunity to work with a number of gifted scholars, many of whom have become close and valued friends. Thanks to Alex Keller, Roy Grundmann, Kirsten Thompson, Lisa Gail Collins, and Michael Gillespie, whose comments and suggestions, on this project and other subjects, have helped shape this study and my scholarship as a whole. I value their friendship, generosity of spirit, and intellectual enthusiasm. They have reminded me, in different ways, that work is important, but friendship sustains the soul. Thanks also to Cindy Lucia, Antje Ascheid, David Lugowski, Marcos Becquer, and Bruce Brasell, all of whom provided comments, editorial advice, and friendship early in the writing process.

I extend my gratitude to the participants in the 1999 National Endowment for the Humanities Summer Institute in Black Film Studies, directed by Gladstone Yearwood and hosted by the University of Central Florida. I began to formulate chapter 2 while I was a participant in the institute, and many of my thoughts were first discussed with the extraordinary group of scholars gathered together in the shocking heat of a central Florida summer. I'm especially grateful to Dr. Yearwood, Mark Reid, Phyllis Klotman, Gerald Butters, and Matt Henry for helping me to form some of my thoughts regarding both silent and sound race films. While the NEH did not offer direct funding for this project, I wish to acknowledge their support in funding the institute.

Partial funding for chapter 2 was provided by a PSC-CUNY Research Award, and I'm thankful to both the Research Foundation of the City University of New York and the readers of my proposal for offering much needed financial and intellectual support. My gratitude also extends to the members of the Department of Film at Brooklyn College, who provided an environment in which I could nurture and rehearse many of the thoughts and theories related to this book.

I would like to acknowledge the staff of the George P. Johnson Collection, Department of Special Collections at UCLA, the Film Stills Archive at the Museum of Modern Art, and the Black Film Center/Archive at Indiana University. In particular, Jeffrey Rankin at UCLA and Mary Corliss at MOMA made the process of tracking down information and stills both exciting and easy.

Over the course of preparing this work, I've had the pleasure to present my ideas to some of the toughest audiences of all: my students. I'm thankful to the participants in my classes at Marymount Manhattan, Hunter, and Vassar colleges for their prescient discussions and questions. I also owe an enormous debt to my students at Brooklyn College for their insights into many of the films discussed herein. Their overwhelming enthusiasm toward the subject encouraged me during the final stages of writing, and their anticipation of this study provided my readers with names and faces.

My appreciation to the editorial staff at Temple University Press, in particular Janet Francendese and Micah Kleit, for their support of this project. I'm grateful also to Robert Sklar, editor of the *Culture and the Moving Image* series, for his helpful comments on the manuscript. To my reader, J. Ronald Green, I'm grateful for his insightful suggestions, all of which went into making this a stronger book.

It goes without saying that none of this could have been accomplished without the support of my family. My parents, Theresa and Arthur Massood, have always believed in me, and this project would never have been completed without their encouragement and love. Thanks also to Rosemary and Charles Goldie, whose interest in the book has meant so much and has made me feel as though I have at least two readers in New Zealand.

Finally, thank you to Matthew Boyd Goldie, who has lived every step of this process with me, reading hundreds of pages, editing sentences, arguing points, looking at films, and supporting me both intellectually and emotionally.

Portions of chapter 6 have appeared in *African American Review* 32.2 (Summer 2001).

Introduction: Migrations, Movies, and African American Cities on the Screen

Space, in contemporary discourse, as in lived experience, has taken on an almost palpable existence. Its contours, boundaries, and geographies are called upon to stand in for all the contested realms of identity, from the national to the ethnic; its hollows and voids are occupied by bodies that replicate internally the external conditions of political and social struggle, and are likewise assumed to stand for, and identify, the sites of such a struggle.

Anthony Vidler (1992)[1]

During the last half of the twentieth century, African American film was increasingly identified as city film in the public imagination. Its narratives were commonly assigned to specific urban settings, with New York's Harlem and Brooklyn neighborhoods associated with African American East Coast life and Los Angeles' South Central and Watts neighborhoods with the West Coast. The two most common genres associated with African American city spaces are blaxploitation films from the 1970s and, most recently, hood films from the 1990s. In both examples, genre is defined by urban visual and aural iconography, which is often engaged in a dialogue with its immediate socioeconomic, political, and industrial contexts.

1

The release in 1991 of Mario Van Peebles' *New Jack City*, John Singleton's *Boyz N the Hood*, and Matty Rich's *Straight Out of Brooklyn*, along with the increased popularity and visibility of rap and hip-hop music, sparked renewed critical, intellectual, and aesthetic focus on African American urban-based popular culture. The popularity and profitability of hood films and rap music galvanized the production and release of an extraordinary number of films between 1991 and 1993 in particular, all of which capitalized on inner-city settings and a focus on male youth culture, and which referenced the films' fashion, the music, the personalities, and the look of contemporary African American urban life for both black and crossover audiences. The films' self-conscious presentation of black city spaces redefined both national and international cinematic and musical forms, and their influence continues even a decade later across a variety of genres.

One of the most striking elements of hood films like *Boyz N the Hood* was that their narratives were thoroughly anchored in the immediate moment. The fashion, music, and extradiegetic references to outside political and social personalities and events, like the Reagan and Bush (Sr.) presidencies and the LAPD's infamous beating of Rodney King in 1992, commentated on contemporary African American life. And yet the films rarely explored the history of black city spaces beyond the time frame of the 1990s. On occasion, such as the inclusion of footage of the Watts Rebellion in Allen and Albert Hugheses' *Menace II Society* (1993), the films referenced the relatively recent past. While such references acknowledged the sources of contemporary urban conditions, their historical analysis rarely extended beyond the life spans of their characters, their directors, or their primary audiences, which consisted of a cross-section of young people. Often, historical events were linked to the biography of a given character, like the Watts Rebellion for *Menace II Society*'s Caine in chapter 5. For many young African American and white filmmakers in the 1990s, therefore, black city spaces existed within limited historical parameters in which the city had always existed in its present form, or, perhaps, as it appeared in blaxploitation films from the 1970s.

In this book I expand the historical and the aesthetic borders of black city films beyond hood films and blaxploitation and argue that cities are highly politicized locations with a long history in African American and American culture. The roots of the most recent cinematic constructions of black city spaces stretch back through the history of black cinematic signification to early race-film production during the silent era, and are closely connected to African American experiences of movement and migration throughout the twentieth century, just as film is a twentieth century technology and "the urban art par excellance."[2] This study outlines the relationship of African American film to migration and the growth of black urban populations, focusing on key periods and genres in film history: black-cast musicals produced between 1929 and 1943; race films from the early sound era; blaxploitation and related films from the 1970s; hood films from the 1990s; and African American filmmaking from the late 1990s, including Maya Angelou's *Down in the Delta* (1998) and John Singleton's *Shaft* (2000). I also discuss two periods in Spike Lee's filmmaking career; I trace the influence of his films on the city representations constructed by hood films in the 1990s in chapter 4, and, in a separate discussion of *Clockers* (1995) in chapter 6, the ways in which Lee, of all the contemporary black filmmakers, acknowledges the crucial influence that movement, especially migration (forced, coerced, and chosen), has had on African American cultural production.

I begin with Hollywood all-black musicals made between 1929 and 1943 and race films from the late 1930s in the first two chapters to provide insight into both the cinematic and literary responses to the massive movements of people in the early decades of the twentieth century which resulted in the majority of the country's African American population taking up residence in northern industrial centers like New York and Chicago. The two groups of film provide very different responses to this phenomenon, with Hollywood films failing to recognize the sociopolitical landscape by producing folk musicals that placed their black characters in a pastoral idyll, resembling a southern antebellum plantation, instead of the city. Race films, on the other hand, existed in a segregated independent sector that was adjunct to Hollywood and were made for black audiences who often screened the films in separate exhibition sites. While silent race films spoke of the ills of city life in order to warn the newly-arrived migrants in their audiences of potential urban evils, sound-era race films addressed, for the first time, the presence and the promise of the city, primarily Harlem, in contemporary black culture in ways that only previously had been seen in African American literature from the Harlem Renaissance and in black newspapers like *The Crisis*. These early chapters provide the historical foundations for my discussions of the later genres and filmmakers.

Although my chief interest is films directed by African American filmmakers, I also consider films that were not black-directed, just as I consider some texts that are not set in the city. This is especially the case in the first chapter, which analyzes films with "black-focused" themes and all-black casts. An examination of films such as Vincente Minnelli's *Cabin in the Sky* (1943) allows me to gauge assumptions about the country's growing African American urban presence by examining its inclusions, exclusions, and distortions in a wide variety of films and visualizations of American city spaces. This approach also offers a more complex understanding of the strategies behind historical stereotypes of African American people by relating them more closely to Hollywood's resistance to acknowledging the active engagement of the country's black population in the industrial growth of the United States. No film, even when a product of the segregated race film industry, is separable from a larger context; frequently, African American films responded to and dialogued with Hollywood images and, in the latter half of the century, vice versa. Therefore, an analysis of a cross-section of films provides the best understanding of the ways in which significations of black urban spaces transformed along with changes in their historical, political, and industrial contexts.

African American Film: Cinematic Fusions of Space and Time

My approach to examining the intersections between space and time, and between text and context, engages Mikhail Bakhtin's concept of the chronotope as a model "for studying texts according to the ratio and nature of the temporal and spatial categories represented."[3] It is, as the term suggests, a *topos* (a place, person, figure) that embodies (or is embodied by) *chronos* (time). Places as disparate as roads, castles, salons, thresholds, and trains function as "materialized history," where temporal relationships are literalized by the objects, spaces, or persons with which they intersect.[4] In *Clockers*, for example, Lee's decision to add trains (both model trains and Amtrak) to Richard Price's original story was the director's way of referencing the history of African American social and geographic mobility. At the same time, the trains have a practical function in the film's narrative present—they move the characters from one place to another. This will be part of the focus of my discussion of Lee's film in chapter 6, which also examines the increasing shift into historical narratives in black film during the mid-1990s.

Bakhtin's theory explaining how texts embody space and time is applicable to cinematic as well as literary narratives.[5] Besides the "time/space" of its actual materiality (film speed, for instance, is twenty-four frames per second), the cinema offers an expanded way of understanding Bakhtin's concept of dialogism or "the relation of any utterance to other utterances," because it acknowledges cinematic discourses, such as casting, performance, costume, setting, and sound, which are not as readily available to written texts.[6] In the cinema such discursive signifying strategies illuminate a text; for example, elements of the sound track play a major referential role in the construction of certain cinematic spaces and times, such as in black-cast musicals where the city is symbolically referenced through jazz-based musical motifs and the rural through spirituals. During the 1970s, the sound tracks for blaxploitation films became extradiegetic marketing devices that brought the rhythms and melodies of the films into the city, and vice versa (a strategy that was also used by hood films). In all these examples, the play between visual and aural signifiers contributes meaning to a film, anchors the narrative in an historical moment, and acknowledges the existence of complementary or contradictory spaces and times in a single text.

The chronotope's links to genre make it a salient theoretical construct for this study because particular African American genres are defined or enabled by certain spatiotemporal tropes, such as the antebellum South in black-cast musicals or the contemporary city in hood films. The places and times in which they are set often wholly define the genres I consider—so much so, in fact, that by the time we get to the hood film in chapter 5, the genre is explicitly named by the spaces mapped out in its films. Even earlier, blaxploitation films (as discussed in chapter 3) used particular constructions of the city, ones related directly to the contemporary urban conditions of the time period that had labeled black city spaces as "ghettoes." Without such a rendering of the city space, these genres would have had little meaning for their audiences who responded as much to the films' settings as they did to the films' plots. In what follows, the only exception to this pattern will appear in the Westerns made by race film producers in the thirties. Films like *Two Gun Man From Harlem* (Richard C. Kahn, 1938), use the trope of "Harlem" symbolically to place African American stories in the immediate context experienced by the film's urban audiences rather than the historical space and time more commonly associated with the Western genre. The films sometimes referenced Harlem merely in name alone, and yet they addressed an urban audience in their contemporary look and sound. (This strategy was also used, as we will see in chapter 6, by Melvin Van Peebles in *Posse*.)

The chronotope offers a more complex understanding of the relationship between the actual world and the spatiotemporal systems that generate cinematic genres. For Bakhtin, there is a distinct relationship between the world *outside* the text and that *created by* the text. As he notes, "out of the actual chronotopes of our world (which serve as the source of representation) emerge the reflected and *created* chronotopes of the world represented in the work (in the text)."[7] This feature of Bakhtin's concept is relevant to a consideration of filmic representation, which for much of its history has been bound up with interrogations of the relationship of the cinematic apparatus to reality. It is even more pertinent to the current discussion when we take into account the discourses of authenticity and "realness"[8] that frequently circulate around black film, as well as the concern for representational verisimilitude as related to a history of stereotype and caricature that stretches back to the beginnings of African American visual representation and that has been so effectively documented in Spike Lee's *Bamboozled* (2000).

While Bakhtin's theoretical construct links the actual world and the text, he cautions against confusing one for the other, because to blur the distinction between the two would result in a form of "naïve realism."[9] This caution bears directly on my consideration of African American film because it acknowledges the influence that exterior reality may have on a text—for example, the relationship between the Moynihan report and the Kerner Commission on Civil Disorders and blaxploitation film in the 1970s—without mistaking cinematic representation for actual extradiegetic circumstance. Many of the filmmakers themselves caution against this naïve realism; for example, Spike Lee, Mario and Melvin Van Peebles, and Allen and Albert Hughes consciously underscore the constructed nature of their films in techniques such as montage editing, direct address, and the mixing of film and video stocks. These strategies remind audiences that what they are witnessing is not actuality, but a "refraction of a refraction" of reality.[10] In my consideration of the roles that African American history (migration, the growth of urban areas, civil rights, and the film industry) and American social policy (the Moynihan report and William Julius Wilson's discussions of race and the "underclass") have played in the films under discussion, I stress that what is put on screen is a dialogue with and a refraction of the actual material world.

Particular cinematic chronotopes—antebellum idyll, Harlem, black ghetto, and the hood—are "historically situated 'utterance[s]' . . . addressed by one socially constituted subject or subjects [the filmmaker, the cinematic apparatus, the conditions of production] to other socially constituted subjects, all of whom are deeply immersed in historical circumstance and social contingency."[11] Ultimately, the films and the spatiotemporal tropes that define them help us to understand the pressures and the constraints that context brings to representation and its analysis. Yet they also remind us that the world presented onscreen by their diegesis should never be mistaken for the real world. Instead, the "spatiotemporal structures" of the films "mold a discursive simulacrum of life and the world."[12] No matter how accurate or realistic the films are in visualizing black urban life, they are always (to a greater or lesser extent) self-conscious, highly-mediated acts.

While part of this work examines how certain periods in film history are marked by the visualization of a specific rural- or urbanscape, a significant portion of my analysis considers that films may contain a variety of traces or motifs of other spaces and times in dialogue with one another. That chronotopes coexist and dialogue with one another in such a manner suggests an active relationship among discourses. As Bakhtin explains, a fundamental characteristic of chronotopes is that they are "mutually inclusive, they co-exist, they may be interwoven with, replace, or oppose one another, contradict one another or find themselves in ever more complex relationships."[13] In *Clockers*, for example, the train echoes the past, yet it also dialogues with the hood's contemporary spaces, expanding the borders of what, by 1995, had become a dominant and claustrophobic cinematic trope. I return to this repeatedly in my discussion of films across the decades, because such spatiotemporal polyphony is not simply a characteristic of Lee's films, but of a number of films with African American themes.

The films' relationships to social and film history are crucial considerations in this study because they help us to understand the ways in which African American cinema, especially many of the texts discussed here, engages with the world around it. Whether the films are "saturated with historical time,"[14] as in the antebellum idyll of black-cast musicals and the southern space of *Down in the Delta* in the epilogue, or with the immediate moment, such as that found in either the black films from the 1970s or in hood films from the 1990s, they are political acts in which the city becomes the symbol of—sometimes the synecdoche for—African American political life. Over the course of this study, we will see the ways in which black city cinema initialized a change in African American filmic representation from ahistorical and static to a force that was fully imbricated in the modern, industrial progress of the nation. From early film production on, black films used narratives set in city spaces such as Harlem to pose "a challenge to contemporary limits and cultural terms within which personal being for both blacks and whites were imagined and defined."[15] City settings, therefore, are complex strategies which, in their interplay of space and time, comment upon the exclusions of film history in general and American history as a whole.

The transformations of the filmic representations of African American city spaces are linked to larger historical factors. At the same time that the black population of the United States was redefining itself through various migrations, from a mostly rural to a predominantly urban population and culture, American film was also transforming from novelty and nickelodeon to art and industry. African American films were also changing from their early forced status as segregated industry with very few resources to a box office powerhouse, with concomitant shifts in production values and audiences. The history of African American migration and urban life and its links to American and African American film history is, therefore, essential to our understanding of films by black directors or films featuring African American people in the twentieth and twenty-first centuries.

A focus on the city, the cinema and African American representation also tells us much about the mythology of transformation that is so integral to American life. In their often conflicted attitudes toward the city as either promised land or dystopian hell, African American texts (film, literature, music, painting) explore themes of hope, mobility, and escape. City spaces such as Harlem were often meccas that, in their promise of decreased racial discrimination, offered social, economic, and political mobility. And yet these very same places trapped migrants who found themselves, at different historical moments, surrounded by poverty, crime, filth, and the lack of any concerted local or national policies to alleviate sub-standard living conditions. These extradiegetic circumstances ripple out from the texts, at various times and in different forms, and remind us that the city is never, simply, the city. It has been an immense force in shaping American life and culture during the twentieth century. It also has been a crucial influence on African American life and culture and, as such, an analysis of the changing roles and presence of urban space in black city cinema can only expand and make even more complex the questions we ask about the power of cinematic representation.

1

The Antebellum Idyll and Hollywood's Black-Cast Musicals

Gillis set down his tan-cardboard extension-case and wiped his black, shining brow. Then slowly, spreadingly, he grinned at what he saw: Negroes at every turn; up and down Lenox Avenue, up and down One Hundred and Thirty-fifth Street; big, lanky Negroes, short, squat Negroes, black ones, brown ones, yellow ones; men standing idle on the curb, women, bundle-laden, trudging reluctantly homeward, children rattle-trapping about the sidewalks; but Negroes predominantly, overwhelmingly everywhere. There was assuredly no doubt of his where-abouts. This was Negro Harlem.
—Rudolph Fisher (1925)[1]

From the bondage of the Middle Passage to present-day re-ports of the return of many northern blacks to the South, movement has defined the African American presence in the United States. This presence has also been linked to the ter-minal points of these movements and shifts, whether they are the antebellum South or the industrialized North or West. In a related and often paradoxical manner, African Ameri-can images have been framed, marked, and understood in relation to these migrations and their destinations, such as Harlem, at particular times. This chapter considers one such

11

movement, the Great Migration, and its relationship to a selection of all-black musicals produced by Hollywood studios between 1929 and 1943: *Hallelujah* (King Vidor, 1929), *The Green Pastures* (Marc Connelly and William Keighley, 1936), *Cabin in the Sky* (Vincente Minnelli, 1943), and *Stormy Weather* (Andrew Stone, 1943).

The Great Migration radically redefined the nation's African American population, nearly reversing the ratio of urban and rural residents and removing some 40 percent of black residents from the Old South.[2] Between 1910 and 1930, an estimated 1.2 million African American migrants moved to the North, increasing the black populations in northern urban centers by 300 percent.[3] Northern industrial cities such as Chicago, Detroit, Cleveland, Pittsburgh, and New York often were final destinations because they were directly located on main rail lines. Also, their industries explicitly courted black workers as a source of cheap and abundant labor, especially as companies retooled for World War I. For southern blacks, northern wages, even when they were lower than the rate for white workers, were still substantially higher than what could be earned in the depressed agricultural market at home, a market beleaguered by boll weevil infestation, overfarming, and a feudal sharecropping system.

At the height of African American migration to the North, the city—Harlem in particular—was associated with a promised land, or, as Charles S. Johnson observed in 1925 in Alain Locke's *The New Negro*, "the Mecca of the Negroes the country over."[4] At the same time, the area's more negative attributes were becoming evident, especially to the newly arrived migrants. The tensions among different urban experiences were exemplified in Harlem Renaissance writing from the 1920s and 1930s. On the one hand, the central core of writers during this time concentrated on the liberatory potential of the city. Harlem Renaissance writers, mostly migrants themselves, "felt joined, not estranged, by their wanderings [prior to settling in Harlem], because they were part of the great migration of black people to the urban northeast. . . . Collectively, they developed a hopeful vision of an urban home that was at once an organic place, a birthright community, and a cultural aspiration."[5] This optimism belied the very real poverty, racial prejudice, and crime that many of Harlem's newly arrived residents encountered, and yet "the migrants themselves often came from backgrounds of such extreme poverty and oppression that Harlem, in contrast, seemed the promised land."[6] Soon, an attitude linking the city with a dystopia replaced celebratory renderings of Harlem, as its residents, "generally precariously clinging to the bottom rung of the economic ladder, suffered especially hard" during the Depression.[7] Writers, artists, and working people were united in their disillusionment.

Even if much of the literary attention was focused on urban life, a rural presence continued to exist and define the "New Negro's" experience of the city. An interesting example can be found in the selection from Rudolph Fisher's short story, "City of Refuge," introducing this chapter. King Solomon Gillis travels to Harlem, fleeing the prejudice and poverty of his North Carolina home, as well as the police, who are seeking him in connection with the murder of a white man. King Solomon views Harlem as the one place where he can start fresh, maybe even become a policeman. Unfortunately, the first person he meets upon arrival is Mouse Uggams, a vaguely familiar and remarkably "helpful" man from down home. King Solomon succumbs to Mouse's charming influence, and is eventually caught by the police for unwittingly carrying Mouse's drugs.

The plot revolves around two central concerns from this time period, both of which will ultimately lead to King Solomon's downfall. First, King Solomon's attitude toward Harlem was common for the time, especially his awe at seeing so many black people in one place going about their business, a feeling echoed in Langston Hughes' memories of arriving in Harlem for the first time in *The Big Sea*: "Hundreds of colored people! I wanted to shake hands with them, speak to them."[8] Even more striking for King Solomon, however, is the sight of a "cullid policeman," who represents the defining difference between the North and the South.[9] The policeman's presence is so significant to King Solomon that when he is finally caught, he surrenders with a grin that "had something exultant about it" because he is led away by a uniformed, *black* policeman.[10] Second, King Solomon—most likely an urbane man in North Carolina—is felled by his naiveté and his willingness to put his trust in Mouse just because "he's from my state. Maybe I know him or some of his people."[11] Even though, as the story suggests, down-home mores are not easily translatable in Harlem, they are universal enough to be used at least as the foundation for a con game, a fact that fuels Mouse's plans.

King Solomon's fear of the southern white police, carried over to New York, identifies racial violence as another reason for many migrants' willingness to leave the South. While economic opportunity may have been the primary "pull" for African American migrants, violence, especially lynching, had been on the rise in southern states during and after World War I and operated as a persuasive "push" factor. King Solomon's fear and hatred of northern white police points to one of the continuities of the migrants' lives; it implies that his biggest mistake might have been to regard the black policeman as different from his white brethren. What he learns is that the law is not for African Americans, regardless of who is wearing the badge.

Although African American literary production echoed the complexity of the tensions attending the massive population shifts in the early part of the century, Hollywood films from 1929 to 1943 utterly failed to recognize the sociopolitical changes in the American landscape. In black-cast musicals in particular, African American characters and stories most often appeared within a picturesque southern setting, largely ignoring the black city space and culture that figured in the lives and the imaginations of the vast majority of African Americans. For instance, in *Hallelujah*, *The Green Pastures*, and *Cabin in the Sky*, the bulk of the narrative unfolds within variations of a pastoral, southern setting. In these films the story space and time is overdetermined by a seemingly static rural space—the antebellum idyll—in which an indeterminate yet bygone past is signified through iconography of a rural, preindustrial southern agricultural economy. *Stormy Weather* ends the stream of antebellum idyll films, referencing the trope of the idyll but foregrounding issues of migration and the subsequent "modernization" of many black performative codes, including music, dance, costume, dialect, and filmmaking in general.

The Antebellum Idyll: Down-Home Space and Time

The antebellum idyll is specifically southern and rural, and is segregated from the remainder of the United States as represented in cinema. It is linked to Mikhail Bakhtin's theorization of the idyllic chronotope, especially in the relationship that time has with space in idyllic narratives. Idylls are self-contained and have the distinct characteristic of "not being related to the rest of the world,"[12] suggesting that their space is separated and segregated from other spaces. While the South, especially the "Old South," figured in many films, particularly in the late 1930s and early 1940s and culminating with *Gone With the Wind* (Victor Fleming, 1939), it was not a dominant setting for Hollywood productions, as popular genres from the time included the Western (which is coded as rural but not southern), gangster films, melodramas, and a variety of musicals. Films directed toward crossover or white audiences sometimes contained all-black sequences or African American performers within a larger, often unrelated narrative, thereby further segregating black performers and stories. This liminal position had its practical aspects; by confining African American performers to a separate narrative, "offending" subject matter could be removed if deemed "inappropriate" by southern censors.

During the same period that the United States condoned the practice of segregation, black-cast films were the norm, echoing the larger, national ideology. In 1896 (coinciding with the first projected film programs in the United States), the Supreme Court's decision in *Plessy v. Ferguson* legalized the separate (but "equal") existence of the races. Ostensibly targeting railroad facilities, the ruling was also interpreted and expanded to include housing and educational facilities, and provided the foundation for southern Jim Crow policies. This judicial environment was extended to the practice of segregation in exhibition: by separating part of the theater (the "nigger heaven" of the balcony, for instance), by screening "colored only" shows, or by limiting runs to theaters located in the "colored" sections of town. The segregated space on the screen was replicated in the experiences of black audiences in the theater. With *Brown v. Board of Education*, the decision was reversed in 1954, coinciding with the release of *Carmen Jones*, the last of the black-cast musicals.[13]

Films with idyllic settings, such as *Hallelujah*, contain a complex construction of time that blurs the boundaries between temporal moments. Many of the films shift between rural and more urban spaces, and while the narratives are located in the idyll they are set in an unspecified post-Emancipation time frame. Nevertheless, the films, especially the earlier musicals, hearken back to the antebellum era with images associated with the plantation system. For example, *Hallelujah* opens with shots of black workers hunched over and picking cotton in vast cotton fields. Without explicitly identifying the time frame, the image identifies the narrative in a specific historical moment by referencing forms of preindustrial, and antebellum, labor, thereby erasing the distinctions between historical moments: it could be the early nineteenth century or it could be the early twentieth century.

In contrast to literary and (as we will see) race film representations of contemporary black life, black-cast musicals removed blacks from the historical context that was witnessing the redefinition of a majority of African Americans as urban rather than rural. The result of positioning African American subject matter in the past was "an almost metaphysical stasis," in which "the black . . . is seen as eternal, unchanging, unchangeable" rather than as a part of the nation's progress.[14] This is more than a matter of stereotypes; ignoring discourses of progress and change, which were so central to African American life between the two World Wars, the musicals' overall effect was to reconfirm ideology that removed African Americans, and all peoples of African descent, from a "civilized" world that was urban and therefore modern. Urban black workers remained liminal to the expansion of an industrial economy.

Hallelujah and the Idyllic Promised Land

Three black-cast musicals in particular—*Hallelujah*, *The Green Pastures*, and *Cabin in the Sky*—are set in the time and space of the antebellum idyll and each incorporates some form of city motifs into its more rural spaces in order to construct a moral contrast between them.[15] Ostensibly set in some variation of the antebellum idyll, each film contains its own particular references to the city through iconography and motifs. That is, they incorporate motifs that "carry the [stylistic] aura of the earlier genre into the new one."[16] In these films the particular signifiers that function as motifs for the urban—through music, clothing, and behaviors such as gambling—would undoubtedly be read as such: by the time *Hallelujah* appeared in 1929, the city and the tensions between the urban and the rural were already familiar tropes in African American literature and journalism, in Hollywood film, and in race films aimed at black audiences.

Hallelujah tends toward realism. King Vidor made accuracy and attention to detail his personal project, inspiring him to shoot the film on location in Tennessee and Arkansas and to hire Harold Garrison, an African American studio employee, as assistant director, to ensure that southern black life would be rendered "faithfully."[17] The film's footage of actual cotton fields and sharecropper shanties adds to its mimetic qualities, and suggests Vidor's concern with creating an "accurate" rendering of "Negro life," one that was presented as real and was believed to be so even by Vidor himself, who felt that he knew black culture because he "used to watch the Negroes in the South," where he was raised.[18] Presented with a look based more on the tradition of documentary realism than on the fantasy world of the musical space that would define later black-cast musicals, *Hallelujah*'s white audiences were "appreciative of some sort of faithful rendering of black folk life."[19]

Hallelujah's plot narrates the temptation, downfall, and eventual redemption of Zeke (Daniel L. Haynes). The film presents a series of thematic oppositions—good versus evil, country versus city—which fascinated Hollywood at the time and appeared across genres. In keeping with the traditional Hollywood fascination, these oppositions are embodied by the two female rivals for Zeke's attention, Missy Rose (Victoria Spivey) and Chick (Nina Mae McKinney), representatives, respectively, of rural goodness and urban evil. In this the film recalls F. W. Murnau's *Sunrise*, released just two years earlier, in its focus on the hero's split loyalties between his rural wife and his city mistress. Combined with Vidor's efforts to achieve verisimilitude, these oppositions suggest two very different African American lifestyles, the country and the city, and in this cautionary tale, it is clear who and what will triumph at the film's conclusion.

Hallelujah's antebellum idyll articulates certain features of Bakhtin's idyllic chronotope in its focus on family and home, and it posits the regenerative value of family and agriculture through the activities performed in its rural spaces.[20] Zeke is introduced as he works with his family. Their labor, smiles, and performance of spirituals immediately signify that the family is hard-working, happy, and pious, even within their impoverished surroundings. While African American song and dance has a long history as political commentary on the conditions endured under slavery, there is no rebellious subtext here and, in fact, there are even a few scenes that echo the minstrelsy of early Edison shorts, as, for example, when Zeke's youngest brothers literally stop the narrative with a tap dance performance that bears little relation to the story. Additionally, the family sings whether they are working or at rest, suggesting that labor is as pleasurable as leisure.

The city makes no definite appearance in the film, but is implied synedochically through the women, music, clothing, and attitudes toward family contained within a rural southern town. The town is nothing more than a river boat landing and a single street featuring a bar; however, it both contradicts the antebellum idyll and contains all the evils of the big city. This symbolic rendering of city space continued with other black-cast musicals, like *The Green Pastures* and *Cabin in the Sky*, which attached city signifiers to places more closely resembling

The Pleasures of King Cotton (*Hallelujah*, MGM, 1929). Courtesy of the Museum of Modern Art Film Stills Archive.

towns or, in the latter film, to a single site. The lack of an actual city space did not detract from Hollywood's packaging of *Hallelujah* as an urban film through suggestions of the city pleasures contained in its diegesis. The urban lures are exemplified in the film's original poster, which advertises *Hallelujah* on the basis of its symbolic relationship to the city.

Unlike the town, the antebellum idyll is a pure space, and this purity is personified in Missy Rose (the "good" girl), Mammy's and Pappy's adopted daughter, and Zeke's love interest. It is also symbolized in the family's religious piety, and is especially foregrounded in their singing of spirituals. Besides work songs and one Irving Berlin song (added late in the production), spirituals are the only music heard in this space. The piety suggested by the music is not only a running theme in the film, it also indicates that religion serves as both Zeke's nemesis and his savior. This role played by the spirituals will continue (to a greater or lesser extent, depending on the film) in all of the films located in the

The importance of the city in *Hallelujah*
(MGM, 1929). Courtesy of Separate
Cinema Archive™.

antebellum idyll, with the performance of spirituals becoming a part of
the conventions of the broader cinematic idyll.

Religion tempts and eventually saves Zeke from his desire for Chick,
who represents the city in looks and action. After gambling away his
family's money and (accidentally) shooting his brother, Zeke becomes
a traveling preacher in an attempt to atone for his sins. Chick attends
one of his revival meetings and is turned toward the path of righteous-
ness by Zeke's words. Vidor makes the erotic pull between Zeke and
Chick evident through editing, point-of-view shots, and the exchange of
glances. Chick's rebirth, therefore, links religious and sexual ecstasy—a
connection that is reiterated twice more: during her baptism and during another revival meeting later the same day. The "relationship between religious fervor and sexuality" is the "fundamental metaphor
upon which the film depends."[21] It comes as no surprise, then, that the
third time they meet, Zeke literally carries Chick off; they leave the
church to start an ill-fated relationship (which includes living together
out of wedlock).

The film's eroticized articulation of religion indicated in Zeke and Chick's attraction blurs the juxtaposition between the tainted and the pure and undercuts the antebellum idyll's piety by indicating the presence of temptation and sin in both characters. The merging of religious ecstasy with the urban is most explicit in a sermon Zeke delivers during Chick's conversion. In it he describes, in allegorical form, a train ride to the promised land (Zeke even dons an engineer's cap before beginning). In this example, the promised land is heaven, not the real-world space of northern cities, as it would be in many migration stories and novels of the time. The train symbolizes Zeke's dueling desires: the pulls of redemption and the pulls of the city (Chick serving as a representative of the city). Thus, in a sermon intended to convert sinners, Zeke succeeds in distancing himself, Chick, and the parishioners from the rural rather than bringing them closer to its idyllic spaces. In fact, he abandons the pulpit for Chick (and the city). This is one of the most interesting scenes in the film, for it is through one of the objects most associated with the Great Migration, the train, that Zeke's moral retreat from the antebellum idyll is symbolized, as if suggesting that even thinking of the urban leads to downfall. But this movement away does not last long because Chick betrays him, subsequently forcing Zeke back into the arms of Missy Rose and back within the borders of the antebellum idyll.

The town is marked by the visual and aural iconography of the Jazz Age, and Chick, as a town resident, exemplifies these factors. The jazz and blues-based musical numbers that are performed in the town (and by Chick) differ from the spirituals and work songs of the antebellum idyll. The town music is secular. Added to the music of the antebellum idyll, it supplies two competing versions of black sound that both signify and underscore the difference between the two spaces: the town is the location of evil and temptation while the idyll is a righteous space. The outfits worn by Chick and other town residents also support this dichotomy. Chick's costuming (especially when we are introduced to her) visually connects her with the urban fashions of the late 1920s favored by flappers: a long-waisted, fringed dress, dark stockings, and high-heeled shoes. The men wear flashy suits and porkpie hats. Such apparel is distinct from Zeke's tattered and dirty work clothes, Missy Rose's demure work dresses or Sunday best, or Zeke's mother's mammy-like apron and kerchief-covered head.

Chick reduces the distinctions between urban and rural to moral differences between women. Her aura of sexuality is obvious in her body language and appearance. Her revealing clothes suggest moral laxity and literally associate her with the underworld of bars and gambling dens (she even has playing-card patches sewn into the breast of her dress). Chick wants money and will do and say anything to get it; her desires are evident to everyone but Zeke. As she and her partner, Hot Shot (William Fountaine), cheat Zeke out of all his money, they encourage comparisons between the rural and the urban, suggested by King Solomon's experiences with Mouse in "City of Refuge." For instance, Zeke's country demeanor marks him as an easy target and partially fuels what manifests itself as a sexual rivalry. However, Hot Shot's lack of respect for Zeke isn't directed at Zeke as much as it is at what he represents—a rural, black past known primarily through disenfranchisement and lack of agency. Zeke, like King Solomon, becomes a symbol of everything from which African American city dwellers would like to distance themselves: blackness and segregation. The city, on the other hand, signifies an undefined colorlessness and assimilation.

Hallelujah depicts the urban as an environment in which traditional relationships between family and labor cannot be sustained, and in this way the film undercuts the regenerative possibilities of the idyll that had been previously suggested by Zeke's family and the products of their labor. The family is literally destroyed when Zeke abandons his brother Spunk (Everett McGarrity) after meeting Chick and then accidentally kills him in a barroom brawl. Symbolically referencing the story of Cain and Abel (a running trope throughout African American city-based narratives in print and on screen), Spunk's murder banishes the family from the city space and suggests that the city leads brothers to kill brothers. What is even more significant about the absence of family in this space is that it is not only Zeke's family who cease to exist but *all* families because Zeke and Spunk were the sole representatives of family in the town.

The absence of the family is also illustrated by Chick's nontraditional role in the household. Neither Chick nor anyone else in this urban space is nurturing. Instead, Chick's energies are concentrated in her overt sexuality. Yet this sexuality is not directed toward reproduction (and therefore regeneration) but toward pleasure and personal gain, first with Hot Shot and then with Zeke. When Chick and Zeke live together, she fails to fulfill the traditional gender role of caretaker and plots to run off with Hot Shot, leaving one immoral relationship for another. In contrast, Missy Rose is shown repeatedly tending to Zeke's younger brothers as well as cooking and cleaning. Thus the city woman is barren, selfish, and aggressive, whereas the rural woman is nurturing, selfless, and accommodating.

In the southern rural idyll, labor is defined in terms of production and renewal and this is supported as we see Zeke's family work the land and reap the benefits of their labor through the sale of cotton. The city space, on the other hand, is defined in terms of consumption rather than production. No one works in the town, and all efforts are directed toward making a quick and easy buck. This is illustrated by Zeke's experiences when first arriving in the town. He loses the family's hard-earned money when he is duped by a scheme he is told will double it. Also, Zeke accidentally shoots his brother while they are both in the town, in effect killing off one of the family's producers. Furthermore, Zeke's relationship with Chick, started within the town, bears no offspring. The heavy-handed moral message of this episode, which will be repeated in Zeke's interactions with Chick, asserts the value of honest work and the dire consequences of succumbing to the temptations of the city.

In the end Zeke recognizes his errors, leaves Chick, and returns to the family. In effect, he takes the redemptive train leading him to, as he outlined in his earlier sermon, the promised land. *Hallelujah* equates the promised land with the antebellum idyll, and while it doesn't fully identify the idyll with heaven, the space's purity and morality, exemplified by Missy Rose, is suggestive of a pure space. These links may be merely symbolic, but they begin a trend of demonizing the city that concurrently functions as a warning to possible migrants to city centers and ignores the wealth of urban culture that had begun to filter into the imaginations of African Americans, both northern and southern, and American culture in general (the 1920s were, after all, the Jazz Age). This trend continued in *The Green Pastures*, the next black-cast musical released. In *The Green Pastures*, however, Zeke's sermon prophecy becomes real, and the antebellum idyll is transformed into heaven.

The Green Pastures: The Antebellum Idyll as Heaven

The Green Pastures, a loose adaptation of a selection of biblical tales retold in the context of a black heaven, has more in common with our understanding of representations of the rural South than it does with more conventional representations of heaven. It combines the characteristics of traditional Hollywood renderings of heaven with a "heav-enly" mise-en-scène resembling a plantation. Although the angels are dressed traditionally (for angels, that is) in white gowns and wings, they also smoke ten-cent "cee-gars" and spend their time fishing and pic-nicking on fried fish and egg creams. The space is defined by highly stylized rural, southern signifiers, most specifically, an abundance of trees draped with Spanish moss and suggestive of the stately landscape of a plantation. It is also first introduced through an iris-shaped frame of fluffy white clouds resembling cotton. Almost immediately, the film places its black bodies in a southern milieu defined by a plantation econ-omy and the presence of its most lucrative crop, cotton.

The film's comparisons between heaven and earth use themes I have already discussed—especially religion, music, gender, and sexuality—to define the diegesis. The film opens with shots revealing a rural, south-ern community on a Sunday morning, including a church (the film's establishing shot) to which the community's young children are head-ing for Bible studies. The events in this small town are the framing device for the larger portion of *The Green Pastures*, using the preacher's Bible lessons to shift the action away from this space to an antebellum idyll in the sky. The framing story repeatedly locates its community in Louisiana by naming the state, the Delta, and New Orleans prior to the transition to heaven, suggesting that the heavenly space is related to either the Delta or Louisiana. For urban African American audiences, many of whom had migrated from the Delta region, the message was clear: southern space is heavenly space.

The Green Pastures first appeared on stage as a successful Broadway play by Marc Connelly before it was adapted for the screen by Connelly and William Keighley in 1936.[22] The stylization of the heavenly set shifts away from *Hallelujah*'s more documentary-like spaces, and resem-bles the unreal or fantasy space that is consistent with other Hollywood musicals of the time. It also differs from the framing story's mise-en-scène. Like *Hallelujah*, the frame attempts realism, at least regarding the exteriors, which appear to be shot on location. With the change to heaven, and the subsequent tales within this part of the diegesis, the cinematography and mise-en-scène become highly stylized. Part of this may have been due to the studio's parsimony regarding location shoot-ing, while part of it may also have been due to Connelly's own roots in theater.[23] The result, however, was to separate heaven from the earthly space opening the film.

The Heavenly Plantation in *The Green Pastures* (Warner Brothers, 1936).
Courtesy of the Museum of Modern Art Film Stills Archive.

The heavenly portion of the film starts with De Lawd's (Rex Ingram)
decision to create the earth, the moon, and humankind. Initially, earthly
space resembles heavenly space, as its first manifestation consists of the
Garden of Eden and Adam, whom De Lawd creates in his own image
(made literal by Ingram, who plays both De Lawd and Adam). However, it is not long before humans discover sin. This discovery launches
a series of tales—separated by inserts either to the framing story or to
heaven—narrating humankind's misdeeds, De Lawd's fact-finding visits to earth, and his struggle to make his creations behave "properly."
The stories loosely follow well-known Old Testament events and individuals such as Cain and Abel, Noah, Moses, the king of Babylon,
and Hezdrel, the modern (New Testament) man, modeled after Alain
Locke's "New Negro."

Heavenly time is both cyclical and static in its relationship to earthly
time, as is exemplified in the different temporal orders defining the two
spaces. In heaven, the "great hereafter," everything exists in a temporal

vacuum in which time is eternal. In much the same way that Bakhtin's idyll constructs a circularity of time fueled by a relationship with family and nature, heavenly time is circular in the repetition of actions relating to the angels' sustenance. Days are taken up by fishing, cooking, and eating, or, as De Lawd says, "fishermen fish, cooks cook, children play, adults pass the time of day, the choir sings." On the other hand, the earthly portions progress in a linear structure, with De Lawd's visits to earth replicating the narrative progression of the Bible.

While heaven's temporal cycles are mostly symbolic because they are attached to the lives of angels, there are still suggestions of multigenerational families and regenerating time. For example, there are several generations of angels. The film does not suggest that the community is made up of biological family members or that any new generations of angels result from biological reproduction. It does suggest, however, a system of familial and communal support in the angels' interactions with each other. The angels form a community that isn't an actual extended family but acts as a "substitute family."[24] For example, the "mother" angel chastises and threatens a young angel with a beating for misbehaving. Perhaps this is merely an example of "ersatz Negro folk culture,"[25] but it suggests a communality that is similar in look and organization to the family gatherings in *Hallelujah*. Here, of course, the extended family is bound by ties of purity and piety rather than blood.

Similarly, the rhythms of nature make their appearance in *The Green Pastures* symbolically rather than literally. For instance, the angels appear in a heaven resembling a natural setting of trees, grass, and rolling hills. They never work the fields like Zeke's family, yet they rely on nature and the earth in other ways that are integral to the community's existence. The male angels spend their time fishing in order to supply the community with food, and all the angels drink a custard concoction made from "firmament," a thick substance similar in appearance to a dense fog. In fact, it is De Lawd's need for a place to drain off the overabundance of heavenly firmament that inspires him to create earth.

The Green Pastures' heaven raises interesting questions regarding the intersection of piety with idyllic space and time. While in *Hallelujah* (and, as we will see, in *Cabin in the Sky*), religion often forms the core of the antebellum idyll, both defining it and offering it cohesion, here the links are overt. Whereas the community's faith and purity were just two of many elements defining the idyll in *Hallelujah*, the faith and goodness of the idyll are *The Green Pastures'* most prominent factors. The antebellum idyll, consistently constructed as an idealized space (timeless, rural, and southern), is now transformed into heaven, complete with angels and De Lawd. What had only been suggested before is now realized. But this also initiates a series of contradictions, the most telling being that heaven remains a privileged site that cannot harbor any urban characteristics.

The film fits with the pattern already identified in *Hallelujah*, setting up a series of dichotomies in which the earthly is associated with the urban, which is then contrasted to the antebellum idyll. The city appears symbolically rather than as "real" urban space. In earlier films, the urban appeared symbolically as town-like spaces; in *The Green Pastures*, the iconography of the city appears in what is defined only as "earth" rather than in a strictly delineated town- or cityscape and in the presence of such elements as juke joints, alcohol, flashy clothing, loose women, knives and guns, crap games, and jazz. All of the activities, individuals, and spaces identified as urban are connected to sin and with the specific cultural signifiers of a black city, thus providing a moral warning about big city behavior and further solidifying the association of illegal and immoral behaviors with African Americans. While urban iconography appears in almost all of the sections of the film, two episodes in particular reveal the tension between the rural and the urban most explicitly: Noah's story and the fall of Babylon.

Noah's section opens with the sound of a woman humming a jazz-based melody and strumming a banjo. This woman, Zeba (Edna Mae Harris), is the first person De Lawd meets on his visit. She is immediately identified as urban through her song, her brazenness, her use of slang, her appearance (tight skirt and shirt, beret, and bobbed hair), and her behavior; she mistakenly interprets De Lawd's interest in her soul as sexually motivated. "Her man," Cain the Sixth (James Fuller), is dressed in urban fashion similar to Zeba's, with stylish suit and straw hat, and he carries a gun, which he draws on De Lawd as a sign of virility.

While these icons suggest the presence of the city, the way that the pair interacts with De Lawd more fully indicates the split between heaven and earth and, by extension, sacred and secular, rural and city. Neither Zeba nor Cain the Sixth treats De Lawd with any respect, even though he resembles a preacher and he is an elder. They even refer to him, separately, as "country boy," behavior that underscores the symbolic presence of the city. (There has been thus far no discernible difference between the mise-en-scène in heaven and where we find Zeba and

Cain the Sixth, who are sitting on grass and under a tree very similar in appearance to those found in heaven.) Zeba's behavior also symbolically indicates the differences between women in heaven and those on earth. In heaven, women engage in traditional gender roles, such as cooking, mothering, cleaning, and being respectful to De Lawd. On earth, women (at least the bad ones) are overtly sexual and disrespectful, as they were in *Hallelujah*.

Zeba and Cain the Sixth disrespect De Lawd in *The Green Pastures* (Warner Brothers, 1936). Courtesy of the Museum of Modern Art Film Stills Archive.

The story continues with De Lawd walking through the countryside and hearing his name being called on by someone in prayer. It is a young boy calling on De Lawd in the vain hope of winning a game of dice. When De Lawd questions the boy regarding his behavior, he is again treated disrespectfully. When De Lawd asks the boy where his mother is, he learns that she ran off with a man, deserting her child. Again, the earthly and urban is contrasted with the heavenly and idyllic through the conduct of women, as it is implied that the boy's behavior is somehow his absent mother's fault (a suggestion that foreshadows the sociological "culture of poverty" discourses focusing on the black family as aberration in the 1960s). Combined with Zeba's sexualized and disrespectful behavior, this exchange indicates that the family either does not exist at all or exists in a deviant form in this space.

De Lawd next meets Noah, who explains humankind's shortcomings: the men fight, drink, and gamble, and the women are "worse than the men." As the pair converse, they stroll through a space that has the appearance of a city street. The camera tracks along with them, showing in this space the film's starkest system of oppositions between goodness and sin. The street overflows with juke joints, people drinking, dancing, and fighting, and the sounds of music, summing up "the life of riffraff . . . in a single truck shot along a sin-wracked street."[26] As with Zeba and Cain the Sixth, the people in this shot are dressed in contemporary fashions and they listen to jazz. In heaven, on the other hand, the Hall Johnson Choir performs traditional spirituals. The religious piety of the spirituals is opposed to the sin of the jazz-based melodies associated with the urban, and "gospel or church music is inscribed as good, while the more powerful and universal Black idioms, Jazz and Blues, are evil."[27] Therefore, the sound track reinforces the dichotomies already presented by the mise-en-scène.

This section of the film suggests that humankind's most serious sin is sloth—Noah attributes all of the earth's troubles to idle hands. This theme complicates the binary oppositions between heaven and earth because no one in either space is ever truly involved in labor (except maybe De Lawd). Labor is *implied* in the heavenly space through the symbolic rendering of the plantation economy. The angels are surrounded by cotton, but they don't literally pick it. On earth, people are not even involved in a symbolic system of labor. Instead, they pursue all the vices that have been collapsed into the city—drinking, dancing, gambling, and sex—and, like the city in *Hallelujah*, nothing is produced. De Lawd decides to destroy the earth (except for Noah and Noah's family), suggesting that the humans have brought this punishment on themselves.

After De Lawd's decision, the film shifts back to the framing story before moving into the second story about the king and people of Babylon. This section is much briefer than Noah's story, yet it employs similar urban iconography. Babylon is not a city. Instead, it is a fashionable nightclub, similar in appearance to those in vogue during the height of the Harlem Renaissance, such as the Cotton Club (although this club allows black patrons). Again, jazz fills the sound track; however, in an interesting inversion, the band is playing a jazzed-up version of "Let My People Go," which was previously performed by the angels in heaven; in this context, it provides an immediate indication of the space's perversion of heavenly values.

"Club Babylon" is filled with richly appointed patrons who are dancing, drinking, and enjoying themselves. In another sign of the perversion of piety, there is a high priest, whom the king of Babylon calls a "fashion plate." The music and the priest reveal urbanism's appropriation of signifiers of the antebellum idyll as a bastardization, not a positive borrowing. A prophet dressed as a sharecropper enters the space and implies that the high priest is a fraud. The prophet warns the people of Babylon to stop sinning before it is "too late." The king, outraged by the prophet's words, orders him shot (by what appears to be Cain the Sixth's gun from the earlier scene), thus removing the incongruous and pure presence of the antebellum idyll from this space. The section ends with De Lawd's voice-over renouncing the people of Babylon for their behavior. While the film continues with one more section in which De Lawd learns to forgive humankind with the help of Hezdrel, this is the final section in which the urban makes any appearance in the narrative of *The Green Pastures*. De Lawd's renunciation of the people of Babylon denies the possibility of anything positive coming out of spaces identified with the city. In fact, it implies that humans can only continue to exist by leaving its spaces.

In its dichotomy between heaven and earth, *The Green Pastures* suggests that rural, southern space is a paradise in comparison to the city. Although the actual conditions faced by urban African Americans during the Depression may have contributed to this comparison, the film's escapist narrative and fantastic mise-en-scène was more in line with conventional Depression-era forms of entertainment that opted for fantasy over social commentary. Additionally, the film's heavenly idyll bears no relationship to the continuing economic, social, and racial hardships faced by African American migrants in the South. Instead, *The Green Pastures*, in its narrative removal of the African American urban population from earth, can be understood as Hollywood's symbolic erasure of the country's urban black population.

The film's constellation of oppositions revolves around behaviors and practices that were historically and stereotypically marked as "black" (playing dice, drinking alcohol, frequenting juke joints, listening to jazz), not only within the diegesis of this film but of most Hollywood films and cartoons with an African American presence and within their minstrel precursors from the nineteenth and early twentieth centuries. This system implies that being black (and thus both a sinner and an urban dweller) or merely taking part in those behaviors associated with being black is cause for punishment. In this manner De Lawd functions more as an overseer than as a God, for it is he who claims responsibility on two different occasions for the enslavement of his people, and he declares that humankind was responsible for their own punishment because of their actions.[28] Just how much of this attitude is related to the social and political impact of a growing urban population in general and how much was related to Hollywood's translation of uplift narratives directed to black audiences in particular (see chapter 2) remains to be seen. Turning to the two musicals produced during World War II, we see the same dominant themes, but a stronger urban presence and a somewhat weaker moral contrast, suggesting the different ideological focus during the war years, one that concentrated on unity (even if symbolically so) in support of the war effort.

Club Paradise Moves to the Country

In the years between the release of *The Green Pastures* in 1936 and the production of *Cabin in the Sky* and *Stormy Weather* in 1943, a number of forces changed Hollywood and subsequently the construction of the antebellum idyll. In the first half of the century, mainstream screen renderings of African American life bore no sign of influential discourses, such as urbanism and migration, which had become central to black experiences in the twentieth century. Most notably, Hollywood's black-cast musicals did not register the effects of the demographic shifts that occurred during and after World War I, migration that redefined the U.S. black population as urban and northern rather than rural and southern. With the two musicals released in 1943, however, a shift can be detected in Hollywood's attitudes toward the African American city. Each film, in different ways and to different degrees, reinterprets not only the role of the city and its concomitant influences, but also the role of the antebellum idyll.

Cabin in the Sky, the first black-cast musical released following *The Green Pastures*, shares a number of elements with the earlier film. Both were adapted from Broadway musicals, and thus had already acquired artistic legitimacy through their association with the stage prior to being adapted for the screen. MGM hired Marc Connelly, author and co-director of the earlier film, to help with the screen adaptation of *Cabin*, adding another level of prestige to the product. Both films hinged on moral themes and Connelly, who had already successfully translated the tensions between good and evil to the screen, was likely to do it again—after all, the Hollywood genre film was built upon successful repetition of formulas. Both films, among others, feature the same performers, such as Rex Ingram, Eddie Anderson, and Oscar Polk. Not only did such casting suggest a continuity between the two films, it also guaranteed an African American audience. Anderson and Ingram also drew a relatively large white audience, and their casting might have been an attempt to give the film crossover appeal in the more integrationist environment spawned by the country's war efforts.

By the time *Cabin* was released in 1943, many key events had oc-curred that would have long-lasting effects on the industry. The first was the entry of the United States into World War II in 1941. With the country's involvement in the war, enlistment in the armed forces was considered an act of patriotism, but many black men were ambiva-lent toward the war effort. The military was still segregated, and many African Americans regarded the government as hypocritical for requir-ing their aid in fighting fascism and racism abroad while granting racism and segregation official status on U.S. soil. Black workers were also cut off from the war effort at home through the racism and exclusion they faced in the defense industry. Even though the industry's ship- and plane-building companies had been hiring in large numbers before the United States entered the war, they refused to employ black work-ers. This situation continued until A. Philip Randolph and the Broth-erhood of Sleeping Car Porters proposed a march on Washington to protest against this system of unfair employment practices. Ultimately, President Franklin D. Roosevelt signed Executive Order 8802 (1941), establishing the Fair Employment Practices Committee and outlawing discrimination in the defense industry.

The surge of African American migration that occurred during World War II was as important and as vast as the movement follow-ing World War I. As with the earlier movement, the migration patterns during the 1940s were directly linked to where workers could find prof-itable employment. California, especially the communities surrounding Los Angeles and San Diego in the south and San Francisco and Oakland in the north, became the final destination for many migrants because this was where the newly opened defense plants were clustered. The reasons for the state's emergence as the center of defense were not only clear-cut, but were also related to the same factors that had induced the film industry's move to the West Coast: "climate, open spaces, and natural resources made it [California] an ideal site for military production. Thus, the government decided to invest almost half of its $70 million national defense budget in the Golden State."[29] The infusion of so much cash, coupled with the increased demand for workers, motivated both poor and middle-class southern blacks to flock to the area seeking employment.

In 1942, the NAACP, led by Walter White, challenged the film industry to change its hiring practices and the archetypal screen images of African Americans. With the NAACP's efforts, an expanding urban black audience, and wartime calls for integration, Hollywood altered (at least temporarily) its treatment of African American performers and personnel. For the first time the industry released films that showcased big-name black personalities and high production values, committing larger budgets and placing skilled personnel both in front of and behind the camera. *Cabin* was a relatively major release compared to the earlier films, which were made with a minimum of outlay from the studios.[30] Utilizing all the resources of MGM's musical unit led by Arthur Freed, *Cabin* features set designs inspired by Vincente Minnelli, who made his directorial debut with the film. Minnelli's and Freed's influence runs throughout *Cabin* and indicates a shift away from the production values of earlier black-cast musicals toward the look and feel of a Hollywood studio production. Since Hollywood had been cutting back on its pre-war extravagances, *Cabin*'s stylization was in line with the studios' more modest war musicals. This is not to suggest that this was the first time that audiences were to see the South portrayed with higher production values, as its representations, especially the antebellum South, were recognizable in Hollywood by this time. *Cabin* appeared four years after the release of *Gone With the Wind* and *Jezebel*, two products of the studio system that continued the mythology of the genteel, patrician, southern white planter class and the contented "darkies" imprinted upon American popular consciousness by D. W. Griffith's *Birth of a Nation* in 1915.

With its constructed sets, the film differs from the more documentary-style renderings of a black southern pastoral as in *Hallelujah*. *Cabin*'s sets are somewhat similar to those used for *The Green Pastures*, especially the earlier film's construction of a fantasy space (specifically in the early rural sets and Little Joe and Petunia's cabin). All three films, *Hallelujah*, *The Green Pastures*, and *Cabin*, follow familiar plot lines. *Cabin* is about the struggle for Little Joe's (Eddie "Rochester" Anderson) soul by the forces of good, in the form of the General, and evil, in the person of Lucifer Jr. (in a remarkable reversal in casting played by Rex Ingram). In keeping with the earlier films' gender politics, the moral cathexis is embodied by the women—Petunia (Ethel Waters), Little Joe's devout and devoted wife, and Georgia Brown (Lena Horne), the femme fatale figure. Furthermore, the women personify tensions between the country and the city; Petunia lives in the antebellum idyll, while Georgia inhabits and is inhabited by urban iconography. *Cabin* differs most significantly from earlier films in the way that elements of one space appear in the other.

The film's mise-en-scène, especially its costumes and setting, depicts the system of oppositions represented by Petunia and Georgia. First, the connection between Petunia and the idyllic, already apparent through her name, is emphasized by what she wears.[31] Her simple, everyday work/house dresses are light in color and usually tight-fitting, but not in order to reveal a sexualized or sensuous body. Instead, they emphasize Petunia's large physique, which while not exactly conforming to the physical conventions of most mammies, resembles the archetype. On the other hand, Georgia wears form-fitting dresses and gowns in dark colors that are more suggestive of urban life. Her purpose is to snare Little Joe in her web and, significantly, she is shown more than once engaged in dressing, making up, and preparing herself. Petunia never engages in such activities—even when she explicitly dresses to lure Little Joe away from his temptations. Petunia's efforts are focused on domesticity, especially as they relate to Joe's comfort and the comfort of others; she also earns her living by taking in other people's laundry. She is both domestic and a domestic. Ironically, Petunia's characterization is progress over earlier depictions of black domestics. Unlike most, she has a private life and a love interest.

Petunia is doubly inscribed within the antebellum idyll's association of women with family and domestic space. Except for her initial appearance in church, and one at Club Paradise near the close of the film, Petunia stays at home. Significantly, even though she is almost always house-bound, Petunia is only twice seen in the bedroom, a space that defines Georgia. It is the *way* in which each woman inhabits this space that reveals the fundamental differences between them and their relationships with Little Joe. Petunia shares her bedroom with Little Joe, but she resides in it only when she is fulfilling the role of caretaker—for instance, when watching over Little Joe's sick body (twice because of the film's dream structure). Petunia's labor is centered around the maintenance of the marital bond. All her efforts are directed toward Joe; she is devoted to him. This can be seen in the arrangement of figures in the bedroom space. Both times that Petunia watches over Joe, her attention, body, and point of view are pointed in his direction to the right.

Petunia only has eyes for Little Joe in *Cabin in the Sky* (MGM, 1943). Courtesy of the Museum of Modern Art Film Stills Archive.

Georgia, on the other hand, is introduced in and defined by a different kind of bedroom. The space itself does not significantly differ from Petunia's (it contains a slightly more ornate bed and dresser, and its mirror takes up most of the space), yet Georgia's use of the space is very different. Her intention is to seduce Little Joe away from Petunia and the domestic space Petunia represents. While Little Joe is never seen in Georgia's bedroom (after all, the film had to conform to the Production Code), Lucifer Jr. is. Additionally, in a clearly conventional way of signifying female filmic narcissism and duplicity, especially the femme fatale's, Georgia's attentions are directed solely toward herself as she repeatedly looks at her image in the mirror. The arrangement of characters here is opposite from that of Petunia's bedroom (and, by association, to the antebellum idyll): Petunia looks toward the right in the direction of Joe, while the direction Georgia glances is left, to her own image. The direction of these looks indicates the fundamental oppositions structuring the two spaces, the two women, and the two ideologies.

Petunia and Little Joe's house is in a rural location, outside town, yet close enough for the pair to shop, labor, and (in Little Joe's case) drink and gamble there. The house and yard are idyllic; the white picket fence, flowers, and interior furnishings hiding the reality of rural pov-

Georgia only has eyes for Georgia in *Cabin in the Sky* (MGM, 1943). Courtesy of the Museum of Modern Art Film Stills Archive.

erty. James Naremore suggests that Minnelli didn't want the cabin to be "dirty" or "slovenly," and thus part of this particular version of the antebellum idyll might spring from Minnelli's own idealism.[32] And yet while the cabin is idyllic, the city intrudes on the domestic space in the form of an automatic washing machine Little Joe brings home as a birthday gift for Petunia. The machine indicates the pair's aspirations to prosperity, but is much more interesting as a form of conspicuous consumption. Little Joe signals his wish to improve their living conditions with the purchase of a prestigious appliance, but the cabin does not have electricity. The machine has no practical function, but its prominent position on the front porch creates a false display of wealth for the community's eyes. Second, the machine's link with the modern raises the possibility of transferring Petunia out of the antebellum idyll into a more urban space. At the same time, it shuts down this possibility by maintaining Petunia's association with the antebellum idyll in continuing her affiliation with the domestic labor already defining her character. Unlike Georgia, Petunia has no leisure time.

As a whole, the film conforms to the temporal boundaries that are characteristic of the antebellum idyll: stasis and circularity. Rather than confining these attributes to the idyllic space, which would be typical, *Cabin*'s narrative blurs these boundaries by marking all the spaces of the film with idyllic time. The narrative follows a seemingly simple structure, with events taking place in a logical, chronological sequence based upon cause and effect. The narrative is much more complicated than first appears, however, and it follows a complex dream-within-a-dream structure. Little Joe gains consciousness for the first time near the beginning of the film, but when he regains consciousness the second time, we realize that the (supposedly waking) events have not taken place at all. Time begins and ends in Joe's head, and is circular rather linear; narrative progression is illusory. As Little Joe lies in the bedroom of his rural house, he has only *imagined* a different sort of time.

As in the earlier musicals, *Cabin*'s city space is neither a real city nor even a developed town, but it signifies itself as urban through particular features. In ways that are similar to *Hallelujah*, "urbanness" is suggested through a mise-en-scène that includes miscellaneous buildings, a street, and the most important focal point, Club Paradise. While the surrounding buildings and the street are important signifiers of the city, Club Paradise acts as the synecdoche for urban experience. The interior of the club is similar in appearance to the Babylonian sequence of

The Green Pastures with its connotations of a high-society cabaret environment. In Club Paradise we find Georgia, Little Joe's problems all begin (he meets Georgia, he gambles and drinks, and he is shot by a rival for his money and Georgia's attentions), and the climax of the film commences—a climax that, significantly, involves the antebellum idyll penetrating its borders. Furthermore, in *Cabin* the cabaret atmosphere is heightened by the presence and performances of Duke Ellington and his orchestra and Louis Armstrong as one of Lucifer Jr.'s helpers, again linking jazz with the city and with temptation.

Instead of the city creating problems in the country, as in *Hallelujah* or *The Green Pastures*, Petunia's entry into Club Paradise causes the major turning point in the narrative. Previously in *Cabin*, the urban had entered the antebellum idyll, mostly in the forms of Georgia, Little Joe's gambling friends, and the washing machine, all of whom visit Petunia and Little Joe's house. Except for the washing machine, figures of the city enter the idyllic space in order to lure Little Joe to Club Paradise, rather than to contribute to or change its spatiotemporal parameters. Yet when the antebellum idyll enters the city, it appropriates certain urban elements for its own use, taking away what it can and shifting alliances if necessary.

Club Paradise does not make an appearance until almost three-quarters into the film. Until then, it has only entered the narrative through dialogue. When Petunia enters Club Paradise in an attempt to rekindle her relationship with Little Joe, the iconography identifying good and evil, and by connection the antebellum idyll and the city, changes. Until this point, Petunia had been contained within spaces exclusively defined in familial, domestic, and idyllic terms. In addition, her piety, her appearance, and her asexuality were markers of the antebellum idyll. When she enters the club, she is a changed woman—she drinks, she wears a tight-fitting gown, and she is overtly sexual (especially with Domino, Little Joe's rival). More important, she talks about money for the first time as she demands her "cut" of her husband's gambling winnings, consequently using her marital status for financial gain and power, something absent from the antebellum idyll, where her relationship with Little Joe placed her in a subservient position.

Georgia's coding also changes in this scene. Her attributes as the alluring temptress all but disappear the moment Petunia enters her space. Georgia's costuming and relationships with men prefigure this shift because she is clad in a long white gown, a marked departure from her previous costumes (ironically, it is now she who looks like a bride). Additionally, as Petunia's power increases, Georgia loses her influence over Domino and Little Joe. Prior to Petunia's arrival, the tension is between the two rivals for Georgia's attentions. Domino has returned to town, having served a prison sentence for shooting Little Joe at the beginning of the film. When Petunia arrives, the attention shifts from Georgia, the temptress, to Petunia, the wife. In a replication of earlier events, Domino shoots Little Joe again as they vie for Petunia. By the end of the club sequence, Petunia, Little Joe, and Georgia die and enter heaven, but ultimately the film reveals that all the events were part of Little Joe's dream.

According to Naremore, *Cabin* "has a paradoxical effect, as if it wanted to dissolve binary oppositions between the town and the country, thereby unsettling the strategy of containment that usually operated in Hollywood's folkoric narratives."[33] Naremore is correct insofar as there is definitely more of a dialogue between the city and the antebellum idyll in this film compared to the others discussed. In fact, the city enters the antebellum idyll as a motif, most specifically with the washing machine, and in Georgia's and Little Joe's border crossings. Similarly, the idyll is a motif—or aura of the South—when Petunia enters Club Paradise. Yet Naremore's overall purpose, endemic to his auteurist project, is to argue that Minnelli's skill as an artist was the reason for *Cabin*'s more contemporary aspects. Instead, the film's more open acknowledgment of an African American urbanity is connected to the combined effects of World War II, Executive Order 8802, the agitation of the NAACP, migration, and the modernity associated with many of the film's African American performers that enabled (and perhaps even forced) the beginnings of such a dialogue. And yet, for all this, we must not overlook the fact that what appears to be Little Joe's bad dream is still, in the final analysis, a nightmare in which the African American city leads directly to hell.

Stormy Weather and Allegories of Migration

A more successful attempt to redefine the spatiotemporal boundaries of the antebellum idyll is found in the other major black-cast release of 1943. *Stormy Weather* signaled an important move away from the depictions of good and evil and city and country that were so central to the earlier all-black musicals. This is not to suggest that the antebellum idyll does not periodically make an appearance in the diegesis, especially as a motif in the film's depictions of a suburban Los Angeles. But the antebellum idyll, and the city for that matter, no longer function according to older tropes and oppositions. In fact, the film explicitly acknowledges African American migration, with its narrative structured as an allegory of African American movement (geographic and aesthetic) between World Wars I and II.

Loosely based on the life story of Bill "Bojangles" Robinson (Robinson plays the protagonist), *Stormy Weather* tracks "Bill Williamson's" progress from a returning World War I veteran to his success on the stage, and his (and his dance style's) gradual replacement by the more contemporary performance modes of the 1940s. As the story unfolds, Bill returns from the war, where he was part of Jim Europe's 15th (African American) Regiment. He temporarily stops in Harlem before heading down the Mississippi River to Memphis. From there, he travels with an African American stage troupe to Chicago, and back to New York, before finally settling down outside Los Angeles, where he works in the film industry. In its most practical sense, this structure allows for a variety of performances and an historical overview of African American musical forms, from the minstrels on a Mississippi riverboat, to the blackface routines of Flournoy E. Miller, to the jive spectacles of Cab Calloway and his band. More metaphorically, Bill's travels loosely retrace the route taken by many southern migrants between the wars, many of whom moved to southern cities (Memphis) before continuing north (Chicago, New York) and finally west (Los Angeles). Thus, in *Stormy Weather* both migration and the city, while not the subjects of the film, operate as given parts of black experience rather than being denied, pushed to the margins, or relegated to hell.

Of all the black-cast musicals produced by major studios, *Stormy Weather* has received the least critical attention, and even has been dismissed as having a plot that "did not amount to much," "was shamelessly illogical," or was "unexceptional."[34] Many of these criticisms are based on the fact that the film's narrative is a backstage story, using Bill's experiences and his onscreen love relationship with Selina Rogers (Lena Horne) as an excuse for the inclusion of performances by notable African American entertainers, such as Fats Waller, Ada Brown, Cab Calloway, Katherine Dunham, and the Nicholas Brothers, all of whom appear as themselves. In this, we see *Stormy Weather* moving out of the folk musical style of earlier black-cast musicals and conforming more closely to the conventions of the show musical—films that "construct their plot[s] around the creation of a show . . . with the making of a romantic couple both symbolically and causally related to [the show's] success."[35] Because of the scope of the narrative, any system of oppositions it contains is focused around two issues: the show and the couple. Thus, questions of good and evil do not enter *Stormy Weather*'s plot unless they interfere with a show or with the romance between Selina and Bill. While the main conflict of the film is related to the various problems Bill faces on his rise to success, it is also the union, dissolution, and reunion of the pair that provides tension.

The most significant facets of the film are the construction of Selina's character and the way in which the film acknowledges a new, more contemporary spectatorial position in its allusions to history and the contemporary world, particularly through the women's roles. Whereas Georgia's femme fatale image was constructed to reference the evils of the city in *Cabin in the Sky*, Selina is coded in a dramatically different manner. Selena is a city woman (she is introduced in Harlem, where she was born and raised), and yet she is not evil. In fact, she is coded in an almost angelic manner, and is often draped in white or pale evening gowns and furs. Like Georgia with Little Joe, Selina exerts an influence over Bill, but only in relation to his performance: she helps Bill's career first by asking Chick Bailey (Emmett Wallace) to hire him, and then by joining ranks with Bill when he starts his own show. This sort of coupling conforms to the treatment of the romantic pair in the show musical, in which there is a merging between "the couple in the narrative and the same couple as actors in the show."[36] This plot culminates in Bill and Selina's final performance, in which they reunite after a long separation.

Bill, Selina, and the rest of the performers exist in a space and time that is more symbolically a contemporary city than any real space, even though the film names specific places—New York, Memphis, Chicago, Los Angeles—which were also known as African American urban centers. Most of the film's action, however, is confined to spaces related to performance, such as the dance hall, the interior of a Beale Street bar, and backstage areas. In fact, almost all we glimpse of city space is restricted to the backstage areas of various theaters.

While the city makes few appearances in the film, the idyll nevertheless continues as a strong motif, defining the relationship of the central couple. Although Selina is not coded as the bad city woman, she initially rejects a life in the antebellum idyll. Selina does not accept an idyllic house that Bill dreams of and designs for them and, significantly, for their future children. With all this, she also refuses a life of domesticity and motherhood, preferring instead life on the stage in the more "decadent" space of Paris, in the process referencing a long ex-patriot tradition and enlarging the scope of the film to include the African diaspora. Bill, however, does not leave this more idyllic life but quickly moves into his dream house in the suburbs of Los Angeles, in the process making literal the connections between the cinema and the antebellum idyll by signing a contract with a Hollywood studio.

The film, like *Cabin in the Sky*, was shot almost entirely on a set, and thus many of its locations have a constructed appearance. Yet in the similarities between Bill's house and the domestic space in *Cabin* we can see the traces of the antebellum idyll in *Stormy Weather*. Ostensibly located in or around Los Angeles, the house is much more rural than suburban. Furthermore, it is completely removed from any identifiable city space, and even though Bill mentions that he has neighbors, their houses do not appear in the frame. The area does not lack a community, however, because Bill is surrounded by children from the neighborhood. Thus, the spatiotemporal characteristics found here are very similar to those in earlier black-cast musicals: an idyllic, rural space (not southern, but southern California), defined by nature, community, and regeneration. The city enters this space very rarely and when it does—once in the form of mail from Bill's performing friends and once in the figure of Cab Calloway, who enters the idyll only to draw Bill out of it—it does not create havoc, but rather provides narrative closure.

When he attends a benefit for African American soldiers departing for World War II, Bill realizes just how different he is from the new urban world. First, he has trouble understanding the jive banter of Cab Calloway and Gabe (Dooley Wilson). This difference is further clarified by contrasting costumes: Bill wears a standard tuxedo, while Calloway and Gabe dress in zoot suits. The significance of costume must be stressed; 1943 was the same year of the "Zoot Suit Riots" in Los Angeles, which began as a dispute between a group of Mexican American youths and white sailors but expanded to include young black men as well. The suits, first a form of stylistic excess, soon became signifiers of a subtle form of race rebellion because they were considered unpatriotic in a time of cloth rationing. Second, the performance that closes the show and the film points to the ways in which Bill's tap style seems outmoded in comparison to the rhythms of Cab Calloway, the acrobatics of the Nicholas Brothers, and the hybrid ballet-vernacular movements of Katherine Dunham and her dancers. Yet, it is also in this final scene that Bill and Selina reunite after she has changed her mind about domesticity and motherhood. The nostalgic characteristics of this climactic coupling are reinforced by a stage performance in which Selina appears wearing a nineteenth-century gown, signifying her willing acceptance of a life in the idyll.

The film relies on self-conscious references to performance styles to position itself in a particular context, especially when the narrative reaches the contemporary 1940s. Yet it also acknowledges American history and roles of African Americans in that history in other ways. Spanning the years from the end of World War I to the beginning of World War II, the narrative begins and ends with movement, opening with Bill's return home and closing with "Cab Calloway Jr.'s" (Robert Felder) departure for battle during World War II. These events place the narrative in a real-world context that none of the previous films had succeeded in doing. The immediate urgency of actual events is even further underscored by the inclusion of documentary footage at the beginning of the film in which returning African American soldiers are shown parading through the streets of New York City after World War I. Thus, in a genre of film as far removed from actuality as possible, *Stormy Weather* acknowledges the world beyond its spatiotemporal borders and uses documentary footage to do so (unlike King Vidor's use of documentary style to imply actuality in *Hallelujah*). At the same time it stresses patriotism, encouraging African American enlistment. While the film's spaces may be still largely defined by the musical genre, its people and places indicate that the antebellum idyll was making way or, at the very least, dialoguing with the African American city despite the backward glance of its romantic conclusion.

From *Hearts in Dixie* (Paul Sloane, 1929) on, Hollywood's black-cast musicals experienced a twofold containment: they were segregated from other musicals produced by Hollywood by virtue of their all-black casts, and they were defined by the antebellum idyll, a space and time far removed from a contemporary context. As I've shown, the city often appeared as motifs and traces in the larger organizing system of the antebellum idyll, but more often than not it was in a cautionary manner—as evil, as sin, and finally, as hell. This would change in the early 1940s, under the combined influences of the NAACP, Executive Order 8802, and the nation's entry into World War II. Except for *Carmen Jones*, released in 1954, black-cast musical production would cease as the industry integrated. While Hollywood gradually began to acknowledge the growing presence of an African American population in American cities, black production companies also grappled with definitions of the city. The following chapter addresses independent African American films, often referred to as "race films," from the early sound period in order to examine the role that the city played in films directly influenced by and made for black audiences.

2

Harlem is Heaven:
City Motifs in Race Films
from the Early Sound Era

**The day of "aunties," "uncles," and "mammies" is . . . gone.
Uncle Tom and Sambo have passed on. . . . The popular
melodrama has about played itself out, and it is time to scrap
the fictions, garret the bogeys and settle down to a realistic
facing of facts.**
—Alain Locke (1925)[1]

African American film production dates to 1912 and the release of the Foster Photoplay Company's *The Railroad Porter*, but African American subjects and subject matter can be traced back to the beginnings of American filmmaking. As early as 1895, Thomas Edison and his assistants filmed and projected the first images of American blacks on the screen in a variety of shorts. Featuring titles such as *Watermelon Contest* (1899), *The Gator and the Pickaninny* (1903), *Ten Pickaninnies* (1904), and *The Wooing and the Wedding of a Coon* (1905), the films continued the treatment of African American subject matter that had first appeared in literature and in the theatrical genres of vaudeville and minstrelsy.[2] This practice further expanded with the development of film narrative in the multiple adaptations of *Uncle Tom's Cabin* in the early years of American filmmaking, and most notoriously in D. W. Griffith's infamous *Birth of a Nation* (1915).

45

During the early years of filmmaking, African American filmmakers realized that the emerging American film aesthetics and politics were such that their involvement would be minimal and that the treatment of black stories would be distorted at best. As early as the first filmic inscriptions of Uncle Tom and Topsy, there were corresponding protest movements among African Americans, who voiced concern and outrage over the images they were witnessing on screen. As part of the marches and boycotts that accompanied the release of Griffith's film, a group of entrepreneurs and political figures literally picked up the camera and began making their own films, most specifically the ill-fated *Birth of a Race* (1918), which fell victim to a shortage of funds and competing political visions. From the very beginnings of its existence, therefore, African American film production had a liminal relationship to the American film industry, existing independently of what would quickly become a centralized and streamlined group of businesses located first on the East Coast and then in Hollywood. Born of social protest and a desire to provide an antidote to already inscribed stereotypes, African American filmmaking has roots in a comparative discourse often determined by an anxiety over the images manufactured by mainstream filmmaking.

This chapter offers a brief overview of the history of early African American filmmaking, covering silent film production from the 1920s to the transition to sound and the development of a cross-section of genre films in the mid-to-late 1930s and early 1940s. I focus in particular on this latter stage of filmmaking, the post-Depression, pre–World War II moment during which producers of films geared toward an African American market changed their theme and focus in order to compete with Hollywood. Rather than concentrating on uplift, the sound-era race film producers adapted popular genres like the gangster film and the Western. More important, during this time, which ran currently with Hollywood's production of all-black musicals, African American city spaces, especially Harlem, appear for the first time as cinematic tropes in the films. Furthermore, these realizations of urbanity exist independently rather than in relationship to more idyllic rural spaces, which so often dominated the narratives of Hollywood films. What developed in this latter stage of race film production, therefore, is a Harlem chronotope, a contemporary, although often symbolic city space connoting African American modernity.

"The Realization of a Negro's Ambition": Early Race Films and the Politics of Uplift

In the decade following the establishment of the Foster Photoplay Company, many other production companies incorporated with the intention of making race films—films intended for all-black audiences, starring all-black casts and featuring black subject matter. Often, but not always, the companies were aided by whites, whether for financing or technical advice, an involvement that would lead some film historians to discount them from being considered "black independent films" on the basis that they were not exclusively made by African American filmmakers and technicians. On the opposite end of the spectrum stood a figure like Oscar Micheaux. Micheaux self-financed his early films, retaining complete control over every stage in their production, distribution, and exhibition. He remained fiercely independent, refusing to accept white financial aid until he declared bankruptcy in the post-Depression 1930s, when he was forced to solicit outside backing. While the issue of white involvement and African American independence has always been a crucial one in determining black film aesthetics, the focus in this chapter is on both the intended purposes of the films and their desired audiences, for it was at this early stage of filmmaking that there was the first acknowledgment of a black box office, especially one located in the urban North. African American venues for film predate even the Foster Company's incorporation in 1910, indicating that from its very beginnings, a black audience existed, and this audience, like the films to follow, emerged in a segregated environment.[3] More important, this audience was increasingly targeted by film producers.

Companies such as the Lincoln Motion Picture Company (established in 1916 by George and Noble Johnson), The Micheaux Book and Motion Picture Company, The Colored Players, and many lesser-known outfits produced films that were rejoinders to white-produced caricatures and stereotypes of black people. But this was just one of their purposes, as many figures, like William Foster and Oscar Micheaux, were entrepreneurs who, along with being race men, were also showmen, concerned with making a profit. Perhaps the most compelling reason for the industry's early development was its frequent focus on uplift, which arose out of and was dependent on the expanding urban black population. The years before, during, and after World War I saw the massive migration of the country's African American population from the rural South to the urban, industrialized North, resulting in the appearance of what Charles S. Johnson described as a "new type of Negro . . . a city Negro."[4] Early African American independent production was in part a tool of protest and education for urban audiences that were increasingly populated by relocated migrants from the rural South. For the northern African American bourgeoisie, who, according to Jane Gaines, considered themselves reputable "merely by virtue of having lived longer in the North,"[5] respectability was a precarious position threatened by their less-polished southern brethren. The filmmakers' response, especially since many of the migrants could neither read nor write, was to use film as a means of education and to create narratives espousing middle-class ideology. A cursory look at some of the early race film titles indicates this focus—*The Realization of a Negro's Ambition* (Lincoln, 1916), *A Giant of His Race* (North State, 1921), and *The Call of His People* (Reol, 1922). Critics soon recognized the pedagogical power of film; for example, Lester Walton of the *New York Age* observed in 1920 that the "screen is not only functioning as a great entertainment, but is great education as well. . . . It therefore is the duty of our own producers to gladden our hearts and inspire us by presenting characters typifying the better element of Negroes."[6] This legacy continues to influence African American film aesthetics today as many independent filmmakers in particular are drawn to film's overtly pedagogical and political potential.

While the growth of urban audiences played a crucial role in the production of silent race films, and could even be argued to be their raison d'être, the city itself was not the central narrative focus of the films. In other words, while many of the race film producers were based in urban areas—the Johnsons in Los Angeles, Foster in Chicago and then Los Angeles, Micheaux in Chicago and Harlem, The Colored Players in Philadelphia, and Reol in New York City—and were dealing with issues relevant to their urban audiences, city living was not really their subject matter. In fact, many of the early narratives in, for example, films like Micheaux's *The Symbol of the Unconquered* (1920) or Reol's *The Call of His People* focused on passing narratives that were not dependent on specific locations. Other films focused on advancement through hard work and industry. In these films the city was often simply background for the narrative, if it appeared at all. But sometimes the city appeared in cautionary tales warning against the evils of urban life. The view of the city as temptation or downfall was similar to the way in which the city functioned as threat in many of the black-cast musicals Hollywood produced between the 1920s and the 1940s, the difference being that in the Hollywood musicals the city would most often only enter and threaten the principally idyllic setting of the films. Two examples, Oscar Micheaux's *Within Our Gates* (1920) and The Colored Players' *The Scar of Shame* (1929), will illustrate the very different meanings of African American urbanscapes in race films from this time.

Oscar Micheaux stands apart from some of the more bourgeois race film producers like George and Noble Johnson, for example, who, after an unsuccessful attempt at securing the rights to one of Micheaux's novels, *The Homesteader*, dismissed him as a "rough Negro who got his hands on some cash."[7] Micheaux's career was longer than that of any other race film producer making films at this early time—in fact, it spanned from 1919 to the release of his ill-fated *The Betrayal* in 1948. One of the reasons for Micheaux's survival was his business acumen, which included his insistence on complete control over the production, distribution, exhibition, and marketing phases of his filmmaking. The Johnsons made almost a film a year between 1916 and 1922, all of which were "filled with individualist heroes, who promised blacks the hope of success and the conquest of despair."[8] In contrast, Micheaux's films were more controversial and drew criticism from both the white and African American middle classes. Whites objected because he took on such taboo subject matter as lynching (*Within Our Gates*) and the Ku Klux Klan (*The Symbol of the Unconquered*); black critics had similar objections and also were upset because Micheaux often directed critiques toward the black community (for instance, the black clergy in *Body and Soul*) or practiced a form of color casting (which was rampant throughout the production of race films, not simply Micheaux productions).

In many of Micheaux's early silent features the city is little more than background for melodramatic narratives. However, on occasion, the city's contradictory roles in African American life are suggested. *Body and Soul* (1925), for example, posits the city as both a refuge and a tomb for Isabelle, its shamed female protagonist. *Within Our Gates*, Micheaux's second feature following *The Homesteader* (1919), offers an even more compelling understanding of the role of the city in African American life and in film from this time period.[9] *Within Our Gates* is most often discussed in terms of the problems the director encountered because of the film's content and the recent discovery of the only extant print in Spain in 1990, but the film most clearly explores the shifting definitions of African American life at the moment it was produced, dialoguing with and refracting the actual world.

While Micheaux's films upheld bourgeois ideals of individualism and ambition, they were often the target of criticism from both black and white social and religious groups. *Within Our Gates* immediately came under fire when Micheaux planned to screen the film in Chicago in early 1920. Ostensibly a melodrama detailing the attempts of the heroine, Sylvia Landry (Evelyn Preer), to save an all-black southern school (Piney Woods) from insolvency, the narrative follows Sylvia from the South to Boston (replicating the migration of many middle-class African Americans) in search of philanthropists. In Boston, Sylvia meets both the worst and the best of the urban populace: a young black man who attempts to snatch her purse and a young doctor (Dr. Vivian), a member of the "Blue Vein Aristocrats," who retrieves her purse and with whom she eventually falls in love. Sylvia also meets a northern white suffragette and patron who eventually donates the needed money to the school. Most of the film is focused on this story; however, it is a backstory, tacked on near the end of the film, which was the cause of concern for Micheaux's critics. In this section Sylvia's lover, Dr. Vivian (Charles D. Lucas), learns that members of Sylvia's adopted family were the victims of a lynching in the South and that Sylvia herself is the product of an interracial relationship—which might have been a legitimate marriage. In this section Micheaux inserts images of the lynching, showing a crowd consisting of men, women, and children who plan and carry out the act over a few days. In addition to the political impact of the lynching itself, the inclusion of all genders and generations as part of the lynch mob throws doubt on the purity of southern white womanhood in particular. Moreover, the film includes a scene in which Sylvia is almost raped by a man who is ultimately revealed to be her father. Even with some confusing plot twists, the film's message is clear; unlike Griffith's version of events in *Birth of a Nation*, racially motivated violence directed at African Americans was often caused by economic jealousy or lust rather than any actual illegal acts perpetrated by its victims.

Within Our Gates was subject to especially vehement criticism in Chicago from both the African American and the white communities because of the continuing unrest caused by a wave of riots that had erupted on the city's predominantly black South Side the previous summer. In order to understand the fears sparked by the "riot-lynching linkage which characterized American race relations in the 1920s,"[10] one has to grasp the connection between southern racially motivated violence and the growth of northern urban areas. In fact, Lawrence Rodgers has identified lynching in particular as the "keynote incident" in many migration novels set in the city.[11] By the "Red Summer of 1919," Chicago's African American population had expanded threefold as migrants arrived daily from the Mississippi Delta region and other areas of the South in the classic push-pull of migration—fleeing southern poverty and violence and being pulled toward the promise of economic and social progress. At the time race relations were tense in Chicago due to a decline in suitable housing on the South Side (a result of the growing number of southern migrants), an increase in racially motivated incidents like the bombings of African American residences as blacks moved into traditionally white neighborhoods, and the continued resistance of white labor unions to black workers. When a young African American man was stoned to death in July for crossing an invisible, although very real, boundary line dividing the races on a city beach and the police stood by rather than apprehend the murderers, black Chicago erupted, resulting in thirty-eight deaths and hundreds of injuries. In this environment the fear was less that Micheaux's film, released in early 1920, would spark African American protest because of what had happened only months earlier and more that the film would stoke the rage smoldering in the community from even before these events. According to Gaines, "Micheaux's spectacle of lynching was rhetorically organized to encourage the feeling of righteous indignation in the Black spectator,"[12] not only directed at the horror of lynching in the South, but at the continuation of social, political, and economic inequalities in northern cities. In addition, this fear was not limited to Chicago. Other communities protested against the film and agitated for either its outright ban or the removal of "offensive" images.

Within Our Gates contains few actual scenes set in a city space, but what it says about the city and the representational power of black city spaces is the key to understanding its historical significance. First, the city is both salvation and damnation for African Americans, especially rural migrants. Sylvia is accosted while in the city and exposed to its "lower" elements, and yet Boston is where she succeeds in finding both the funding to save Piney Woods and a suitable husband.[13] Second, there is a link between the actual living conditions of urban areas and the spaces and narratives explored in the film. The fact that Micheaux's film spoke to the contemporary moment in Chicago (1919–1920) and this was considered enough of a threat that even the black bourgeoisie would call for censorship is an important early example of the connections between African American films' representation of urbanscapes and contemporary social protest, a connection that endures today. In the chapters that follow, I discuss how films responded to the "riot-lynching linkage" that continued in the 1970s and 1990s, and which connects films' power to spark indignation to the fear of urban rebellion.

Unlike *Within Our Gates*, a greater percentage of The Colored Players' *The Scar of Shame* takes place in an urban space and it offers a more cautionary narrative about the city than the former film, which for all its controversial content ends on a positive note when Sylvia reunites with Dr. Vivian and the two characters look forward to a post–World War I environment of hope and progress based on African American participation in the war. *The Scar of Shame*, on the other hand, is about the ill-fated marriage of Alvin Hillyard (Harry Henderson) and Louise Howard (Lucia Lynn Moses), who meet in a Philadelphia boarding house. The boarding house, in this film as well in literature from this time period, is often a space that brings together a cross-section of African American classes, from middle-class strivers to urban hustlers, a heteroglossia enabled by the movements and dislocations of the Great Migration. Alvin meets Louise when rescuing her from a beating at the hands of her stepfather, an alcoholic named Strike Howard (William E. Pettus). After delivering her from two more attacks, first by Strike and then by his friend Eddie Blake (Norman Johnstone), Alvin marries Louise. The result is a novel union that pairs Alvin's bourgeois blood and ambitions with Louise's less admirable family tree. In this marriage, the film implies, Alvin is saving Sylvia from her birthright.

The Scar of Shame is most commonly understood in terms of its caste—both color and class—dynamics. For example, Thomas Cripps argues that the film's tensions are clustered around class and that its narrative "affirmed and dramatized" the "new Negro ideal" that blacks from all walks of life could move into the black middle class as long as they worked hard enough.[14] Gaines offers a more compelling reading of the film, which falls into two lines of argument. First, she argues that the film's intertitles and narrative focus on the intraracial differences among blacks of different classes. On a more oblique, but just as important level, she reads the film, and especially its rendering of mise-en-scène, as a subtle critique of the color consciousness of both black society and race movies from the time.[15] In this latter argument,

Gaines identifies what she sees an "antagonism" between the deference for and the criticism of color cast,[16] which was directly connected to the preferences of the black middle classes.

Both of these arguments are provocative, but what is also interesting is the way in which the film, like *Within Our Gates*, charts the contradictory roles of the city in black life. Furthermore, *The Scar of Shame* achieves this by introducing an entirely novel set of oppositions to African American—and American—film: the differences between the city and the suburbs. While the film details the multifaceted environment in the expanding urban areas through the microcosm of the boarding house, whose occupants run the spectrum of African American subjectivity, it is not celebrating this as much as it is cautioning against what exists in the city. The narrative opposes this urban underworld, exemplified by Strike and Eddie, to suburban-inflected Alvin's lifestyle.

The film's emphasis on space is introduced in the very first frames in which a title card reads:

> Environment—Surroundings,—Childhood training and companions often is [sic] the deciding factor in our lives.—It shapes our destinies and guides our ambitions.—If early in life some knowing, loving hand, lights the lamp of knowledge and with tender care keeps it burning, then our course will run true 'til the end of our useful time on this earth, but, if that lamp should fail through lack of tender care, through lack of loving hands to feed its hungry flame—then will come sorrow and SHAME.

This strangely articulated opening conflates environment with education and aspiration, and these intertwined factors fuel the narrative. On the one hand, we have Alvin Hillyard, a pianist living in Mrs. Lucretia Green's "select" boarding house. Alvin embodies the aspirations of the black bourgeoisie; he is a skilled concert pianist who signifies high culture through his clothes, surroundings, and past times. Additionally, once he is fooled by Eddie into visiting his mother in Morton, a suburb outside Philadelphia, we learn that Alvin is also a product of this suburban environment and is therefore himself a new migrant to the city, there to acquire the necessary skills and contacts he needs to succeed.

On the other hand, Eddie and Strike are products of the city who frequent the very same underworld establishments that the bourgeoisie warned audiences against. Eddie's aspirations code him as "low class," as his business pursuits include operating a cabaret and enlisting Louise's help in some unspecified role that hints at prostitution. Strike's aspirations include nothing more than finding his next drink. Unfortunately,

Louise is shuttled between the two opposing forces: her desire to live a better life and her desire to get away from her stepfather. These forces consolidate in her relationship with Alvin even though she has very different roots. Louise, also a product of the city, seems to have the potential to change, but her only act of agency comes when she attempts to leave Alvin once she realizes that she'll never be accepted by "his set." However, even this attempt at agency is thwarted because both Eddie and Alvin interrupt her plans to flee.

One of the interesting characteristics of the film is the way in which it defines and presents black urban space. Its exterior shots, all filmed on location in Philadelphia, incorporate the city into the lives of the characters as they maneuver through its streets and alleyways. We are supplied with a vision of a dynamic African American cityscape of well-kept brownstones and tidy streets. This image is replicated in the exterior shots of the suburbs, again characterized by well-kept buildings and yards. While the narrative sets up a human opposition between these two places, in looks they are not that different. But what the suburbs lack are the bars, cabarets, and gambling dens of the city, the elements that define the urbanscape's bad environment and drag down individuals like Eddie, Strike, and, eventually, Louise.

The film uses interiors to define the differences between the city and the suburbs rather than relying on exterior shots. While initially both Alvin and Eddie live in Mrs. Green's boarding house, it is not long before Eddie is asked to leave because his behavior is deemed inappropriate (that is, not "select" enough). Alvin often appears in well-appointed interiors (in the boarding house and then in his studio)—environments befitting his status as a pianist and piano teacher, someone who is pursuing the "higher arts." Later in the narrative he is surrounded by the luxurious fittings of his future wife's suburban house. Eddie, however, is almost always placed in different settings, even when he is living in the boarding house. He is shown in the streets, in his bar, or later in his cabaret. Louise, whose status throughout the film changes, resides in both the boarding house, in "Alvin's world of neat, dull furniture,"[17] and then, after her downfall, in the lush rooms of the cabaret where she works. The film's contrast between city and suburban spaces makes an additional point about class. While neither Alvin nor Louise actually lives desirable lives, and, in fact, both options (middle class or working class) "appear as equally evil,"[18] the fact that Alvin survives and thrives while Louise dies points to the film's inevitable moral. Voiced by Louise's new lover Ralph Hathaway (Lawrence Chenault), we learn that Louise's urban environment kept her from achieving her aspirations.

This sort of antagonistic relationship between the bourgeoisie and the working classes existed in the treatment of urban subject matter by race film producers in the 1920s and by the poets, novelists, and artists affiliated with the Harlem Renaissance. Throughout the decade, what it meant to be a New Negro was to be associated with the city—according to Locke, Johnson, and W.E.B. DuBois—but it also meant being associated with an "elite" class of African American urban dweller, one who was educated, experienced, and belonging to what Walton identified earlier in this chapter as a "better element of Negroes." According to Rodgers, many of the Renaissance writers were reluctant to tap into the working-class or cabaret aspects of their environment because the individuals there did not possess "the same assimilationist goals and values" as their middle-class counterparts, who acted as "exemplary models of racial uplift."[19] And yet the existence of this "lesser" element could not be denied, as is most powerfully evidenced in Langston Hughes' poems and prose, including his lament from "The Negro Artist and the Racial Mountain," originally published in 1926:

> Let the blare of Negro jazz bands and the bellowing voice of Bessie Smith singing Blues penetrate the closed ears of the colored near-intellectuals until they listen and perhaps understand. Let Paul Robeson singing "Water Boy," and Rudolph Fisher writing about the streets of Harlem, and Jean Toomer holding the heart of Georgia in his hands, and Aaron Douglas drawing strange black fantasies cause the smug Negro middle class to turn from their white, respectable, ordinary books and papers to catch a glimmer of their own beauty.[20]

For Hughes, jazz, the blues, the urban North, and the rural South were all part of African American culture. Films like *The Scar of Shame*, as products of a bourgeois worldview, worked directly against Hughes' definition by indicting one element of urban society in order to agitate for a specific construction of the African American city—one that was middle-class, educated, and refined. A change of focus did not occur until the development of sound-era race films, which took a more celebratory approach to all aspects of urban life, if not for the reasons stated by Hughes then for economic necessity

Two events occurred in the late 1920s that had long-standing repercussions for independent African American film production. First was the transition to sound in 1927 with the release of *The Jazz Singer*. The film continued the legacy of minstrelsy first seen in the shorts of Edison and other early companies; however, it also influenced an almost immediate vogue for African American performances, especially those from singers and dancers because of the promise of an aural "harmony in general."[21] Entertainers from the cabaret and nightclub circuit, as well as performers in race films, were drawn into the production of "soundies," short musical performances made for specially equipped players such as *The St. Louis Blues* (1929) starring Bessie Smith as well as longer feature films, such as *Hallelujah*. Along with a slightly more liberal casting environment, enabled by the dual forces of the performers' popularity and post–World War I protests by the NAACP, Hollywood opened its doors to African American talent. Subsequently, race film producers had less talent with whom to work because they could not compete with Hollywood's salaries which, while still paltry, were extravagant in comparison to what the independent producers could pay.

The second event, the stock market crash of 1929, had longer-lasting effects on African American filmmaking and African American urban life in general. Race film companies were usually undercapitalized ventures, producing product on a film-by-film basis. Often companies did not survive the production of more than one film, and sometimes they didn't even make it to the successful release of a single film. In this already marginal industry, the effects of the Depression would prove devastating, with most producers going bankrupt. Additionally, theaters catering to all-black films and audiences were almost always financially unable to make the transition to sound, even before the crash. The effects of the Depression and sound technology on exhibition sites alone indicate the state of the industry in the early 1930s: in 1925, approximately 200 black-owned theaters were in existence; by 1942, only seven theaters owned and operated by blacks remained.[22] African American audiences could see black performers in Hollywood productions with better technical qualities, and they could see them in theaters wired for sound regardless of whether they had to sit in restricted seating or attend all-black screenings. The demand rose for films that could compete with the look and sound of Hollywood products, an exigency that would not be met until the second half of the 1930s and the beginning of the production of sound race films.

Gangsters, Cowboys, and Thieves:
Black Independent Sound Film

During the early 1930s, race film production decreased, with Micheaux one of the few remaining individuals making films—and then only with the help of outside financiers. Independent black film production entered a period of identity crisis, in which it struggled to redefine itself in the wake of economic, technological, and social changes.[23] Besides sound technology, post-1935 race films are distinguished from their predecessors in other significant ways. First, as has often been mentioned (and even more often lamented), race film producers shifted their focus from uplift melodramas, social dramas, and morality tales to adaptations of the already familiar Hollywood genres: the Western, the gangster film, the musical, the comedy, and the sports film. The primary purposes of films like *Dark Manhattan* (1937), a gangster film starring singer-dancer Ralph Cooper, were to entertain and to make a profit against the greater appeal of Hollywood releases. But gangster films in particular, and other genres as well, appealed to the sensibilities of the urban African American audience, which by this point made up a large percentage of its box office. The films addressed a spectatorship that was, according to Clyde Taylor, "urban, industrial, and modern," and they used familiar iconography to do so.[24]

Less identified with uplift discourses, the gangster films and Westerns in particular followed narrative conventions that had already been established by Hollywood and their similarities resulted in the gradual disappearance of the term "race movies." The films began to be defined in different ways, and were thought of in the same vein as the "B" films produced by independent production companies.[25] More telling nomenclature is used by Daniel Leab, who refers to the films as "ghetto films" more because of their projected audiences and exhibition venues than for their settings.[26] And yet what seems like a major difference is actually less so when the films are examined because many of them contained narrative lines similar to those in the earlier race films, supporting bourgeois values such as race pride and aspiration. What changed was the means by which success would come: the films tried "to include blacks in the American myth, through inclusion of the total subculture, rather than integration of individuals, thus suggesting larger contextual concerns toward desegregation."[27] As audiences migrated and transformed, they demanded more urban and therefore more contemporary onscreen images. Silent race films, and the worlds they imagined, were old-fashioned. There was an increasing consciousness among black intellectuals about "the effects of mass culture on black city dwellers. . . . By the 1930s, Hollywood film—that modern image of an earthly city based on material consumption—had become ubiquitous, a presence in black life that could not be ignored."[28] In fact, as the following discussion of *Dark Manhattan* will show, the newer sound films explore the tension between the "old school" approach and the "new way," thematic cruxes that reside at the root of many of the gangster films and that continue in later African American urban films.

Another important difference between the two time periods is the increased participation of white financiers and personnel in the 1930s. As mentioned earlier, many of the early race film companies accepted, with varying degrees of reluctance, the involvement of white money and personnel, including the films produced by The Colored Players, which had an African American frontman, Sherman Dudley, and all-white producers and technical crew behind the cameras. Yet their films, *Ten Nights in a Barroom* (1926) and *The Scar of Shame*, are considered to be models of silent race film production because of their stress on the ideals of the black bourgeoisie, which in many film historians' views was equated with a black aesthetic.[29] Richard Norman, of the highly respected Norman Film Manufacturing Company, is another example of a white filmmaker making silent race movies (for example, *The Flying Ace* [1926]) reflecting the ideology of the black bourgeoisie.[29] The later genre films, therefore, are thought of as abandoning racial uplift as well as a black aesthetic because of their dependence on white personnel and money. The problem with this line of argument is that it equates a black aesthetic solely with a middle-class aesthetic, leaving no room for considerations of the ways in which genre filmmakers adapted and changed generic conventions to fit their own aims, sometimes directly promoting uplift and sometimes promoting nothing more than profit.

A narrower focus on aesthetics is also prejudiced toward the director because it overlooks the important role that African American producers, performers, and writers played in the production of sound race films. Black producers and stars had a strong voice in the films they developed, even though white money and personnel might have been involved. Ralph Cooper, for example, and his partner George Randol joined forces in 1937 to make *Dark Manhattan*. The pair collaborated with Harry and Leo Popkin, West Coast entrepreneurs, to form Million

Dollar Productions after *Dark Manhattan*, and they continued to work together producing gangster vehicles until 1939. Throughout his association with Million Dollar Productions, Cooper was listed as the general manager on the masthead, perhaps, as with Dudley's experiences, acting like nothing more than a front man. But Cooper was also the star of his films and had a direct interest in his screen image, a concern that ultimately caused him to break with Randol and Million Dollar Productions in order to move away from gangster films.[30] A slightly different situation occurred with the series of Westerns produced between 1937 and 1939 starring Herb Jeffries. Made first for producer Jed Buell and then for Richard Kahn, the films starred established African American performers whose resumés included appearances in both race and Hollywood films. One of the films in the series, *Harlem Rides the Range* (1939), for example, was co-scripted by Spencer Williams and Flournoy E. Miller; the former soon established himself as a race film director, a career that continued into the mid-1940s. Overall it is difficult for the historian to determine influence when there were so many personalities involved. What can be stated is that race films changed more as a response to industrial and economic factors than to shifts in the ideology of the race film industry.

But if the films also continue certain seminal themes, what was it about them that caused critics to despair and to claim that "all-colored films are our own worst enemy" at the time of their release?[31] Even in present-day histories of African American film, this valuative attitude remains, if the genre films are discussed at all.[32] The seeds of what appears to be a critical prejudice can be located, again, in the films' differences from their predecessors: they aped Hollywood films, and they were made with the involvement of whites. What I believe is the foundation of some historians' blind spots is the fact that, like the notion of African American urban space as an "earthly city of material consumption," the films were made for "mere" entertainment and profit rather than for edification. It appears as though the shift toward genre filmmaking, a less explicitly "political" form of production, was and still is considered a less noble endeavor.[33] Moreover, it cannot be overlooked that even if they were not continuing bourgeois definitions of a black aesthetic, for several years the films were popular and spoke to many facets of their audiences' experiences. They therefore can illuminate the changing role of the race film in African American popular culture. In the remainder of this chapter, I focus on two examples of this group of films in order to examine the ways in which they construct a certain vision of African American urban life, "shaped by a vast culture of migrants, poor but in place, rather than a relatively small orbit of writers, intellectuals, and artists."[34] In short, the films speak to the contemporary moment in Harlem in ways previously unseen by audiences of either race films or Hollywood's black-cast musicals.

"Black Manhattan—What a Place!": *Dark Manhattan* and the Harlem Chronotope

Throughout the 1920s and spurred along by the literary achievements of a coterie of writers and artists, Harlem was equated with a promised land, a mythology based more on legend than on fact, and which functioned "as the embodiment of an idea" that challenged the "contemporary limits and cultural terms within which personal being for both blacks and whites were [sic] imagined and defined." Harlem represented new possibilities for self-definition for thousands of migrants of all classes who shifted to the area to create new lives. Harlem had a particular appeal to writers that

> lay not in its distinctive details of setting but in its power as a sign. . . .
> The impulse of the first literary generations employing the motif was to
> regard black Harlem as a trope, a received cultural artifact for a writer's
> imaginative re-making as if only through figurative elaboration could
> the novel idea of a great black city in the very heart of America's premier
> metropolis begin to be comprehended and conveyed.[35]

Harlem was the embodiment of an idea, a sign, a motif, and a trope, all of which combined to create a fictive image of a city space through which the possibilities of an African American urban metropolis could exist in the public imagination.

At the same time that Harlem was being elaborated as a crucial African American space in the novels, short stories, and verse of the Harlem Renaissance writers, the urbanscape was curiously absent from either silent race films or Hollywood films from the 1920s. Race films that explored the conditions of the city might have been a means of edification for newly arrived migrants, and yet Harlem was not a named urban space in film to the same extent that it existed in literature. Harlem was an even rarer presence in Hollywood, appearing in *Stormy Weather* of all the black-cast musicals and then not until 1943. This did not change in race films until the late 1930s and the shift to genre production. Ironically, this development coincided with the effects of the Depression, resulting in the deterioration of the actual space of Harlem "into a slum whose abject living conditions would come to embody the continued disenfranchisement of black America."[36] At this point many of the writers of the 1920s had stopped producing, and nothing had come along to fill the void.[37]

With the production of two genres in particular, gangster films and Westerns, we see the continuation from literature to film of the use of Harlem as a trope, an expansion that incorporates certain temporal elements of immediacy, creating a Harlem chronotope that continued throughout the remaining years of race film productions and reappeared again in the 1960s and 1970s. One of the characteristics of this early cinematic Harlem, which has its roots in the silent films set in city spaces, is the acknowledgment of an African American city space that is contemporary with the urban audience's immediate surroundings. In the 1930s, black audiences "hungered for urbanity . . . and sought modernity."[38] Genre films like Ralph Cooper's *Dark Manhattan* obliged by conjoining the urban with the urbane, often through the use of contemporary fashions (not work clothes), urban slang (not rural dialect), and the performance of contemporary music (not spirituals). Besides offering a means of competing with the Hollywood-produced black-cast musicals, the musical performances provided the films with a cultural cachet by calling on the appeal of Harlem's cabaret scene.[39]

When Ralph Cooper joined George Randol in 1937 to produce *Dark Manhattan*, he was no stranger to the entertainment industry, having performed on the stage as a dancer, a singer, and an emcee at the Apollo Theater before moving from New York to Hollywood. Initially contracted to star opposite Shirley Temple, it was decided that the "sleek, bronzed" actor "just wasn't the type"[40] to pair up with the child actress, especially considering that Temple's usual partner was Bill Robinson, who connoted a different time and place through his performance style.[41] Cooper was younger and more hip, and projected an urban and sensual image of African American life, an obvious challenge to Hollywood producers who continued to cast black performers in subservient and often backward roles. After remaining under contract for a short time, Cooper tried to interest Hollywood in the production of all-black films. When the studios showed no interest, he began producing films for himself. Shortly thereafter, Cooper and his company joined with the Popkin brothers' Million Dollar Productions, where Cooper eventually starred in two more gangster films, *Bargain With Bullets* (1938) and *Gang War* (1939), and in a relatively successful musical opposite Lena Horne, *The Duke is Tops* (1938), before breaking with the Popkins and gangster films as a whole.[42]

Cooper's *Dark Manhattan* was not only responsible for ushering in a new style of race film, it was also, as its press releases announced, "the first all-colored cast motion picture with modern story, setting and costumes,"[43] therefore underscoring the precise means by which a contemporary black city space would appear on screen. The action was set in Harlem, and the characters articulate the language and wear the fashion popular at the time. In fact, many of the genre films

> introduced a new rhythm to American cinema. Vocal inflections and intonations set the ears abuzz. The manners, gestures, postures, surprising double takes, swift interplay and communication between the characters is a world unto itself, capturing, despite whatever other distortions or failings, a segment of black American life and culture.[44]

This was a far cry from Hollywood films featuring black casts who were forced to speak in dialect and wear the work clothes of rural sharecroppers even when the entertainers (for example, Lena Horne and Ethel Waters) neither spoke nor dressed this way and signified contemporary performance modes in their association with urban cabaret scenes in Harlem and Chicago. Compared to *The Green Pastures*, released the year before (1936) and set in an heavenly and historically static antebellum idyll, *Dark Manhattan* was modern.

The story follows the conventions of the gangster film in which a slum kid rises through the ranks of a crime organization before experiencing a downfall caused by greed and hubris. Curly Thorpe (Cooper) is promoted from an inconsequential underling to a trusted assistant by L. B. Lee (Clarence Muse), the "squarest numbers banker in Harlem." The differences between the two men, and therefore the conflicts that structure the narrative, become apparent when Curly appears for his first day of work wearing inappropriately flashy attire, a fact commented upon by more than one person in Lee's sedate offices, and laughed at by Lee's girlfriend, a sophisticated cabaret singer. In one of the first exchanges between Curly and Lee, the pair's ideological differences are laid out: Lee's business ethic is based on hard work and a code of morals while Curly has no scruples and even openly admits to being willing to do "whatever it takes" to get ahead. The tension between the two in-

Dark Manhattan promotional poster (Million Dollar Productions, 1937).
Courtesy of the Black Film Center/Archive, Indiana University.

creases until the older Lee falls ill and Curly not only takes over the business, but also takes Lee's girl Flo Grey (Cleo Hernden). Curly's comeuppance is based in part on his own hubris, following the model of Howard Hawks' *Scarface* (1932), but his biggest mistake will be that he breaks with the bankers' association, a business alliance of all the numbers bankers in the city. In other words, he is punished for breaking with the community.

Critics have dismissed *Dark Manhattan* by claiming that its "black vision consisted of [nothing more than] its cast, its precise duplication of a segregated city, and its attempt to depict a small group of blacks in power,"[45] but the film deserves more in-depth analysis. First, it acknowledges a contemporary and heteroglot urban black population consisting of gangsters, business owners, cabaret performers, and everyday people. Second, *Dark Manhattan* offers a detailed exposition of the solidarity of the numbers bankers, a group that acts as a metaphor for African American solidarity as a whole and as a reference to the history of black social movements and the figure of the race man in particular. Lee is presented as an honest and hardworking businessman, even if he is a numbers banker and, therefore, a criminal. Lee is a leading member of the bankers' group, and he conducts his business peacefully with little or no disruption to community life. Curly, on the other hand, is selfishly ambitious; he is punished for this and for rejecting the community for his own individual interests (even if this, ironically, contradicts uplift discourse). Furthermore, the solidarity suggested by the bankers' association might be a reference to the rising influence of the Communist Party in African American city life during the 1930s, an influence described in Richard Ellison's *Invisible Man*, written a decade later but focusing on a similar time frame as the film. Either way, the bankers' group is presented as a legitimate business organization looking out for its own interests and, by relation, those of the community. This pattern recurs in other gangster films, for example, Cooper's *Gang War* and even more explicitly in Edgar Ulmer's *Moon Over Harlem* (1940).

While the temporal dynamics embodied by the Harlem setting tell us a lot about attitudes toward the city at the time, things become even more compelling in the film's construction of city space. Since D. W. Griffith's *The Musketeers of Pig Alley* (1912), the city has functioned as a formal prerequisite for the gangster genre. In the black gangster film, like the Hollywood gangster films and Westerns, we see a "melding of legendary, ritual themes, aspirations, solidarity and pride, set in immediately identifiable locales."[46] In Hollywood gangster films, that setting was most often Chicago and New York. These locations continued to appear in race movies with some variations: Harlem becomes the primary location of the films with a few exceptions, most notably Micheaux's *Underworld* (1936) set in black Chicago. But while the films followed genre conventions fairly faithfully, it is instructive to look at just how they imagined Harlem. While *Dark Manhattan* announces its setting as Harlem, it was neither shot on location nor did it provide many exterior shots of what could be recognized as the area's streets. Instead, it relied on the fact that Harlem was immediately identifiable, if not in image then certainly in word and legend.

At this point it is instructive to return momentarily to the dynamics of the race movie industry from this time. Unlike the silent film producers, who were located throughout the country and often inhabited studio spaces abandoned by white companies, sound film producers were mostly located on the West Coast, adjunct to the major studios. While many of the films were either advertised or discussed upon their release as Hollywood or Black Hollywood films, it was because they were being made in *proximity* to Hollywood, not that they were being made *by* Hollywood. Cooper and Million Dollar Productions were no exception to this rule. Already undercapitalized—for example, the premiere of *Dark Manhattan* was delayed because Cooper and Randol didn't have the $13,000 needed to obtain the print from the processing lab—race film producers worked on minimal budgets and short shooting schedules, hardly enough capital or time to allow them to move cast and crew to shoot on location in Harlem.[47]

Despite the absence of present-day Harlem, everything else about *Dark Manhattan*, including its title, announces its location. The film is apparently set in Harlem, with a few scenes in other locations in Manhattan, all of which are unspecified except for the fact that they are "downtown." The film's establishing shot is a sign advertising Lee's business offices but without an address, and it is not until the next scene that the offices' location is established through dialogue rather than mise-en-scène. Yet setting is important to the narrative because it is not solely generational or stylistic differences that create the tension between Curly and Lee. Midway through the film, Curly explains his ambitions to Flo by acknowledging, calling out, geography: as a kid growing up in what he calls "the jungle" (a neighborhood downtown), Curly had nothing. Moving north to Harlem and into Lee's confidence is both a literal and a symbolic rise: he ascends the organization's ranks and his success allows him access to the people (Flo) and places (Harlem) previously out of reach. His literal migration to Harlem is therefore successful and is metaphorically indicated in Curly's progress from the pool room where he is first seen, to Club Congo where Flo performs; in the change of Curly's working-class outfit of floppy hat and dark jacket, to top hat and tails; and even in the difference between Curly's impromptu song and dance in the pool hall and Flo's fully orchestrated performance in the nightclub. Curly's story, therefore, metaphorically adheres to the idealized migration stories familiar to spectators in the audience with the distinction that most spectators would not be enjoying similar material success.

Almost every scene in the film occurs in interior settings, and for this reason also the city space is established symbolically rather than visually. There are only a few breaks from this pattern and, still, they tell us very little about the urbanscape; for example, there are multiple long shots of the building in which Lee's offices are housed. In these shots the only visible landmarks are the entrance to the building, the sign, and a few other nondescript storefronts. The location could be anywhere from a street in Los Angeles or Kansas City to a studio backlot because there is nothing that makes it specifically "Harlem." Later in the film, while Curly is being pursued by members of a rival gang, a chase ensues through the city streets. Again, there are no distinguishing landmarks and, in fact, the buildings and houses in the background resemble Los Angeles more than Harlem. (Even when it was principally pastureland, Harlem was not known for its single-family bungalows!)

Similarly, in many of the other gangster films from the time, Harlem exists indirectly in the narrative, even if it enables it. When the city appears, it is normally either in montage sequences or in traveling shots used to establish space. It is very rare to see characters interact with one another in recognizable places or in actual locations, as in *The Scar of Shame*. *Gang War*, for example, includes an inserted dolly shot of a street that appears to be in Harlem, or at least some of the signs on the storefronts place it there (for example, Harlem Seafood Lunch, an actual diner from the time). Later, when a group of gangsters goes out on the town, their exploits are intercut with Harlem club signs, the Montecarlo and the Savoy, for example, which anchor their actions in a particular location. But this attempt at verisimilitude is undercut by other portions of the film, usually chase scenes, in which the cityscape again appears to be a part of Los Angeles rather than New York City, a fact, like in *Dark Manhattan*, that is given away by the background architecture. Only a slightly later film, *Moon Over Harlem*, attempts to include the city more fully in the narrative. For example, the film opens with a nighttime establishing shot of 125th Street with the Apollo Theater, the Savoy, and the Baumans signs illuminated in the distance. These shots are repeated, along with street scenes and shots of the elevated subway at night. But, like in the other films, characters neither appear nor do actions occur in these settings.

The absence of Harlem's actual streets and buildings is only a partial indication of the financial, aesthetic, and technical constraints faced by many production companies.[48] It also suggests a facet of this city space that was indicated in the earlier discussion of Harlem's role in Renaissance literature, and that is the power "Harlem" possessed as a sign. Harlem's appeal was not so much that it was an actual space as much as what it suggested for the possibilities of redefinition for individuals, for the African American community, and for American society as a whole. Curly's move up to Harlem is his attempt to better himself, to redefine himself from slum kid to a respected member of society. The film adheres to generic conventions by punishing him for his hubris in the end. But the film is not that different from *The Scar of Shame* in suggesting that it might be Curly's background in the jungle that prevents his success in Harlem and (even more important) in its warnings against inappropriate behavior. In this way, *Dark Manhattan* is just as much an uplift melodrama as *The Scar of Shame*.

Harlem's status as a sign in many of the gangster films from this time is further supported by the way in which the city space is celebrated and yet frozen in time, the effect of which is that "Harlem" connotes a contemporary time frame, but what that means is vague, resulting in what can only be understood as a series of temporal delays. The first delay is in the exclusion of any acknowledgment of the effects of New Negro ideology in Harlem. Alain Locke's anthology, *The New Negro*, was first printed in 1925, and its values and (even more important) language of aspiration and redefinition had flooded African American literature and print journalism throughout the 1920s and 1930s. Yet, besides Lee, who might survive in *Dark Manhattan* but who is, along with the other numbers bankers, almost impotent compared to Curly, there is no sense of how the characters are influenced by a New Negro ideology, which "was taking on mass proportions in the '30s and, in the Northern cities particularly."[49] Furthermore, even the bankers' call for solidarity might be a sign of either the New Deal politics or communist ideology prevailing at the time rather than any race discourses in particular. In *Gang War*, a film in which a jukebox syndicate functions in a manner similar to that of the bankers' alliance in *Dark Manhattan*, the groups' members also do not articulate New Negro discourses. In fact, New Negro values will only appear in *Moon Over Harlem*, where they are a running theme throughout the film; for example, one of the main characters, Bob, is specifically identified as a race man whose goals are to unite Harlem's honest people in a fight against (both black and white) racketeers. For Bob, "Black Manhattan . . . What a Place!" is filled with potential. In *Dark Manhattan*, Harlem's celebratory aspects are relied upon for cultural, although not political, meaning.

The second temporal exclusion is *Dark Manhattan*'s lack of acknowledgment of the actual economic and social circumstances enveloping Depression-struck Harlem, which by the 1930s had been severely crippled and robbed of whatever potential it might have possessed. All of the gangster films, even if they focused on the underworld, still reveled in the idea, expressed by Bob in *Moon Over Harlem*, that Harlem was a place of unlimited possibilities. This same attitude fuels Curly's ambition in *Dark Manhattan*, even if the promise is for personal economic gain. But the film's focus on the celebratory facets of the city—and this includes its nightclubs and cabarets—fails to acknowledge the more negative aspects of the place, especially those brought on or magnified by the Depression. As Jervis Anderson quotes, "The *Herald Tribune* reported in February of 1930 that the stock market collapse had 'produced five times as much unemployment in Harlem as in other parts of the city.' In the summer of 1934, more than 19,000 Harlem families were on home relief."[50] Additionally, Harlem experienced a riot in 1935, the result of rising tensions due to the unemployment, price inflation, and police brutality experienced by residents of the community. Granted, it was not to be expected that films aimed at entertainment would address such issues, and certainly Hollywood's renovation of the Western and the musical genres in the late 1930s suggests an overall escapist desire. Yet the films' claims to contemporaneity and their self-conscious announcement of place would suggest some acknowledgment of the area's present economic conditions. Again, it was *Moon Over Harlem*, rather than *Dark Manhattan* and the other Cooper gangster films, which did this. Perhaps this was because *Moon Over Harlem* was made by a European émigré, Edgar Ulmer, who was not as familiar with Harlem as Cooper (and did not feel a responsibility to the area), but it appears more to be a matter of narrative: many of the gangster films focus exclusively on a criminal milieu whereas *Moon Over Harlem* focuses equally on racketeers and the people most affected by them, privileging the point-of-view of the latter over the former.

Gangster films like *Dark Manhattan* were successful in mapping the spatiotemporal contours of Harlem in the 1930s. In such a construction, the space utilized by the films is more a motif than it is a realistic duplication of the streets of the actual city. In these films Harlem connotes a multiplicity of meanings, including the potential for transformation and growth. More important, Harlem also symbolizes a new, modern, and vital black population rather than, as in Hollywood's black-cast musicals, a static rural community existing outside the contemporary moment. While it might seem that such a sense of time and place would be part of the generic conventions of the gangster film, this particular spatiotemporal construction also influenced the musicals, comedies, and, most surprisingly, the Westerns made by race film companies at the time.

From Harlem to the Wild West: Harlem Motifs in the Western

Of the early genres, it is perhaps the gangster film and the Western that are the most dependent on place. In the gangster film, the urban space enables the hero's rise and eventual fall because the urban environment of the early twentieth century facilitated the transformation from newly arrived immigrant to "American" or from one class to another. For African American gangsters, Harlem possessed symbolic meaning as a transformative site. The Western is also reliant on geography, so much so that it derives its name from both the actual, although vague, coordinates in which its films are set and the metaphorical impact of this geography on national legend. For Edward Buscombe, the Western "is not merely a milieu or a way of life, but another world, or at least another country."[51] In African American Westerns the genre's iconography plays a complex role. Already occupying a separate world by virtue of belonging to a segregated industry, black Westerns "tapped the mythic base of the United States, drew on the mainstream of American popular culture, and . . . gave Negroes a place within it."[52] Because the films created another world, the genre was used by race film producers to narrate tales of African American aspiration and, even more important, ownership and settlement of the land in ways not seen in previous race films or supplied in the slave and sharecropping narratives produced by Hollywood (but that had appeared in Hollywood-produced Westerns).[53]

The release of sound Westerns was not the first time that race film producers experimented with the genre. Early in the 1920s, the Norman Film Manufacturing Company released two silent films featuring Bill Pickett, *Crimson Skull* (1921) and *The Bull-Dogger* (1923), both of which combined the conventions of more than one genre but relied on the overwhelming appeal of the Western. This can be seen in the advertising for *Crimson Skull*, as the production poster claimed, a "Baffling Western Mystery" filmed on location in the "All-Colored City of Boley, Oklahoma." Additionally, many of Micheaux's films from *The Homesteader* on also looked to the West, replicating Micheaux's own autobiography. For example, while *The Symbol of the Unconquered* is most often discussed regarding either Micheaux's rendering of the Ku Klux Klan or its passing story, it is just as noteworthy for its explication of the experiences of homesteaders in the American West.[54] With the change to sound, however, the Western disappeared until it was resurrected in a series of films starring nightclub performer Herb Jeffries.

Like the Cooper gangster films, the Jeffries' Westerns were made between 1937 and 1939. The films, in an attempt to appeal to the biggest audience possible, are generic hybrids like the Norman Company films from the 1920s. Billed as "Western Musicals," they featured performances by Jeffries, the Four Tones, the Four Blackbirds, and vaudevillians Flournoy E. Miller, Manton Moreland, and Spencer Williams. Also, Jeffries' character was modeled after other singing cowboys, like Gene Autry and Tex Ritter, who were at the height of their popularity in the late 1930s. As well as indicating a high point in African American production as a whole, the production of black Westerns was part of an all-around increase in the production of Westerns during the late 1930s, most specifically indicated by the release of John Ford's *Stagecoach* in 1939 and thirty other prestige Westerns between 1939 and 1941.[55] Furthermore, all the films in the series were marketed to a crossover audience, a rarity in race film production, but an indication of both the appeal of the genre and the increasing integration of audiences that occurred on the eve of World War II.

The four Jeffries films can be divided into two groups, the first film produced by Jed Buell and distributed by Associated Features in 1937, and the remaining films produced by Richard C. Kahn's Hollywood Pictures and distributed by Sack Amusement Enterprises in 1938–1939. While Buell's film, *Harlem on the Prairie*, introduced the series of "sepia cowboys" and is important for its use of the trope of "Harlem" in its title, the remaining Kahn films form the core of the series. The first of these, *Two Gun Man From Harlem* (1938), introduced the characters and the story lines that continued throughout the remaining films, *The Bronze Buckaroo* (1939) and *Harlem Rides the Range* (1939). In each of the Kahn films Jeffries plays a heroic wandering cowboy named Bob Blake who, along with assorted sidekicks, helps protect land holdings and save assorted damsels in distress.

While a series of Westerns would seem a strange focus in a discussion geared toward examining the construction of city spaces in film, it is important that we consider the ways in which the Harlem chronotope functions in the films as a motif, an "aura" of another genre, or as a reminder of another place and time.[56] While Harlem appears in the titles of three of the Westerns, it only shows up as an actual space in one, *Two Gun Man From Harlem*. In this film, Blake (Jeffries), falsely accused of murder, flees east to Harlem before returning home and subsequently clearing his name. In all of the other films, it is unclear whether the Harlem of the title is intended to refer to Jeffries' character or to the entire cast. What is clear, however, is that through the 1920s and the 1930s the city, Harlem in particular, had developed an important temporal function, signifying modernity. As such, the use of "Harlem" in the titles was intended to be read as a sign for a contemporary black space and presence, thus satisfying two needs: the need for updated black images on screen and the need for a "hook" that would draw audiences into the theaters. If a New Negro was a city Negro, then the city Negro was a Harlem Negro. By utilizing the motif of Harlem, the films create an immediacy of time frame in a genre that was, until the 1960s, almost exclusively associated with the past. Like *Dark Manhattan*, *Two Gun Man From Harlem* is indisputably modern.

To understand the particular ways in which Harlem functions as a motif in this group of films, it is important to examine two things: casting choices and the appearance of the area as an actual space in *Two Gun Man From Harlem*, for both indicate the ways in which the films are just as contemporary as the gangster films produced at the same time. First, it is unclear who was primarily responsible for Jeffries' involvement in the films. While Buell was the first to cast him in *Harlem Rides the Range*, in interviews, Jeffries claimed that the idea of a series of black Westerns that would provide role models for African American boys was his.[57] Regardless of the idea's provenance, Jeffries brought name recognition to the films because he already possessed an established reputation as a vocalist for the Earl Hines Band, a group that had traveled the cabaret and nightclub circuits on both coasts, and for Duke Ellington's Band. Unlike the silent cowboy Bill Pickett, who was an actual cowboy, Jeffries could boast of credentials that included being a performer associated with urban forms of entertainment, a fact pointed out by the press for *Harlem on the Prairie*: "The cast is an interesting cross-section of the upper crust of Los Angeles' South Central Avenue's Negro District" as well as veterans of Broadway.[58] As this indicates, this was also the case with most of the other performers in the film, who brought with them, like Moreland and Miller, name recognition from the stage and screen.

Jeffries' celebrity as a cabaret performer is interesting when he is compared to other singing cowboys of the time. In his history of the singing cowboy in film, Peter Stanfield argues that performers like Gene Autry came from a musical tradition that "had its roots in the rural South" rather than the western frontier. According to Stanfield, the musical forms used by singing cowboys in film arose out of the performance modes, such as yodeling, associated with blackface minstrelsy and southern rural folk music.[59] Autry's films, as an extension of his music, "addressed the difficulties his audience confronted in making the socio-economic change from subsistence farming to a culture of consumption, from self-employment to industrial practices and wage dependency, from rural to urban living. . . . Autry's films represent a confrontation, magnified by the Great Depression, with modernity."[60] But while for black migrants the overwhelming issue they continued to confront upon moving North was race, for many poor white migrants the issue was class, and the predominant form of southern rural music, country music, went through a process of stripping itself of any derogatory connotations from its redneck or hillbilly past. The singing cowboys' performances offered a sanitized and modernized version of rural southern performance modes that "carried none of the overt race or class connotations of the hillbilly or his White Trash cousin."[61] While white musical Westerns allowed for a certain form of nostalgia for a now-sanitized past, that nostalgia was absent in the Jeffries' performances because they utilized contemporary jazz-based rhythms and his presence fully signified modernity even in the Western setting. There is no nostalgia in Jeffries' films, just a celebration of contemporary urban performance modes.

The temporal immediacy in the Jeffries films was fueled by the fact that, even though the narratives could have been set at any point in the movement west (usually the nineteenth century), the film's fashions and dialogue place it in the contemporary moment of the late 1930s. While all the male characters are outfitted in cowboy clothing, including boots and wide-brimmed hats, the women wear fashions (particularly knee-length dresses) from the immediate moment rather than the past. Additionally, whereas Hollywood was making all-black films that almost always utilized vernacular, all of the films in the series were marked by an absence of dialect spoken by their main characters, a fact noted by more than one reviewer: as Leab quotes, "An Atlanta review of *Harlem Rides the Range* pointed out that its 'actors pretty much talked like other folks' and, to use *Variety*'s words, 'colored audiences like[d] to see themselves treated in the same manner as white folks.' "[62] The cast rarely even spoke in "Western dialect," instead mixing it with more contemporary slang, resulting in a "stylish way in which Western lingo and manner . . . blended with the cool vigor of the ad lib black talk."[63] Not only were African American cowboys modern, they were also urban and cool.

Besides the title, Harlem only appears in *Two Gun Man From Harlem*, which like *Dark Manhattan*, constructs a city space that is symbolic rather than actual. Once Blake is wrongly accused of murder, he heads east, first to Chicago and then to New York. The first indication that we are moving out of the boundaries of the Western is that Blake hitchhikes east rather than riding his horse, Stardusk, as if suggesting that a different, mechanized mode of transportation is more appropriate for his trip into the city. Two other changes also signify the shift in setting: first, screen movement, which had heretofore been primarily right-to-left, switches to left-to-right. This will be the direction and angle of all shots from Blake's first hitchhiking to the introduction of Harlem's nightclub space. The second change is that Blake, who had been part of his environment while in the West, disappears from the space in the montage sequence between the West and Harlem. While simply a function of the montage sequence and the use of what was undoubtedly stock

Two Gun Man From Harlem promotional poster (Sack Amusement Enterprises, 1939). Courtesy of Separate Cinema Archive™.

footage, it also removes Blake from the intervening spaces, locating him solely on the frontier or in the city and minimizing the experience of actual migration.

Harlem's city space is introduced in the film gradually through the montage sequence, with points called out along the route of Blake's trip: Chicago, New York, Harlem. This is accomplished through titles superimposed over nighttime long shots of urban street scenes. As Blake nears his final destination, the titles grow in size, with Harlem, HARLEM, virtually shouting its presence on screen. Besides the titles of this series of films, this moment probably best exemplifies the way in which Harlem acts as a motif rather than an actual space. While Harlem is more significant than Chicago or even New York in the narrative, it is the size of its name that matters, not the actual shots in the background, as the long shots establishing space for both Chicago and Harlem are exact duplicates. While this may be nothing more than Kahn's way of using stock footage to economize, nevertheless it points out the importance of suggesting the space through signs rather than through actual location shooting, a convention that will continue, in expanded form, in later decades. Unlike the gangster films, the Westerns were actually shot on location, at Murray's Dude Ranch in Victorville, California. Once the story switches to the city, the location shooting ends and the city is a set.

After the introductory title, the city of Harlem is introduced with a song and dance act performed in a nightclub setting. Like the change in location shooting, there is an overall shift in technique as the performer is framed in a medium shot with a static camera. Except for a few cutaways to Blake in the audience, there is very little camera or subject movement (everything is filmed to appear in the center of the frame). The Harlem sequence officially starts with this performance and, along with lasting a short six minutes in a sixty-minute film referencing its name, is set entirely within the nightclub space. This setting allows for the addition of musical numbers, similar to the cabaret sequences in the gangster films, an additional draw for audiences. Surprisingly, there is very little change in musical style between the performances in the city and the performances on the range because the vocal styles of the Four Tones, who accompany Jeffries at the beginning of the film, and the Four Blackbirds, who appear here, are almost exact. What these similarities accomplish, however, is to connect the frontier to the city.

Two Gun Man From Harlem and *Dark Manhattan* are similar in the transformative potential suggested by their Harlem settings. Once in the city, Blake meets the Deacon, a Harlem gangster and killer who, as his name suggests, wears the clothes of a Church-going man. The Deacon also bears a remarkable resemblance to Blake. While it is unclear how or why Blake decides to impersonate the Deacon, he returns to the range disguised as such and prepares to clear his name. Using the Deacon's notoriety, he manages to reveal the true identity of the killer and win the girl Betty (Margaret Whitten) in the end. Even though this ending shares its simplicity of resolution with many other B-Westerns (African American and white) produced at the time, it again points to the possibilities for redefinition promised by Harlem. It is only after Blake has reached Harlem that he formulates a plan, and it is only after he transforms—and takes on urban characteristics—that he succeeds in both clearing his name and pursuing romance.

If we agree with Buscombe's view that B-Westerns, even if they include a placename in the title, "operate in a fantasy no-man's-land in which specific geographical reference is subordinate to plot and action,"[64] then the fact that Harlem appears in the titles and narratives of the Jeffries' films is insignificant. But Buscombe's observation overlooks the specific place that is being called out in these African American Westerns and Harlem's resonance for the audience for which the films were made; in short, he doesn't account for the ways in which an African American context influences generic conventions. Stanfield is more accurate, even if he's speaking of the appeal of Westerns to white migrants, when he states that the "Western proved to be solid and familiar enough to be understood by all and fluid enough to contain all kinds of contradictory messages. More than anything, the Western provided a home for those who felt dispossessed and dislocated."[65] By referencing Harlem, the Jeffries Westerns prompted a chain of signifiers that were already familiar to African American audiences. While the use of Harlem as a motif might have been nothing more than an appeal to urban audiences as a means of making a profit, it also, by calling on the spatiotemporal characteristics of a contemporary urbanscape, confirmed its audience's transformation from rural farmers to urban industrial workers. The films addressed their audiences in the present tense, and in doing so, affirmed the redefinition of African Americans from static and ahistorical to vibrant and modern, a redefinition that had already been addressed in literature but which lagged in filmmaking.

As the United States geared up for entry into World War II, race film producers faced another crisis. Raw film stock began to be parceled out by the Office of War Information, and independent producers suffered in comparison to the studios which, as a means of economic survival, began to produce war films. Additionally, the political climate was altering, and race films began to fall out of favor because they were viewed as vestiges of Jim Crow in a society that was moving toward desegregation. By the end of the war, the production of race films had all but ceased, with most producers moving rapidly into other areas of production or dropping out altogether and the studios providing some opportunities for African American personnel in, especially, the production of "problem pictures." It was at least two more decades before black city spaces again appeared on screen, as highly transformed settings, shot on location and signifying very different messages than the Harlem motifs used in early sound-era race films. But what we see in the early African American genre films is an attempt to place black visual narratives in the contemporary city, a space and time that was familiar to their audiences.

3

Cotton in the City: The Black Ghetto, Blaxploitation, and Beyond

All over the country, in key areas of city after city, black people dominate in numbers; and the general opinion is that within a few years they will dominate to a degree that will make them the persons who matter in those areas.

—C.L.R. James (1970)[1]

The release of *Stormy Weather* in 1943 was the beginning of Hollywood's shift from the segregated geography and the static etiology of the antebellum idyll toward a more apparently integrated cinema. This shift resulted less from an overt desire to change than from a combination of industrial, political, and cultural circumstances. These included the passage of Executive Order 8802 and the creation of the President's Commission on Fair Employment, Walter White's and the NAACP's pressure on the studios, and African American participation in World War II. The results of these developments ranged from the decrease in the number of all-black films produced by Hollywood, to a drop in the production and the gradual extinction of race films, to the slight increase in the number of roles played by African American performers in Hollywood productions.

For all this, there wasn't a considerable change in the content of Hollywood films. While the industry made cursory moves toward hiring more black performers, roles were

79

often insignificant. At the time African American subject matter most often appeared in films made outside Hollywood altogether or in "message movies." Variously referred to as "problem pictures" and "Negro-cycle" films, message movies explored the social inequities of American race relations. As such, the films spoke to the rising tide of integrationist politics from the late 1940s through the early 1960s. Additionally, many of the message movies, such as *Home of the Brave* (Mark Robson, 1949) and *Lost Boundaries* (Alfred L. Werker, 1949), were modest in both budget and cast, nothing like the Hollywood spectacles of the time.

The bulk of message movies avoided the black city (or any *specifically* black space) as a location, a practice again directly related to the integrationist discourses of the time. In the majority of films featuring African American characters, plots were neither directly set in an African American urbanscape nor concerned with issues faced by the nation's burgeoning urban black population, a practice similar to the black-cast musicals produced during the height of the studio system. Instead, plots focused on isolated issues like racism in the Army (*Home of the Brave*) or with black professionals facing prejudice in an all-white workplace (*No Way Out*, Joseph L. Mankiewicz, 1950). While this may have been Hollywood's attempt to confront racism, it also indicated the industry's continuing inability to place black stories and characters outside prescribed parameters. In other words, while the message movies offered an alternative to the antebellum idyll, they still struggled to find a "suitable" setting for their subject matter. This situation would not change until the mid- to late 1960s with the release of *A Man Called Adam* (Leo Penn, 1965) and *Up Tight* (Jules Dassin, 1968), both of which were set in identifiably black, inner-city spaces (New York and Cleveland, respectively).

While message movies were heralded as a positive change from earlier representations of African Americans, they also influenced the Sweetbacks and Super Flies (and even the O-Dogs and Doughboys) that followed. Message movies introduced characters who were almost always male (and almost always played by Sidney Poitier and, to a lesser extent, Harry Belafonte) and almost always middle-class or professional. Additionally, sexuality played an important role in the civil rights era representations of black characters, not for its presence, but rather for its absence, as exemplified by the characters played by Poitier. Thus, the portrait of the African American male painted by the problem pictures was asexual, middle-class, and more rural or suburban than urban.

What appeared in the early 1970s, as a response to these emasculated tropes and related to changes in American race politics as a whole, was an African American screen hero who was male, urban, sexually and socially virile, and often problematic for his middle-class critics—both African American and white.

Message movies signify a crucial transitional phase in American cinematic production. Not only do they redefine the spaces in which African Americans had previously appeared, they also acknowledge the social environment surrounding and enabling them through the inclusion of discourses of racism and integration. Nevertheless, it cannot be overlooked that most of the message movies of the late 1940s to early 1960s depicted a world and conditions that existed outside those faced by the majority of rural and urban African Americans alike. As with the black-cast musicals and their strategies of containment for their characters, and just like the race films' segregation from the industry as a whole, message movies constructed a world that acknowledged neither southern living conditions nor the continuing black migration to northern and western urban spaces. Nor were they to acknowledge the increasing association of the black city with a ghetto.

The subsequent appearance of contemporary ghetto settings in the late 1960s emerged at the same moment as important civil rights discourses. From the 1940s through early 1960s (the height of the popularity of the problem pictures), civil rights activists primarily focused their efforts in the South and were concerned with integrationist issues such as desegregation and voter registration. However, this changed in the mid-1960s when the civil rights movement and the black nationalism that followed turned their attention to the urban poor in the inner cities. Bearing this in mind, in the remainder of this chapter I focus on an examination of the ways in which the black (inner) city was defined and imagined on screen in what I call the black ghetto chronotope, and how this is related to political context.

From Problem to Box Office Powerhouse

Until now this study has concentrated on two specific periods of migration, the Great Migration and the demographic changes associated with the opening of defense industries to black workers during World War II. Yet African American movement continued unabated in the following decades, with at least 1.5 million people leaving the South for the North and West between the 1960s and 1970s.[2] Such large-scale demographic shifts, combined with white flight from the cities to the newly emerging suburbs, changed many metropolitan areas, with the African American population reaching, as James notes at the beginning of this chapter, near majority numbers in some cities. The result of this continuing migration was that African Americans became increasingly identified with urban spaces in the national imagination.

These new demographics had long-term effects on African American film production. At the same time that the black population became identified with the city in mainstream popular culture, the black audience was targeted as a potential money maker in the box office. By the late 1960s, Hollywood, in the midst of a financial collapse, was desperate for an influx of cash. It began to target an African American audience, in part because it was estimated that the black box office generated somewhere between 30 and 40 percent of the total American box office.[3] A related determinant was the location of this audience in urban centers, as this afforded ease of exhibition. What started out as the identification of a specific market sector with a high profit potential ironically resulted in the first acknowledgment by the industry of an urban African American population (echoing race film producers' strategies from decades before).

Since its emergence in the 1970s, blaxploitation has been studied in detail by a number of scholars.[4] While it is not my project to reiterate the multiplicity of causes that enabled this influential genre, it is important, nonetheless, to lay out a few factors that had a direct bearing on the specific urban imagery manufactured and reified by these films. One of the most oft-cited circumstances leading to the genre's popularity was the specific constitution of its primary audience—young, black, male, urban. This audience was increasingly dissatisfied with the emasculated and isolated characters played most often by Poitier, the actor who symbolically represented "the cultural presence, the aspirations, and the social psychology of the largest minority in the United States" for white America.[5] By this time, roles for African American men were already in transition, with the increasing appeal of the more powerful characters played by a rising cadre of black sports-heroes-turned-actors, like Jim Brown and Fred Williamson. With their transformation into the even more powerful Sweetbacks, Shafts, and Superflies of the 1970s, the actors began to project "an emergent assertive, sometimes violent, black manhood" that "exudes a sexual expressiveness long denied blacks on screen."[6] Moreover, there was an increasing dissatisfaction with Hollywood's treatment of black subject matter, culminating in renewed attempts by the NAACP in 1965 to pressure the industry once again for increased African American involvement.

This is not to suggest that blaxploitation's urbanscape simply appeared out of nowhere. As I have maintained throughout this study, the city was a presence in African American print and visual culture, even occasionally making its way in various forms into Hollywood productions. And certainly, the male characters weren't new, as they contain traces of what Mel Watkins refers to as "Bad Niggers," heroes that include such figures as Shine and Staggerlee.[7] Black film of the 1970s referenced familiar tropes, even if cinematic representations of the city lagged behind other African American cultural forms, especially folklore, literature, and art. Between this and the number of urban black moviegoers, it should come as no surprise that films that addressed the black audience's contemporary "socio-cultural reality" would be such a success.[8]

By 1968, blaxploitation's African American audience "had experienced three major assassinations including that of Martin Luther King, a failure of old-line black leadership, a loss of collective black focus on shared goals, a retreat into black nationalism, and a waning attention to poverty in the cities on the part of national white politicians."[9] Yet, while all of the elements of black urban life played a central role in the formation of these films, one of the most important circumstances influencing the creation of specific urban cinematic codes was the wave of urban rebellions that shook the nation from 1965 through 1968. Unlike earlier uprisings, like Chicago in 1919 and Harlem in 1935, the rebellions of the 1960s were televised and acted as a momentary "warp" in the surface of the nation's racial repressed. The images served dual purposes; for white suburban America,

> images of black inner city life were formed or reinforced by the television images that portrayed blacks looting neighborhood stores while buildings burned. Destruction and the destructive seemed to define the black community. The combination of televised news coverage of the urban uprisings and the militant rhetoric of black armed resistance intensified white middle-class America's opinions of blacks as violent people.[10]

Where white suburban America saw violence and destruction, black audiences saw resistance to specific wrongs of the inner city—disenfranchisement, poverty, decay, and unchecked police brutality.[11] The controversy surrounding most blaxploitation films exhibits these contradictions: the films were accused of being one-dimensional and needlessly violent by many reviewers, yet they addressed a facet of their audience's experience, even to the extent of quoting imagery similar to that seen on television.

From Idyll to the Ghetto

> I don't see any American dream; I see an American nightmare!
>
> —Malcolm X (1964)[12]

My decision to call the prevailing spatiotemporal system in African American film from the 1970s a black *ghetto* chronotope is deliberate because the phrase is indicative of the sociological discourses of the time. Spearheaded by Robert Park and social scientists at the University of Chicago, the term "ghetto" was redefined to refer specifically to urban, usually slum, areas inhabited by minority populations.[13] This shift in thinking about the inner city and race culminated in three seminal publications in the mid-1960s: Daniel P. Moynihan's *The Negro Family* (1965), Kenneth Clark's *Dark Ghetto* (1965), and Oscar Lewis' "The Culture of Poverty" (1966), each of which, in related ways, labeled black ghetto culture as pathological. For example, Clark described urban ghettoes as characterized by "overcrowded and deteriorated housing, high infant mortality, crime and disease . . . resentment, hostility, despair, apathy, self-depreciation, and . . . compensatory grandiose behavior."[14] These models formed the basis of American social policy toward its inner cities, most famously in Moynihan's infamous report, which described crime and drug-infested ghettoes populated by black welfare mothers and absent fathers.[15] These discourses formed such an integral part of the government's urban policy that the trope of the black ghetto defined the American urbanscape as a whole. It is therefore important to examine how the films that envision a black cityscape dialogue with this political environment.

While traces of the antebellum idyll and historic Harlem remained in some black-directed films from the 1970s, most films from the time were set in contemporary urban ghettoes. The characteristics of black ghetto films include a specific and highly identifiable urbanscape, normally associated with places such as Harlem and the Watts section of

Los Angeles, although other cities with significant African American populations, such as Chicago and Oakland, also play key roles.[16] These were areas with high concentrations of African American residents, and they were influential in defining the African American urban scene, especially its look and sound. Other characteristics include the self-conscious use of cultural and political references and an immediacy of time frame produced, in part, by extradiegetic references and cinematic technique.

The spatiotemporal parameters of the filmic ghetto were framed by an almost near-obsession with providing details of the cityscape, a project facilitated in part by the fact that the majority of films were shot on location. More important, part of what gave black ghetto films their impact was their inclusion of clearly identifiable urban, black monuments, even to uninitiated audiences. For example, in many films set in New York—such as *Cotton Comes to Harlem* (Ossie Davis, 1970) and *Shaft* (Gordon Parks Sr., 1971)—there is an almost obligatory walk down, or a least a shot of, well-known Harlem landmarks, such as 125th Street, the Apollo Theater, Small's Paradise, or The Cotton Club. These "tours" of the city were often used as devices in films featuring detectives, like Shaft, where the detective's search often was the catalyst for a moving montage through the streets of the city, like Baudelaire's flâneur walking the arcades of Paris.[17] Additionally, the films' verité explorations of the city offered their audiences undeniable voyeuristic (fetishistic and narcissistic) pleasure, either acting as anthropological documents for audiences unfamiliar with the ghetto or as sources of identification for those who were familiar with it.

The use of the city in this way was not solely to add "local color" to the diegesis. It also indicates an integral feature of representations of the black ghetto in film. The ghetto mise-en-scène is not only background for the narrative but also is active in influencing the events unfolding onscreen.[18] The complicated and interwoven dynamics of these films become clearer when it is understood that the city *enables* events. Consequently, discourses of poverty, unemployment, governmental abandonment, and the increasing presence of drugs and crime shape many of the narratives. This is why, unlike *Dark Manhattan*, characters are so much of a part of their environment.[19]

Besides supplying details of the urbanscape, the black ghetto's temporal characteristics provide an indication of what sort of city is envisioned by the films. Previously, Hollywood films set in the antebellum idyll were characterized by a static temporality in which time "has no advancing historical moment."[20] In race films, especially crime films like *Dark Manhattan*, the contemporary black city began to appear, no matter how liminal the situation or delayed its references. The films set in ghetto spaces in the 1970s present the black city as an entirely *contemporary* phenomenon. The self-conscious references to popular culture and political icons of the day contribute to the films' immediacy: urban African American audiences saw and heard what appeared to be the same worlds on the screen and on the streets. This is not to suggest, however, that the films exclude any acknowledgment of the past, as references to another place and time will figure (in different ways) in some of the films from the decade. This reference to multiple temporal moments results in a complex and polyphonous temporality that is embodied spatially, and is not found in either black-cast or race films from earlier decades.

There is no doubt that African American film from the 1970s is most closely associated with blaxploitation. It is my belief, however, that the highly televised nature of many social movements and protests in the 1960s and 1970s, along with social policy discourses, mean that more than one genre was affected. Therefore, the four films in the following discussion represent a cross-section of filmmaking styles from the 1970s: two seminal films from blaxploitation, *Sweet Sweetback's Baadasssss Song* (Melvin Van Peebles, 1971) and *Superfly* (Gordon Parks Jr., 1972) and two others, *Cotton Comes to Harlem* and *Bush Mama* (Haile Gerima, 1976). My intention is to examine the use of city space as more than just mise-en-scène, as it is often considered by film historians. In fact, I will assert that the city is an active presence in the films, playing a central role like any other character.

Cotton Comes to Harlem and the Ghetto Chronotope

Cotton Comes to Harlem opened in the summer of 1971. The film, a comedy-mystery, is set in Harlem, and introduced the area's streets and faces on the mainstream cinematic screen. The film, Ossie Davis' directorial debut, engendered mixed critical responses: critiqued for its use of "stereotypes of black life," *Cotton* was also praised for its "exuberant irreverence toward just about everything."[21] Perhaps it was the fact that it opened at almost the same time as Poitier's *They Call Me Mister Tibbs* (Gordon Douglas, 1970), or perhaps it was the film's "irreverent" mix of comedy and criminality that contrasted with the more commonly televised images of inner-city violence, but the film was overlooked when it was first released. Actually, it wasn't until the release of *Sweetback* and *Shaft* the following year and the subsequent black movie boom that critics would more seriously consider *Cotton*.

The decision to include *Cotton* in the present discussion is based upon a desire to alter the discourses surrounding the conventions of blaxploitation by indicating characteristics normally associated with the genre that appeared prior to and concurrent with it. While most critical discussions of blaxploitation start with the question of whether *Sweetback* is or isn't an example of the genre, they make little or no reference to *Cotton*, which was released approximately nine months earlier. The exception to this is Ed Guerrero, who states in *Framing Blackness* that *Cotton* "influenced the pacing and the formal visual-musical elements that would go into the construction of the crime-action-ghetto Blaxploitation features to follow."[22] In addition, many elements associated with blaxploitation appeared earlier in African American literature, especially in the work of Richard Wright, Ralph Ellison, and Chester Himes. With *Cotton Comes to Harlem*, an adaptation of Himes' 1965 novel of the same name (published in France in 1964 as *Retour en Afrique*), we see the translation of these literary tropes into cinema.[23]

Cotton remains fairly faithful to the novel, with few changes made to the substance of the story. However, one noteworthy change was Davis' decision to downplay the threat posed by the novelistic Harlem. The film is a self-conscious attempt to reinterpret what by that point was Harlem's reputation as a "sociological problem." Davis wanted audiences to understand that Harlem "is a complete world, one which includes moments of joy and laughter as well as misery and discontent. We hope to show the entire scope of the picture, not just a facet of it."[24]

The contemporary ghetto's spatiotemporal parameters define *Cotton*'s narrative. The film's central mystery is a heist, in which $87,000 is stolen from Deke O'Malley's Back-to-Africa Movement. A subplot involves a bale of cotton, which has mysteriously appeared and then disappeared from Harlem's streets. Detectives Jones (Godfrey Cambridge) and Johnson (Raymond St. Jacques) are called in to help find the missing money and possibly to solve the puzzle of the cotton bale. Their search leads them throughout the streets and buildings of Harlem, and acts as a "black travelogue."[25] In particular, a car chase near the beginning of the film provides a high-speed, extended view of Harlem's neighborhoods. Additionally, the Apollo Theater features prominently. The first time we go there it is because O'Malley's girlfriend, Iris (Judy Pace), has sought out her friend Billie (Mabel Robinson) in an attempt to flee from the police. Beyond offering shots of the Apollo and introducing Billie, this scene fails to advance the plot, but it helps anchor the narrative in its setting.

The film is unquestionably set in the aesthetic and social environment of late 1960s Harlem. The car chase, the detectives' search, and most of the exterior scenes are shot on location and they establish Harlem's city space. The streets, buildings, signs, characters, costumes, and even speech idioms illustrate what LeRoi Jones (Amiri Baraka) calls "The City of Harlem":

> Harlem, as it is, as it exists for its people, as an actual place where actual humans live—that is a very different thing. . . . Harlem is a place—a city really . . . but like any other city, it must escape *any* blank generalization simply because it is alive, and changing each second with each breath any of its citizens take.[26]

The streets, and the characters' costumes and dialect, especially urban slang, signify a "presentness," as well as a retort to any generalizations about the city by policymakers. It is also these things that indicate the changeability of which Jones/Baraka speaks.

Cotton opens with a gathering of Harlem residents waiting for the arrival of Reverend Deke O'Malley (Calvin Lockhart) and his Back-to-Africa Company. Gathered on the corner are neighborhood residents, all of whom signify the diversity of urban black subjectivity. Certain characters are demarcated from the crowd, primarily through what they are wearing and their behavior. For example, the detectives' attire is in keeping with the codification of most cinematic police detectives (African American or white). The group of unnamed black nationalists, called simply the "Black Berets" in the cast list, signify a younger, more hip generation. The Black Berets are linked with the Black Power movement more for what they are wearing than anything they say or do (thus the identifying nomenclature), although, ironically, their berets are green. Initially, members of the group are literally tossed aside by Jones and Johnson before they disrupt the Back-to-Africa meeting. However, they make two more appearances in small, although significant roles. First, when the detectives are searching for a potential witness to the robbery, they visit a known drug house only to learn that it has been converted into the black nationalist meeting rooms (a similar location recurs in *Shaft*). The Black Berets have switched from a life of crime to a life of community activism. The group's involvement in actual events is minimal, but their inclusion in the film indicates the growing familiarity with and influence of nationalism in the American social landscape.

O'Malley also signifies a younger, urban-identified generation, although he is most remarkable for the number of roles he fills. O'Malley's call-and-response sermon echoes 125th Street's history as a series of soapbox corners—as locations where leaders such as Marcus Garvey and Malcolm X spoke to Harlem residents. O'Malley's clothing and Back-to-Africa Movement consciously reference both the African diaspora's and Harlem's history through links with Garvey. At the same time, O'Malley is a bridge to the present with the growing Afrocentrism in the contemporary African American community: the Back-to-Africa movement and even more so in his donning of a dashiki at one point in the film. While O'Malley may be part old-school religious charlatan, he is also part urban trickster in the mold of Staggerlee, and, as we'll see, Sweetback and Priest from *Superfly*. O'Malley may, in fact, have much more in common with Sweetback and Priest than is first apparent. All three are outsiders in the community, work (primarily) for themselves, and use the law to their own advantage. O'Malley is fearless when confronted by the police, but he is also taking the community for everything he can get (mostly money and women). But O'Malley differs from heroes like Shaft because he shares the narrative with other strong characters, disallowing for the sort of exclusive identification the audience will enjoy with later blaxploitation heroes.

The central female characters in the film—Iris, Mabel Hill (Emily Yancy), and Billie—occupy less significant positions, yet their clothing and street-savvy contribute to the film's overall atmosphere of urban chic. When first introduced, Iris is wearing a chain-metal sheath, with slits up the sides, over sheer cocktail pants. Mabel spends much less time onscreen (and is in fact murdered by Iris in a fight over O'Malley), but is dressed just as fashionably, albeit more conservatively than Iris. This costuming changes in her last scene, when she wears a dashiki and Afrocentric-patterned headdress. Combined with her dead husband's dashiki, borrowed by O'Malley, Mabel's outfit emphasizes the film's already open acknowledgment of the growing Afrocentrism of the African American community.[27] But as with O'Malley's use of the dashiki, Afrocentrism takes the form of fashion-coding and nothing more.

Billie, like Mabel, spends little time in the narrative. Ironically, while dressed for her vaudeville-like performances at the Apollo, Billie is more politicized than most of the characters. This link between the Revue and ideology is not contradictory, however, as Billie explicitly states a desire to add a political dimension to her routines, thus referencing the black arts movement, and self-reflexively commenting on the film's own aesthetic system. Billie's political motivations result in her climactic routine, a striptease performed on top of a bale of cotton. Significantly, she strips down from her pickaninny's wig and rags (resembling Topsy from the many cinematic versions of *Uncle Tom's Cabin*), to pasties and a bikini bottom, made out of cotton balls.[28] While an overt spectacle eliciting a double system of voyeuristic pleasure, Billie's performance defines the interconnections between the antebellum idyll and contemporary ghetto spaces by suggesting the legacy of the rural South in the modern northern city. At the same time, the routine indicates how sexuality and cinematic history are also implicated in these interconnections: the sexual ecstasy of King Cotton and its links to capitalism, the sexual repressed in the history of U.S. race relations, and the complicity of cinematic history in all of this.

The fact that the women play such secondary roles in the narrative speaks to the growing male focus of both African American political and sociological treatises of the time, an ironic outgrowth of the mixture of civil rights discourses with urban sociology. Robin D. G. Kelley observes that "in the midst of urban rebellions, the masculinist rhetoric of black nationalism, the controversy over the Moynihan report, and the uncritical linking of 'agency' and resistance with men, black men took center stage in poverty research."[29] Moreover, black men, with the exceptions of later blaxploitation programmers like *Cleopatra Jones* and *Foxy Brown*, would take center stage in blaxploitation narratives of African American agency. Later, we will see how Haile Gerima offers an alternative view in *Bush Mama*.

Uncle Bud (Redd Foxx) is also first introduced at the Back-to-Africa rally. His clothes, his unkempt appearance, and his self-effacing demeanor demarcate him from the rest of the characters and signify that he is from a different time and place. While Uncle Bud's age should ensure him a position of respect in the community, his economic status and rural ways prevent this and even lead one character to refer to him as an Uncle Tom. Yet the film refrains from using his character solely to symbolize the cinematic and literary past. Instead, Uncle Bud

Billy's performance links sexuality to the cotton industry in *Cotton Comes to Harlem* (United Artists, 1970). Courtesy of the Museum of Modern Art Film Stills Archive.

is an acknowledgment of both the past and the future. Ironically, this is accomplished when a bale of cotton falls out of one of the vehicles during the opening chase. Uncle Bud finds it and immediately recognizes its Mississippi origins. Seeing the opportunity to make some money, he carts it off to Goldman's junkyard. Jones and Johnson, upon discovering traces of the cotton and linking it to the missing money, set about to find the bale, as do O'Malley and a mysterious man named Calhoun (J. D. Cannon).[30] Eventually the cotton is recovered; however, by this point both the money and Uncle Bud are missing. The mystery isn't solved until after O'Malley has been exposed as a fraud at the end of the film: a postcard from Uncle Bud reveals that he's used the money from the cotton to purchase his own cotton plantation in Africa, thereby providing a variation on the novel's original title. Uncle Bud's return is twofold: a return to his rural roots *and* a return to his African roots.

Throughout the film, only Uncle Bud recognizes the value of the bale—premium-quality Mississippi cotton. This is emphasized by Uncle Bud's answer to Mr. Goldman's questions regarding the origins of the cotton, in which Uncle Bud replies that he has picked enough cotton in his lifetime to recognize its origins. All others involved in the search, including Jones and Johnson, see only a bale of cotton, a symbol of a past they have never personally experienced. For example, in an exchange between the detectives it is apparent that the pair, raised in the city, never had to pick cotton and even have a nostalgic attachment to it as a sign of the rural South. The final twist of the plot, then, is that Uncle Bud, the rural fool, outsmarts the urban tricksters, like Deke O'Malley, and uses his southern past to do so.

In this twist resides an exemplary instance of the film's multiplicity of discourses, as Uncle Bud successfully maneuvers his way through the urbanscape. His presence indicates the ways in which the film's contemporary black ghetto setting incorporates and dialogues with different spaces and time periods. In fact, it is the presence of the antebellum idyll in the film that acts as a *memento mori* of sorts, as a memory device that remembers the past and incorporates it into the present, suggesting that "Harlem has always been a southern place—in its talk, its memories, its music, and its religion."[31] Uncle Bud's victory reminds its urban, black audience of its roots, urges the acknowledgment of the country in the city, and provides a "palimpsestic impression, which results in a tension between the city as past and the city as present."[32] It also indicates the ways in which the city space facilitates a "sense of time as it is lived, the relation of that time to the past, and the value of the imminent future to which it is always oriented."[33] Further, through Uncle Bud's character, both the film and the novel suggest that African American cities are what they are because of the South, not in spite of it.

One defining characteristic of African American films from the 1970s is the use of "black-inflected" speech idioms, dialect, and slang. This, as with setting and costumes, provides the films with a ghettocentricity. However, *Cotton*, unlike the blaxploitation films that follow, does not rely on explicating a black street idiom. In fact, most of the characters, such as Mabel, Billie, and Deke, use "dialect-free" speech normally associated with the black bourgeoisie. When dialect is used, it is often set off—placed in quotation marks—from the rest of the film, for instance, in the slang used by the Black Berets. Only Uncle Bud speaks in a strong dialect, implying the influence of the antebellum idyll through the intra-generational and regional differences his words connote. Yet the film's use of language unveils one of its primary concerns: the definition of blackness. On multiple occasions, the question, "Is It Black Enough For You?" is posed between various characters: between O'Malley and the crowd, between the detectives and the militants, and between Uncle Bud and an associate, for example. The use of this question to punctuate so many interactions indicates how extradiegetic concerns again enter the diegesis. In light of the sociopolitical context, informed by the civil rights movement and black nationalism, it is as though the film is self-consciously asking itself the question.

Cotton Comes to Harlem introduces many of the characteristics of the black ghetto chronotope into African American filmmaking of the 1970s. In some ways, *Cotton* is an anomaly compared to what follows: for one, unlike *Sweetback* and *Bush Mama*, its style and technique is more indebted to Hollywood. Additionally, it seems, of the four films included in this chapter, to be the one that is less firmly set in a contemporary present, instead operating in some transitional place in which the antebellum idyll and the celebratory aspects of historic Harlem are engaged in a dialogue with the ghetto. What we will see in the films to come is the refinement of the spatiotemporal characteristics of the black ghetto, so that by the release of *Superfly* two years later the black city has become a familiar space.

Br'er Soul and the City

Due to the combination of Melvin Van Peebles' marketing savvy and his famously outrageous public persona, the history of *Sweet Sweetback's Baadasssss Song*'s critical responses is long, varied, and (often) over-heated. Within a few months of its release, critics were already observing that

> there is no need at this time to restate the theme of *Sweet Sweetback's Baadassss* [sic] *Song*. By this time you've probably seen it, read it, heard it or re-lived it through countless reenactments on the street (brothers are now calling each other 'Sweetback' as if it is something they grabbed from the unknown).[34]

Sweetback is legendary for its innovative production and marketing strategies—it was produced, directed, and scored by Van Peebles, who also performed in the lead role. The film's rental income was supplemented by the sale of a companion sound track album and "making-of" book, which added to the film's legacy by providing Van Peebles' views on filmmaking, politics, and Sweetback. Made on a tiny budget, *Sweetback* went on to become one of the highest-grossing films of the year, with most figures estimating a box office of between $10 million and $12 million. Moreover, the film's success helped cement the financially ailing industry's move toward targeting more films to an African American youth audience.

But *Sweetback*'s content also sparked heated debate. This controversy normally fell between two poles. Labeled "revolutionary" filmmaking by Van Peebles, an attempt to "de-colonize" his audience's minds,[35] he argued that Sweetback's mythic qualities, sexual virility, and political agency empowered African American audiences. This view was supported by Huey Newton of the Black Panthers.[36] An equally common viewpoint, a view more in line with the black middle class, criticized that very same violence, sexism, and the film's insinuation that a revolution could succeed through sexual prowess.[37] While these responses provide insight into the debate raging over a black aesthetics at the time, I am more interested in staging a critical examination of the spaces in the film. The majority of the reviews mention the "ghetto" spaces Sweetback encounters during his flight from the Los Angeles police, however, most overlook the fact that the urbanscape only appears for about half the film. The other half switches to the deserts of southern California and Mexico. In crediting the film for its images of Watts, many critics overlooked its equally important rural scenes. Ironically, the result is that *Sweetback* has only been considered as a city film, and as *the* city film of the time.

Discussions of the film have almost always concentrated on its narrative rather than its technique, but *Sweetback* is also interesting for how it draws from the aesthetics of both international art film and Third Cinema.[38] The 1960s were distinguished by an experimentation with form in which a number of young European directors, like Jean-Luc Godard, attempted a break from conventional Western structures of realism. Starting with Godard's *Breathless* (1958), many films streamlined the use of location shooting, sync-sound, and a mobile camera, along with discontinuous editing to contribute documentary immediacy and an element of reflexivity to their narratives, techniques that would then be utilized by American directors. Third Cinema, especially Cuban Cinema, Brazil's Cinema Nôvo, and African cinemas, had its own reciprocal effect on European cinema which, especially after 1968, used very similar techniques in an attempt to articulate a revolutionary (counter) cinema aesthetics. Van Peebles' discussion of the colonization of his protagonist's mind, as well as *Sweetback*'s guerrilla-like production history, its aesthetics, and its anti-hero, combine all these influences in an attack against hegemonic filmmaking practices.

Taken in by prostitutes as a child, Sweetback (Van Peebles) grows up performing odd jobs and sex acts in a Watts brothel. When the LAPD is in need of somebody to stand in as a murder suspect, Sweetback is "volunteered" by Beetle (Simon Chuchster), his boss. On the way to the precinct, the police pick up Mu-Mu (Hubert Scales), a young black revolutionary, whom they beat (initially while he's still attached with handcuffs to Sweetback) During Mu-Mu's thrashing, Sweetback turns on the cops, beating both unconscious. This moment is Sweetback's political awakening, although it is short-lived and, from then on, intermittent. It is also the beginning of Sweetback's flight from the police—action that will consume the remainder of the narrative, put Sweetback in touch with other residents of the black community, and map out certain areas of urban and rural southern California. Along the way, Sweetback will bed many partners, beat two more cops, and leave the city.

Sweetback's escape provides the excuse for a "tour" of the ghetto. The film is split among three locations: interior and exterior spaces of Los Angeles, rural California, and rural Mexico. Most of the interiors are confined to the brothel and a few places that shelter Sweetback from his pursuers: a neighborhood storefront church and informal drug re-hab center, the house of at least one acquaintance, a gambling club, and a cabin outside the city. Almost all of these spaces are run-down and ill-maintained and envision a much more dystopian space than what we saw previously in *Cotton*. Also, the interiors are dark and claustropho-bic, possibly a result of the film's production values, but more likely an indication of the threat they pose. Sweetback's vulnerability in these locations indicates that they allow only for a temporary haven—he is initially picked up by the police in the brothel, the church offers no sanctuary beyond a "Black Ave Maria," Sweetback's gambling friends can only offer a ride out of the city, and Sweetback and Mu-Mu are discovered by two officers from the Sheriff's Department while hiding out in the cabin.

Sweetback is focused upon a central hero rather than the more decen-tered subject set up in *Cotton*, which encouraged identification with the whole community. Based upon a long history of the trope of the out-sider, Sweetback's characteristics of distance, silence, and independence made him a hero for the youth audiences that filled the theaters.[39] These characteristics also, ironically, make Sweetback the ultimate American hero. Combining the traits of loner and folk hero, Sweetback personi-fies the tension between individualism and collectivism emphasized by American ideology. Sweetback's rejection of authority figures, his sex-ual success, and his proven cunning link him with similar mythic figures played by John Wayne and Clint Eastwood, and, in fact, *Sweetback* in-corporates some of the characteristics of the Western, including the construction of its hero and similarities in setting. Thus, it is no ac-cident that Eastwood would move out of the rural West and into the urban frontier in *Dirty Harry* (Don Siegel, 1971) at roughly the same time as the rise of blaxploitation's heroes. While their characteristics were similar, Sweetback and Dirty Harry were to play opposite roles, a fact emphasized by each film's opening tribute: *Sweetback*'s "to all those brothers and sisters who had enough of The Man," and *Dirty Harry*'s "to the police officers of San Francisco who gave their lives in the line of duty."

The film's exterior spaces are split between Watts and the rural and desert areas stretching south from Los Angeles to the U.S.-Mexico bor-der. Los Angeles' urbanscape unfolds as Sweetback runs through its streets, alleyways, railyards, and industrial terrain. His flight shows Los Angeles as a black ghetto, an area of decaying buildings, empty lots, and industrial waste. It is interesting to note the differences between New York's and Los Angeles' cityscapes. Los Angeles' spaces are much more open than New York's, but this does not result in a less-circumscribed mobility. This difference is further signified by the different landmarks that codify black Los Angeles. Whereas in Harlem the black cityscape was often signified by particular signage, Los Angeles' black city space is denoted by industrial waste and the almost-dry riverbed of the Los Angeles River.

Sweetback does not lack the elements of a recognizable black urbanscape. The film incorporates the streets and faces of Watts into its spaces. But, for instance, while *Cotton*'s neon signs reference specific Harlem landmarks, *Sweetback*'s signage is used more symbolically. For instance, the film returns repeatedly to a neon "Jesus Saves" sign. It first appears at the beginning of the film, when Sweetback is being taken to the precinct, and then later in the film during his flight out of the city. The sign can only be read ironically, as the overall narrative suggests the impotence of the black church to help save Sweetback, a different interpretation of the divine than in the antebellum idyll, for instance, but a view of the church much more in keeping with Oscar Micheaux, one of Van Peebles' models. Similar uses of signs occur elsewhere in the film, notably a recurring orange barrier with "Caution" written across it, which both comments upon narrative events and editorializes about the conditions in Watts and Sweetback's ability to move from place to place. The use of signs in such a manner, especially to comment upon the constraints on mobility placed upon Los Angeles' African American population, will continue in the 1980s and 1990s, for example, in John Singleton's *Boyz N The Hood* (1991).

Although *Cotton*'s and *Sweetback*'s figurations of the black ghetto may differ, they are similar in that the latter incorporates a contemporary time frame into its narrative, most explicitly through extradiegetic references. Because of Los Angeles' more recent and less familiar history of African American migration, Van Peebles did not have a body of local historical references from which to draw upon as would a director in Harlem. Van Peebles instead focused on the more recent history of black Los Angeles, in particular, the Watts Rebellion when "Southcentral Los Angeles exploded in rage against police abuse and institutional racism."[40] In fact, *Sweetback* is a product of the resulting cultural climate of the Rebellion, which was similar to New York's black arts movement in political intensity, and which "established a distinctive Watts idiom in fiction and poetry."[41] The influence of the Watts Rebellion exists in *Sweetback*'s multiple references to the systematic program of brutality maintained by the LAPD toward the city's African American and Mexican American populations, with the beatings of Mu-Mu, Sweetback, and Beetle.

A compelling example of the LAPD's role in Watts occurs when Sweetback is caught by two police officers who put him in their cruiser with the intention of taking him to a secluded place in order to beat him without witnesses. Once in the car the three men are surrounded by neighborhood residents, who set fire to the cruiser. During the ensuing confusion, bystanders emancipate Sweetback, allowing him to escape from the police. Rather than follow him, however, the camera holds on the shot of the burning and exploding patrol car. This image, combined with shots of the crowd of people surrounding the car, serves a number of purposes. First, it is one of the film's few examples of collective action.[42] Up to this point Sweetback has forced himself on the community; here the community willingly comes to his support.

More important, the scene's composition is a reference to recent extradiegetic events. Images such as the burning cruiser spoke directly to the audience because they replicated a "visible, televised actuality" that included images of "enraged, vandalistic, violent young people who appeared on the nation's television screens night after night, sweeping through the streets . . . looting, challenging the police, and effectively repudiating the pacifist tactics of Martin Luther King."[43] Van Peebles not only included such images in his film, but he used moving cameras and location shooting to add to their impact. In this way, the scene refracts a sociocultural reality that was itself already mediated by television, effectively supporting the claim that media "images of Los Angeles refer essentially to the media."[44]

Sweetback references Los Angeles' contemporary situation in a number of other ways, all of which interact and combine to add to the "now" of the film (what so many spectators and reviewers referred to as the film's "reality" quotient). As with *Cotton*, *Sweetback* references the Black Power movement. Sweetback is awakened politically when he stops the police from beating Mu-Mu, a black revolutionary. This awakening is short-lived, however, as Sweetback immediately disassociates himself from Mu-Mu following this episode. This scene has been the subject of much discussion, mostly criticizing Sweetback for his refusal to join the collective.[45] However, what is often overlooked is a later scene in which

Sweetback recognizes and articulates the younger man's importance for the future. Sweetback's acknowledgment of Mu-Mu is the only explicit approval he gives to anyone in the film (and is one of the moments when the otherwise monosyllabic Sweetback actually says more than a few words). Thus, while Sweetback fails significantly to align himself with the movement—to do so would be to undermine his appeal as a "baadasssss nigger"—his disengagement is not total.

Sweetback's lack of a political agenda raises interesting questions regarding the topicality of the film's narrative, and this is one of the reasons why it came under so much criticism. The film's most telling sign of its immediacy is personified in Sweetback himself. As Guerrero notes, *Sweetback*'s "male-focused black nationalist discourse [was] aimed at rediscovering and articulating the mystique of a liberated 'black manhood' during the late 1960s and into the early 1970s."[46] Sweetback oozes an "aesthetique du cool . . . a style meant to convey a Black politics."[47] These characteristics are remarkably close to those already identified as traits of the Bad Nigger. Sweetback wears the same costume throughout most of the narrative, changing only near the conclusion of the film. This outfit—gold crushed-velvet pants and vest (he loses an overcoat and fedora early on) and a brown open-necked shirt—marks him as an urban folk hero. At the same time, Sweetback's clothes acquire a meaning of their own, as they speak a language of resistance similar to zoot suits in the 1940s. In this way, *Sweetback* acknowledges the larger temporal framework in which the narrative takes place, primarily through costume, dialogue, sound track, and references to particular extradiegetic cultural icons; however, the plot is much more concerned with Sweetback's coming of age than with the community's. This tension—between placing Sweetback within a larger context and identifying solely with him—is never fully worked out and because of it the film becomes almost schizophrenic at times.

Sweetback spends about half of the film in the streets of the city. Interspersed between these scenes are his two excursions outside the city limits. First, Sweetback's friends drive Mu-Mu and Sweetback into the hills surrounding Los Angeles. This episode provides the occasion when Sweetback, having been provoked, will "duel" with a gang of bikers and beat two more police officers. These events are followed by Sweetback's inexplicable return to Watts. As the police search intensifies, Sweetback leaves the city again and heads south. His flight into the desert shifts the narrative into a space that includes both traces of the antebellum idyll and African motifs, and it is the interplay among spaces and times—ghetto, Africa, idyll—that gives the film a mythic dimension.

While it is true that Sweetback's flight into the desert isolates him from the community—he is truly alone, and the only assistance he receives is from a white drifter—it also links him to a dimension of the antebellum idyll absent from most of the film's earlier episodes. Once he enters the desert, the film's tenor changes as Sweetback transforms. This metamorphosis is most apparent in costume and sound track. In the desert, Sweetback switches clothing with a vagrant—a fact not revealed until the police run down his stand-in. Sweetback's new outfit of tattered clothes signifies nothing of the city but everything of the rural South. In fact, there exist viable echoes of *Cotton*'s Uncle Bud in Sweetback's new look because he wears very similar clothing.

The traces of the antebellum idyll are more explicit in the "hunt" scenes that close the film. While making his escape to the border, Sweetback is pursued by two men and a group of dogs. The images of Sweetback chased by the dogs resemble those of an escaped slave making a run for the border. But this reference to the antebellum South is stripped of the nostalgia and fantasy of black-cast musicals because its configuration is much more deadly in the links it makes to lynching. In fact, its contours are much more threatening than what was to be found—at least for Sweetback—in the ghetto. In a curious inversion, the Promised Land is not the North as it had previously been, but rather the South and Mexico.

Sweetback's desert scenes address, however slightly, the growing Afrocentrism of the black community in the late 1960s and early 1970s, expanding what appears to be an individual struggle to the entire African diaspora. Earlier in the film the storefront preacher is costumed in African-style "zebra buba and leopard alb,"[48] but the film makes nothing of the costume (similar to *Cotton*'s treatment of O'Malley's dashiki)—and, if anything, problematizes it through the preacher's refusal to shelter Sweetback. In the desert, Sweetback's African "roots" are not so much shown as suggested by action and by the sound track. First, Sweetback's use of folk remedies to help heal a wound in his side is presented as instinctual. Second, the sound track changes notably during these scenes. Previously, it consisted of contemporary R&B songs performed by groups such as Earth, Wind, and Fire. With the location shift the contemporary sounds change to African-based rhythms performed with percussion and wind instruments. The overall effect of this change in music is to connect Sweetback to a diasporic cultural context.

With this move into the desert Sweetback becomes surprisingly similar to figures like Uncle Bud in *Cotton*. Possibly because of their status as tricksters, but even more so because of their actual and symbolic connections with the American South and Africa, they "succeed" in ways not accomplished by other characters. For example, Mu-Mu never exhibits Sweetback's survival instinct, and this may be the reason he is struck down halfway through the film. Similarly, Deke O'Malley, for all his street savvy, also fails in *Cotton*. Additionally, Sweetback's and Uncle Bud's successes intimate one of the more interesting aspects of their characters (and a number of blaxploitation's heroes)—that they actually have much more mobility than is first apparent. Thus, for at least some of the characters, the contemporary black ghetto and its intersections with other spatiotemporal formulations is indicative of a social and political agency because it acknowledges links between past and present, something that will continue in later decades, most notably in Spike Lee's films.

Superfly and the Refinement of Black City Cinema

African American films from the early 1970s charted the spatiotemporal terrain of the ghetto and placed the streets, alleyways, and spaces of the black inner city onto the cinematic screen. While the presence of the antebellum idyll diminished over time, and the representations of the black ghetto would be increasingly refined, it is interesting that in a group of films so wholly identified with the urban, the temporal and spatial characteristics of other spaces could have such an influence. However, with the refinement of blaxploitation, African American narratives focused more on placing an individual hero in a contemporary, urban landscape. In fact, blaxploitation films modeled after *Sweetback* were often reduced to focusing on a single character whose heroic status was enabled as much by the city as by the clothes he or she wears. This is nowhere more explicit than in the plethora of films named after their main characters, for example, *Shaft*, *Foxy Brown*, *Cleopatra Jones*, *Willie Dynamite*, and *Dolemite*.

Gordon Parks Jr.'s *Superfly* was produced at about the midpoint in blaxploitation's development—still early enough that it could be considered one of "the purest formulaic expressions of the new genre," yet late enough that its conventions were familiar.[49] Following the rapid success of *Sweetback*, *Shaft*, and *Superfly*, African American films from the 1970s soon devolved into the short-lived production of poorly realized blaxploitation programmers, sequels of earlier films, and black-cast remakes of other genres, such as horror and the Western. Ironically, *Superfly* enjoys a contradictory status as both the genre's zenith and its nadir. The film is a "pure" example of the conventions of blaxploitation, at the same time that these very characteristics sparked a critical backlash from African American groups protesting the film's images and stereotypes. My discussion focuses on *Superfly*'s description of the ghetto and how this relates to the film's definitions of political agency, specifically mobility.

Superfly's plot is fairly simple and relies on many of the elements of the black cinematic ghetto discussed thus far. The film focuses on Youngblood Priest (Ron O'Neal), a young, successful coke dealer, and his partner Eddie (Carl Lee). In his desire to break free of the drug business, Priest decides to use the pair's $300,000 in savings to bankroll the purchase and sale of enough cocaine to net a $1 million profit. Priest's and Eddie's plans change when their scheme is discovered by the police, and yet the pair is not arrested for the kilo of coke in their possession. Instead, they are enlisted by the corrupt cops to be their drug representatives in the ghetto. The temptation of police protection is too much for Eddie, and he betrays Priest's plans to quit the drug business to the cops. With the help of his girlfriend, Georgia (Sheila Frazier), Priest outwits the cops and Eddie's betrayal and escapes with his share of the money.

While Priest's movements are the catalyst for another tour of the ghetto, we are actually introduced to the city five minutes before his character enters the narrative. The film opens with an extreme high-angle long shot of a Harlem corner as two junkies conspire to commit a robbery. The next few minutes of the film consist of traveling shots of the pair as they walk through the streets on their way to an unspecified destination. The city, as it is introduced here, contains all of the characteristics of the ghetto space we have seen in films like *Sweetback*—its buildings are decayed, burned out, or abandoned; trash covers the sidewalks and gutters; and the majority of the storefronts are boarded up. Furthermore, groups of men are seen milling around with nowhere to go. In short, the Harlem introduced here is not just a means to supply background information or to serve as a canvas for the unfolding events. Instead, the city is introduced as any important character in a film would be, and what is contained in its spaces immediately plays a significant role.

Approximately half of *Superfly*'s interior and exterior scenes were shot on location. The choice of locations, combined with the generous use of moving camera and the film's grainy images, contribute a documentary immediacy, often credited as an aspect of the film's authenticity. In fact, many shots resemble the shaky, hand-held movements of surveillance video that became familiar with reality-based television in the 1980s and 1990s. Donald Bogle notes that "*Super Fly* looks authentic: the Harlem settings, the streets and alleyways, the bars, and the tenements all paint an overriding bleak vision of urban decay, new terrain for commercial cinema."[50] While my previous discussion disputes Bogle's assertion that this was new terrain, I agree that *Superfly*'s images differ in tone from those of either *Cotton* or *Sweetback*. While ostensibly portraying the same city streets, *Cotton*'s humor and lampooning provides a buffer, and Davis' intent to dispel Moynihanized visions of Harlem suggests that the area is much more of a community than allowed by social scientists. The intimacy with which *Superfly*'s streets are shot (partly because of closer shot distances) provides it with a personal dimension not apparent in *Sweetback*'s urban and industrial wastelands. Additionally, the film's construction of Harlem is much more dystopian than in the race films from the 1930s.

Priest is introduced after this scene, in bed with his white lover and drug customer, Cynthia (Polly Niles). It's not actually until after he leaves Cynthia's apartment that *Superfly*'s mise-en-scène expands and places Priest fully within Harlem's urbanscape. Significantly, Priest's movements in and around the city provide the opportunity for its parameters to be more fully delineated. While the film's construction of interior and exterior city spaces furnishes *Superfly* with its particular urban panache, less explicit elements also reinforce the film's ghetto aura. As we have already seen with the urban worlds constructed in *Cotton* and *Sweetback*, *Superfly*'s urbanscape includes a variety of "idioms and fashions of the inner-city black community,"[51] all of which contribute to the film's "city-ness." Additionally, music adds a key element to the city's auralscape and emerges as an important characteristic of the cinematic ghetto, especially because Curtis Mayfield's "Pusherman" plays over combined shots of Priest's trip uptown and the film's opening titles.

A defining moment in establishing the film's setting occurs when Priest leaves Cynthia's apartment and heads uptown. When he arrives, Priest is attacked by the two junkies from the beginning of the film. A scuffle ensues, and Priest chases one of his attackers. This pursuit again exposes the ghetto's streets and alleyways, however, in a much more intimate manner than in those scenes in which Priest travels the streets encased in his Cadillac. In maneuvering through an urbanscape strewn with trash and dotted by abandoned buildings and burned-out cars, Priest is more immediately part of the city. Once the chase moves inside a rundown and claustrophobic Harlem tenement apartment, Priest is fully master of the space. The apartment is similar in style to most of the film's more impoverished spaces, such as the gambling dens and bars that make up the Harlem underworld. However, the apartment's condition, with its mother and children huddled around an open oven door for warmth, is a stark contrast to the more affluent interior spaces occupied by Priest up to this point and to follow. The juxtaposition between the more impoverished spaces of the city and these signs of affluence is also a form of indictment, especially as this scene precedes an immediate cut to Priest's lush residence. Priest, after all, makes money from the community but returns nothing to it. Furthermore, it indicates Priest's contradictions; while united with the city space, he is often distanced from it.

A significant difference between *Cotton* and *Superfly* is that Priest's travels do not rely on specific landmarks such as the Apollo Theater to define location for the audience. In fact, Priest frequents mostly nameless bars and cafés, offering no identifiable sense of place. Whereas in other Harlem-based films like *Cotton* and *Shaft*, references to the Apollo and Small's anchor the film in a specific location, in *Superfly*, Small's only appears in the far background of a shot. The famous bar is not called out as a monument; instead, it is used simply as part of the mise-en-scène, indicating that the treatment of African American urban spaces has shifted from having to be announced to forming a more subtle texture of the city. In fact, one of the few signs that place the film in Harlem advertises the Harlem Studio Museum's mural project that adorned the walls of many area buildings. For the most part, ghetto space has become a recognizable trope; it no longer has to be defined with specific placenames.

At the time *Superfly* was released, mainstream black film had defined the characteristics of a highly identifiable group of urban characters, from *Sweetback*'s pimp to *Shaft*'s detective. This group also included an assortment of prostitutes, junkies, con artists, petty thieves, and drug dealers found mostly in the black city space. By this stage in the genre's development, the characters had acquired metonymic significance; they stand for the city and identify its space with the "parasitic, hustling milieu of the black urban underworld so poetically described by its inhabitants and by [author] Donald Goines as 'the life.' "[52] While Priest was already a recognizable paradigm in the background of the ghetto landscape, *Superfly* moved the pusherman to the foreground. Priest is familiar not simply because he resembles the urban trickster, but also because he dresses in the urban fashion of the time period. Moreover, his suits, long, flowing leather and fur-trimmed coats, and broad-brimmed hats cross over into the archetypal coding of the pimp. Priest shares similarities with Sweetback: they dress alike, but more important, they share a similar outlaw aura, the cause of both their popularity and their opponents' biggest criticisms. Additionally, both Priest and Sweetback share characteristics with most of the black male heroes from the time, in particular, their sexual and physical abilities. In fact, this is what first defines Priest—his character is established as he lies nude in bed with Cynthia.

Superfly includes a whole collection of archetypal characters in addition to Priest. Two types of characters in particular reference the contemporary African American political and social landscape even though they make only brief appearances in the narrative. At one point, Priest is confronted by a group of "militants" (as they are referred to in the cast list) and, like their counterparts in *Cotton* and *Sweetback*, they signify some form of black nationalism. In *Superfly*, the three militants are unnamed and play only a slight role in the narrative, and yet they articulate their position in ways heretofore unseen. For example, upon approaching Priest, they accuse him of becoming rich at the expense of the community and demand that he contribute money to their political cause. Priest refuses to identify with them. Surprisingly, his refusal stems not from ideological differences but more from his disapproval of their methods. As Priest sees it, the militants aren't militant enough, an attitude based upon their failure, in his opinion, to claim full agency by arming themselves (even though Priest never uses a gun). What we've seen is the development of the militant archetype from comedic buffoon in *Cotton* to integral member and voice of the community. Unfortunately, however, since narrative identification rests with Priest, his way of surviving is posited as preferable.

The other character is K.C., a pimp who first appears breaking up a fight between two prostitutes. Later, K.C. reappears in a bar where Priest, Eddie, and two of their men have gone to discuss business. K.C.'s interaction with Priest is incidental, but his presence in the diegesis is important. First, his clothes are almost identical to Priest's. This resemblance is made all the more interesting by the fact that K.C. was an actual pimp (of the same name) working in Harlem at the time the film was made, thus further blurring the line between the diegetic and extradiegetic, and forming a complex dialogue between real and fictional urban landscapes. The fact that Priest's car in the film is K.C.'s actual car further compounds the relationship between the diegesis and the actual world.[53] For *Superfly*'s Harlem audience (it opened in New York), the film utilized more than just the streets of the city, it used actual personalities and recognizable elements of the urbanscape. This casting is another example of the way in which the representation of Harlem differs from what we have seen in *Sweetback*'s Los Angeles, in which the city is represented in a self-referential spiral of media references. However, the result is similar, as each set of references, from actual personalities to newsreel footage, stands in for the real.

These aspects of the ghetto mise-en-scène provide *Superfly* with a temporal immediacy and mimetic quality, two of its principal attractions. As Mark Reid has said about *Sweetback* and blaxploitation as a whole, "black inner-city youths and black street people identified with the film's imaginative reflection of their real lives,"[54] an observation that unconsciously touches upon an issue that has repeatedly surfaced in my discussion of *Superfly*, the tension between reality and fantasy. Most of the films released prior to *Superfly*, especially *Sweetback* and *Shaft*, have similar tensions. Because the films so accurately rendered the spatiotemporal boundaries of the city—even when, as in *Sweetback*'s case, they quoted media representations of the urbanscape—they were thought to represent, rather than refract, reality. This was all the more explicit in the films' strategy of extradiegetic references, or in *Superfly*'s case, by transferring elements of the actual city into the filmic urbanscape. As the references to other spaces, at least ones connoting a past, became rarer and rarer, the films' authenticity seemingly increased. Ironically, for decades African American urbanscapes were absent from more mainstream screens. Once they appeared, and did so with "accurate" renderings, they were mistaken for reality and critiqued for their negative portrayals of black urban life, a similar criticism leveled against idyllic representations and a suggestion that black film was still struggling with questions of positive and negative stereotypes.

Bush Mama in the Ghetto

Having now discussed three relatively "mainstream" examples of film-making from this time period, I want to turn, by way of contrast, to a film that successfully utilizes the complex dialoguing of past and present and rural and urban motifs so much a part of African American films of the 1970s: Haile Gerima's *Bush Mama*. In its intersections with themes of transformation and mobility, Gerima's film provides insights into the cinematic constructions of a black ghetto at this time and it accomplishes this from outside the industrial parameters and generic iconography of blaxploitation. While *Cotton*, *Sweetback*, and *Superfly* were all independently produced (to differing degrees) and released in first-run theaters, Gerima's film was produced in an university setting and exhibited on the festival and academic circuit.

One of the main differences between the previous films and *Bush Mama* is this context of production and reception. Gerima, originally from Ethiopia, wrote, shot, and edited the film while a graduate student at UCLA. In fact, the film was made with equipment and materials provided by UCLA, and was financed with a combination of University and NEA grants as well as Gerima's personal funds and contributions made from various individuals. Gerima was part of a group of African and African American film students, enrolled in the Theater Arts and Film Departments at UCLA, who are referred to as alternately the "LA Rebellion" and the "LA School of Black Filmmakers," and who included people like Charles Burnett, Larry Clark, Billy Woodberry, Alile Sharon Larkin, and Ntongela Masilela.[55] One of the fundamental differences between the LA Rebellion and African American filmmakers working within the mainstream industry is the former's explicit political desire to deconstruct what they viewed as Hollywood's ideological prisonhouse. As Masilela remembers: "The challenge facing this generation of independent Black filmmakers was to find a film form unique to their historical situation and cultural experience, a form that could not be appropriated by Hollywood,"[56] but which was appropriate to the post-civil rights, post-Rebellion context within which they were working. As part of this project, they looked to alternative sources of inspiration rather than replicating the Hollywood form, and unlike the race film producers who preceded them, the LA School created a separate space by choice rather than by necessity.

Bush Mama clearly illustrates the wide-ranging group of thinkers and filmmakers who influenced Gerima's filmmaking. Cinematically, Gerima's style is shaped by a diverse cross-section of filmmakers, ranging from Oscar Micheaux, Dziga Vertov, Italian Neorealists, and the French New Wave, to Third Cinema. Gerima discusses the transformation he underwent as a filmmaker as a result of being exposed to Third Cinema:

> It was unveiling when I saw these Third World films, especially to see Ousmane Sembene's films, where the Africans spoke their own language instead of French or Portuguese or English. They spoke African with all its psychological and sociological ramifications. My restlessness was legitimized by these filmmakers because they were restless like me. And the unrest was calling for different cultural manifestations that I was able to share.[57]

With the additional influence of the black arts movement and such figures as Amilcar Cabral and Franz Fanon, Gerima and others in the LA Rebellion understood the ideological links between film and national culture, especially as it related to colonialism, both in the Third World and in the United States. It is specifically internal colonialism and the human potential for political awakening that is at the core of a number of Gerima's films,[58] especially *Bush Mama*, the story of Dorothy, a welfare mother who gradually comes to political consciousness while facing economic, political, and social oppression. As we have already seen, a similar rhetoric was used by Van Peebles with *Sweetback*. Notwithstanding the similarities in form, members of the LA Rebellion did not look to the film as a model because while "some of *Sweetback*'s techniques and procedures were acceptable to the insurgents . . . its politics were not." Instead, films made by members of the LA Rebellion, especially those by Gerima, Burnett, and Woodberry, focused on "family, women, history, and folklore."[59]

Bush Mama's divergence from blaxploitation is apparent in its nonlinear narrative, its combination of acoustic and visual techniques, and its identification (although not overly privileged) with a female character played by Barbara O. Jones. The film positions Dorothy's struggle as both institutional and intellectual: she endeavors to support herself and her daughter Luann (Susan Williams) while her man, T.C. (Johnny Weathers), is serving a jail sentence for a crime he did not commit; she struggles to maintain dignity in the face of her welfare caseworker; and she struggles to protect her family from the police presence in the Watts section of Los Angeles.

In her extreme circumstances, Dorothy is forced to violent action as a means of protecting Luann against a sexual assault committed by a member of the LAPD. The violence serves a particular purpose in indicating Dorothy's political transformation and, according to Gerima, was not intended for the purpose of glorification.[60] Dorothy resorts to violence to protect the integrity of her family rather than as a means of individual self-defense or as act of physical empowerment. Both Burnett and Gerima were concerned "with the politics of resistance within the family which emerged after the Watts Rebellion."[61] Both filmmakers and others in the LA Rebellion saw the importance of the family in relation to history—saw, in fact, the family as providing the agency and potential for political change.

Bush Mama differs from *Cotton*, *Sweetback*, and *Superfly* in that it is a rare example of the family in the city from this time. While Sweetback's family consisted of the prostitutes who raised him, the potentially nurturing aspects of his situation were problematized by the fact that it was while under their roof that he is sexually molested as a child and turned over to the LAPD as an adult. In both instances, representatives of Sweetback's family disregard his well-being for their own self-interests. On the other hand, Dorothy's actions are undertaken solely to preserve the integrity of her family, as a means of protecting the generations. Thus, *Bush Mama*'s construction of family is an ironic counterpoint to what we saw with the antebellum idyll because, unlike the family in the antebellum idyll that was *removed* from the present, Dorothy's domestic situation is *situated in* the present.

The film's use of setting illustrates the complex intersection between spaces that traditionally have been considered separate: interiors, exteriors, the home (domestic/feminine space), and the city (male-focused space especially in black exploitation films). In many ways the film goes beyond *Sweetback* in developing the visual characteristics of the black ghetto. About half of *Bush Mama* is set in the streets of Watts, and many shots provide detailed documents of storefronts and signs. For instance, a wig store figures prominently in the beginning of the film, never to reappear. In a use of signage similar to *Sweetback*'s, the store's signs also comment on the narrative and foreshadow Dorothy's later transformation, which will be most obviously signified by her removal of her wig and her switch to wearing braids at the end of the film. Furthermore, Dorothy often walks through Watts' streets on her way to the welfare office, the employment office, the clinic, or, sometimes, to nowhere in particular.

Bush Mama expands *Cotton*'s, *Sweetback*'s, and *Superfly*'s depiction of the city by illustrating the poverty, despair, and oppression the residents of Watts experience. Rather than relying on blatantly run-down houses or vacant lots (there's an absence of both in *Bush Mama*) to connote a ghettocentricity, the film verifies urban oppression by highlighting the extent to which the LAPD governs the area and suggests, in combination with the other films, police oppression as an important characteristic of black urban experience. The film is rife with suggestions of the LAPD's presence, from its accounts of African American men being brutalized by police officers to Luann's assault near the end of the film. More noteworthy are the references the film makes to actual, extradiegetic events. The first example of this appears at the film's beginning, which opens with documentary footage of two African American men being searched and harassed by at least four members of the LAPD. This episode is, in fact, Gerima and another member of his crew, who were stopped, searched, and arrested by the LAPD, "who equate Black men with expensive equipment with criminality."[62]

Another example is the poster that Dorothy's young neighbor, Angi (Renna Kraft), hangs on Dorothy and Luann's wall. Referencing an actual incident of police brutality, the poster consists of a photograph of a dead African American man who had been shot and killed (with twenty-five bullets) by the LAPD, and a caption above it reading "Murdered." Both of these references to the actual African American political and cultural landscape, as with the films before, contribute immediacy and authenticity to the fiction. However, rather than employing a romanticized urban outlaw figure such as Priest or Sweetback, *Bush Mama* suggests the danger of the ghetto space and the reality that life in the city is deadly. Instead of suggesting that the source of the violence stems from any dysfunction in the black community, *Bush Mama* points to governmental policies like policing strategies and welfare, and makes the argument against pathologizing black urban neighborhoods.

Bush Mama does not limit its critique to the LAPD. In fact, its purpose is to explore the different forces affecting Dorothy. More than one of these pressures comes from the community itself, as is shown by an incident that occurs early in the film. On her way to the welfare office,

Dorothy is the victim of a purse snatching when a young boy grabs her bag and runs off with it in the middle of a crowded sidewalk during daylight hours. Dorothy is helpless to protect herself at this stage, and has to accept the loss of the purse and what little money she had. At this point she has yet to realize her own potential agency to protect herself and those she loves. However, the scene is also an indictment of the community's passivity as a whole, as no one comes to Dorothy's aid during the incident. Additionally, the fact that the boy is African American is suggestive of the sort of crimes being committed against the residents *by* the residents of this economically depressed community.

The experimental nature of the film's acoustic track differs from the sound tracks of the other films discussed in this chapter. On the one hand, the sound tracks of all the films contribute an immediacy because the music becomes inseparable from the city culture being visualized onscreen. On the other hand, whereas a number of blaxploitation vehicles, *Shaft* and *Superfly* in particular, capitalized on the popularity of their musical tracks by separately producing and selling sound track albums (thus adding to the income of the films), *Bush Mama*'s sound track was not marketed in the same manner. In fact, where *Shaft*'s and *Superfly*'s sound tracks entered actual city spaces, blurring the boundaries between the film and reality, Gerima's tactic was to have the city enter the sound track of the film.

The combination of oppressions is manifested in the juxtaposition of the film's visual and acoustic elements. Described as "a jangling amalgam of urban sound,"[63] *Bush Mama*'s sound track layers a multiplicity of noises on top of each other in a near-deafening urban heteroglossia in which "LAPD helicopters yacket overhead, sirens keen, a glass-voiced social worker intones repeatedly—'Have you ever received any non-cash gifts?'—buses belch, guns explode, babies wail."[64] In addition to this, there are also the sounds of a radio sermon, music by Gil Scott-Heron, and T.C's voice-overs speaking directly to Dorothy and the audience about his political transformation. The sounds are as oppressive as their content, and the pressure building up both Dorothy's external and internal worlds is made tangible through them.

The sounds further enable an understanding of the film's interior and exterior spaces. While much of the narrative takes place in the streets, a large part of it is also shot in the interior spaces most closely associated with Dorothy: her apartment, the welfare office, the Women's Clinic, the neighborhood bar, and T.C.'s cell. Rather than connoting the nurturing aspects of the domestic sphere that are often associated with "women's space," Gerima indicates how interior spaces also become a threat depending on the circumstances involved, a threat that's quite different in meaning than Sweetback faces in interior spaces. For instance, the welfare office is the site of some of the harshest pressures Dorothy faces. It is where she is dehumanized, made to feel ashamed, and told that she must abort her child (the exact opposite of the film's subtext about family). Furthermore, the welfare office trespasses into Dorothy's personal space, as when her social worker visits her apartment, or when it enters Dorothy's internal world via the sound track. As she sits in her apartment, social workers' voices oppressively hammer at her. Like Georgia Brown entering the antebellum idyll in *Cabin in the Sky*, the social worker's visit to the apartment is disruptive (signified by Dorothy's fantasy in which she hits the social worker with a bottle). Dorothy may be a welfare mother, but the pathology is systemic rather than cultural.

There are other blurrings of acoustic boundaries between external and internal spaces. For example, the film repeatedly returns to the letters T.C. writes to Dorothy from jail. Each time Dorothy receives a letter, the sound track switches to his voice-over reading its contents. At certain times, the visuals switch to a medium close-up of T.C. actually speaking the words, as if in a direct address to Dorothy and the audience.[65] The film's sound track and visuals connect T.C.'s literal imprisonment with Dorothy's growing consciousness of her figurative imprisonment. At one point, T.C. discusses the similarities between the prison guards and overseers from slave plantations as the visuals travel over medium shots of different prisoners' faces, pausing on each prisoner staring out at the audience. The effect is to put faces to the victims of the police state.

Finally, the film's treatment of the family directly aligns domestic spaces with exterior, urban spaces. In blurring the boundaries of the internal and external world, *Bush Mama* links Dorothy's oppression with T.C.'s in a manner that acknowledges gender differences but that also stresses the necessity for collective cooperation and addresses the increasing masculinist focus of African American politics. This is an important point if we understand that while Dorothy is ostensibly the "lead" of the film, we are denied exclusive identification with her point of view. In fact, Dorothy is more a symbolic representation of black inner-city humanity than an individual. Her problems are community

T.C. addressing both Dorothy and the audience (*Bush Mama*, Mypheduh Films, 1976). Courtesy of Haile Gerima and Mypheduh Films.

problems; her needs and desires are those shared by the community. This is a characteristic of most of the LA Rebellion films, which posit the viability of men and women working together for all.

The most explicit example of the blurring of interior and exterior boundaries comes in the form of the poster also hung on Dorothy and Luann's wall by Angi. In it, the image of an African woman holding a gun in one hand and a baby in another stares out at and confronts the audience. The poster was produced by the Movimento Popular de Libertacao de Angola (MPLA), which was formed in 1956 and fought for self-determination and the withdrawal of Portuguese troops from Angola. The Portuguese did not leave Angola until 1975, making Portugal one of the last of the European nations to withdraw from its former colonies in Africa. The poster is a much more effective symbolic rendering of Pan-African collectivity than the dashikis and bubas from the earlier films. In this image, revolutionary change is not merely signified through fashion. Instead, direct links are drawn between the oppression experienced by the black community in Watts and that experienced by the African diaspora. In fact, the film ends on a freeze frame with Dorothy in the foreground and the poster in the background, symbolically uniting the two women, providing a clear political and collective reason for why Dorothy resorts to violence at the end of the film.

Throughout the film, Dorothy is buffeted by different pressures, contributing to her gradual metamorphosis from passive victim to active political agent. The film's story of Dorothy's transformation, Clyde Taylor argues, is similar to Sweetback's transformation.[66] I would like to suggest that Dorothy's conversion is more complex, in part because it is still self-consciously tentative and incomplete. Additionally, Dorothy's transformation includes the surrounding community in her own political expediency—a significant difference from Sweetback's and Priest's changes. Dorothy's metamorphosis is fully enabled by her surroundings, suggesting the cooperation and the tensions among individual, collective, and space.

You Can't Get There from Here: Possibilities for Mobility in the Ghetto

Janet Maslin observes of *Bush Mama* that "the sense of these characters' imprisonment and frustration is the film's most vivid message, far more powerful than the angry declaration at which Dorothy finally arrives."[67] There is no denying that Dorothy's world is shaped by physical and psychological imprisonment. After all, T.C. and Dorothy both end up in jail by the end of film. Ironically, this experience contributes, in various ways, to the "unlocking" of their minds, echoing Malcolm X's own jailhouse transformation. However, not all of the characters in the film are liberated from this internal, psychic imprisonment. For instance, Angi's mother refers to the MPLA poster as "militant trash" and Dorothy's friend Molly (Cora Lee Day), one of the film's only traces of a southern, rural past, cannot see the system's culpability in the oppressions surrounding her. Instead, she blames "niggers" for the problems in Watts.

Dorothy's oppression is directly related to her surroundings, especially the role of the police in limiting movement. As Gerima argues, "one of the experiences of being Black in America is not going where you want to go, being stopped."[68] As I have already mentioned, the film's visual and aural tracks replicate this overabundance of surveillance and containment by presenting us with the sights and sounds of control and indicates the "underlying relations of repression, surveillance and exclusion that characterize the fragmented, paranoid spatiality towards which Los Angeles seems to aspire."[69] Toni Cade Bambara notes that "the omnipresence of sirens, cruisers, and cops define the neighborhood(s) as occupied territory."[70] We are reminded, repeatedly, that Dorothy is constrained by her surroundings in an accurate rendering of a "carceral city."[71]

The limitations of the ghetto in *Bush Mama* are quite different from those in other films. In *Cotton*, *Sweetback*, and *Superfly*, the movement of characters is nowhere as constrained as in Gerima's film, and it is often the case that characters move freely within and among neighborhoods. This is perhaps the case because as a woman Dorothy's mobility is constrained by gender whereas the other films focus on male protagonists. Yet, there are significant similarities among all of the films. In each of the films discussed in this chapter, characters' escapes are motivated much more so by political decisions than a desire to leave the city, and where physical escape is impossible, other forms of resistance arise. For instance, Dorothy does not escape Watts; however, by the end of the film she has begun to escape her own internal colonialism. Similar transformations take place, albeit in different ways, in Sweetback and Priest. These characters' concerns with movement and travel must also be understood as psychological and evolutionary rather than merely physical.

Furthermore, if we remember that one of the major African American tropes of the twentieth century was migration, it is no surprise that mobility is one of the core concerns of these narratives. Characters in earlier films, such as black-cast musicals, are denied this movement, truly existing in a "spatial apartheid."[72] In the 1970s, the potential for movement began to appear in films as a result of so many years of migration and a largely dispossessed audience. This emphasis on movement is localized and centered on the characters moving around the city. In this way movement is also optimistic because it is more concerned with flexibility and change of lifestyle, thinking, and social conditions than it is about leaving the city altogether. In other words, mobility is about changing the spaces of the ghetto, of transforming them, not leaving them. In this regard, it must be remembered that even Sweetback, who flees the ghetto, promises to return. This optimism is a result of the time frame in which the films were made. While the general discontent about the impotence of civil rights strategies from the late 1950s to early 1960s may have led to the more active strategies of the Black Panthers and black nationalism, these ideologies rest upon the belief that things could be changed. The city—no matter how destitute—in the films from the 1970s reflects the formation of a new black sociopolitical identity and agency. As we will see, this will change in the 1980s and 1990s when mobility is linked to a literal escape from city space.

We are witness to a complex series of changes and dialogues in African American film from the 1970s. The films are evidence of a move away from earlier representations of African American subject matter as rural, southern, antebellum, or removed entirely from any recognizable context. With this redefinition of space and time came a concurrent reevaluation of images and stereotypes, especially as related to the images of the city constructed by the Moynihan report and other sociological studies. The films struggle to articulate a black aesthetic, one in which the city plays a central role. As a result, the black city became a recognizable trope in both industrial and non-industrial films, to the point in which, by *Superfly*'s release, the city was familiar, though highly contested, terrain.

4

Welcome to Crooklyn: Spike Lee and the Rearticulation of the Black Urbanscape

or a brief period spanning the late 1960s to the mid-1970s, the visualization of an African American cinematic urbanscape was inextricably linked to blaxploitation and other black-focused films. This city space, which I have referred to as a black ghetto chronotope, was characterized by precise spatial and temporal coordinates: African American neighborhoods in New York and Los Angeles in the 1970s. Films such as *Sweet Sweetback's Baadasssss Song* and *Superfly* shared a temporal immediacy and documentary-like realism produced by cinematic devices such as location shooting, handheld camera, and sync-sound. References to the fashions, urban patois, and politics (such as black nationalism) contemporaneous with African American urban experience during the period enriched the films' mimetic qualities. Furthermore, the films' musical scores expanded their overall aura of urban chic by extending blaxploitation's reach from theaters to radio when sound tracks were marketed as separate, although related, entities. Used in this way, music contributed to the films' cultural capital and reified their urban narratives in a reciprocal relationship in which their sound became part of the city's sound track and vice versa.

While ghetto settings were not an exclusive characteristic of blaxploitation—a point I made in my discussion of Haile Gerima's *Bush Mama*—films from the genre authored

and disseminated what were some of the most recognizable constructions of the black city in the early 1970s, examples of which include
Superfly's New York and *Sweetback*'s Los Angeles. Due to their overwhelming popularity, the films defined the contours of the represented
"Black City" for millions of theatergoers. Yet, because of the central
role played by the ghetto in blaxploitation, it is no surprise that as the
genre began to disappear from the cinematic screen, so too did the black
city, if for no other reason than blaxploitation was almost the sole ar-
ticulator of its spaces in commercial cinema. Urban spaces may have
materialized in other black-oriented films like Michael Schultz's *Cooley
High* (1975) and *Car Wash* (1976), as well as in Berry Gordy's *Mahogany*
(1975), but it appeared in increasingly diluted forms, diminishing the
city's importance in the narrative. For instance, in *Mahogany*, Chicago's
South Side is solely a backdrop for the first part of the film, its impoverished inner-city streets becoming nothing more than the literal "local
color" for a fashion shoot.[1]

Ironically, part of the responsibility for blaxploitation's disappearance can be found in its successes. One of the main reasons for the
film industry's initial interest in the production of blaxploitation vehicles like *Shaft*, *Superfly*, and later spin-offs was their profit potential.
They promised to attract what had long been identified as a large proportion of the filmgoing audience—the African American box office.
Facing financial ruin, the result of a number of intersecting causes, such
as anti-monopoly legislation, television, and suburbanization, the industry looked to what would eventually be called blaxploitation and its
promise of significant box office returns for minimal financial output.
Blaxploitation films, in effect, helped pull Hollywood out of a financial
slump. However, when the financial crisis had abated somewhat, the industry shifted back into the production of other genres—importantly,
ones with more of a "crossover" appeal—and decreased the scale of its
investments in black-focused product.[2]

The turn away from blaxploitation was further influenced by the environment of critical contestation engendered by the films. As early as
the appearance of *Sweetback* in 1970, blaxploitation's glorification of
sex, violence, and criminality came under critical scrutiny from different segments of the African American community, indicating the continuing concern with defining a black film aesthetics that had begun
with the first protests against D. W. Griffith's *Birth of a Nation*. Initially
these critiques were limited to the pages of various print media. The

release of *Superfly* in 1972, however, sparked the formation of a number of groups such as Jesse Jackson's People United to Save Humanity (Operation PUSH), an organization determined to change the nature of African American cinematic representations. PUSH's focus echoed those of Walter White's and the NAACP's from decades before in its concern over the lack of African American representation both on the screen and in film production as a whole, a clear indication of what little change had actually occurred in integrating Hollywood since the World War II protests and promises.

It was not long before PUSH was joined by other groups adverse to the genre's use of "negative" stereotypes. For instance, the Coalition Against Blaxploitation (CAB), an alliance of civil rights (NAACP, CORE) and community groups, proposed a ratings system for black action films produced by Hollywood.[3] Furthermore, Marion Barry organized Blacks Against Narcotics and Genocide (BANG) in Washington, D.C. BANG was a response to what Barry saw as the "mind genocide"[4] of *Superfly*'s glorification of criminal life and drug use. Overall, the community's response at this time—at least the middle-class response—was to call for censorship in the form of ratings systems and an all-out economic boycott of the industry. A more significant effect of this pressure was that the industry had an excuse to scale back on its production of blaxploitation films. The result was that the production of negative stereotypes ceased but little was offered in exchange.

The disappearance of black urban spaces from the screen had already been foreshadowed in blaxploitation narratives. The remakes of popular genre vehicles, for instance, *Shaft*, *Superfly*, and *Cleopatra Jones*, shifted the films' story locations away from the city spaces they formerly inhabited—New York and Los Angeles, respectively—and into more "exotic" territory. An example of this appears in the third in the *Shaft* series, *Shaft in Africa* (John Guillermin, 1973), which sent John Shaft to West Africa and to France to break up an illegal immigration and indentured employment ring. *Superfly T.N.T.* (Sig Shore, 1973) reprised the role of Youngblood Priest within a Parisian setting, thus removing him from the Harlem milieu that had previously supplied him with agency. In both of these examples, the heroes, who up to this point had both defined and been defined by the black city, worked in a larger diasporic context, with Shaft in Africa and Priest reprising in fictional and action form the footsteps of many African American ex-patriots, like Langston Hughes, Chester Himes, and Josephine Baker, in Paris.

Lastly, the relatively late release of *Cleopatra Jones and the Casino of Gold* (William Tennant, 1975) relocated one of the female variants of the formula, already a revision of generic conventions, from Los Angeles to Hong Kong. Maybe these changes were made simply as a means of keeping the genre afloat a little longer. Or maybe, as it has been suggested, the changes capitalized on the combined appeal of blaxploitation and martial arts films, another genre popular with African American audiences at the time.[5] It is also feasible that the relocations were more an indication of the industry's attempt to move the genre out of the ghetto, as a response to growing criticisms of its representations. Such a change also made the films less threatening to crossover audiences because a film like *Cleopatra Jones* resembled an African American version of a James Bond film more than it did a blaxploitation film. These later films had nowhere near the success of those located in the social and political landscape of select U.S. cities, an indication of the extent to which blaxploitation's representation, marketing, and audience appeal were deeply connected to the black ghetto. In short, what made the genre so successful, its verité representations of black city space, was also one of the prime causes of its downfall because the city and the characters contained therein threatened segments of both black and white audiences.

These factors, combined with the loss of portions of the black audience and performers to television and Hollywood's growing realization that audiences were beginning to tire of blaxploitation's conventions, reinforced the industry's move away from blaxploitation. The release of films focused on African American subject matter declined after 1974, as "the film industry realized that it did not need an exclusively black vehicle to draw the large black audiences that had saved it from financial disaster."[6] What little production remained was converted into films with even greater crossover appeal, sparked, in part, by the success of *Sounder* in 1972, a film that significantly shifted away from the contemporary black city in its narrative focus on a family of southern sharecroppers in the 1930s. The result was a story set in a less threatening historical moment more closely resembling the antebellum idyll of Hollywood's earliest black-cast musicals.

Studio-financed black film production virtually disappeared in the late 1970s, when the industry revamped its approach to filmmaking with the development of large-scale, big-budget blockbusters. These films had the capacity to draw upon a large audience, a significant proportion of which was made up of African American viewers. Since the appeal of blaxploitation films for Hollywood rested upon the fact that they had a high investment-to-profit ratio—and thus presented little financial risk—it was unlikely that the industry would have financed an expensive film with a black focus. The contradictory ideology against such block-busters was the belief that big-budget films with black themes would not draw white audiences whereas films with smaller budgets could. The result was an overall decline in mainstream African American film production in the late 1970s and the early 1980s. Furthermore, no sig-nificant gains were made in the numbers of black actors and personnel working in Hollywood. With this dearth in production, only a small number of black celebrities, such as Diana Ross, Richard Pryor, and Ed-die Murphy, rose to superstar status in the 1980s, giving the appearance of African American participation in the film industry while, in fact, it was on the wane. This trend continued until the mid-1980s, when a new generation of young filmmakers, one of whom was Spike Lee, appeared. Significant representations of African American city spaces would not reappear until Lee first redefined them in the 1980s and then a whole new generation of filmmakers and rappers associated with a "New Jack" aesthetic transformed them into the hood in the 1990s.[7]

Spike's Joint: Guerrilla Filmmaking and Black Brooklyn

> There are different types of black films. I feel that the same people that saw
> *Krush Groove* and the other rap movies will like this film [*She's Gotta Have
> It*] a lot.
> —Spike Lee (1986)[8]

In the following pages I focus on the role that Spike Lee has played in the rearticulation of the black cinematic city in African American film-making from the black ghetto of the 1970s into the hood of the 1990s. One of Lee's most obvious and significant influences has been in shift-ing the location of East Coast city films from Harlem, the black cultural mecca of the past, to the borough of Brooklyn, a move that acknowl-edges larger African American demographic shifts that took place dur-ing and after World War II and that underscores Brooklyn's geographic significance for present-day African American cultural life. But Lee's films are interesting for more than his vision of a black Brooklyn, for they also reshaped the American independent film sector that followed. Lee is an example of a "Black Commercial Independent," a filmmaker who combines the autonomy of the independent sector with the financial muscle of the commercial realm.[9] This autonomy and agency allow Lee control over his narratives, formal experimentation, and marketing while the commercial elements allow him to make films with relatively substantial budgets. As we will see in the following chapter, all of this influenced (and enabled) a new generation of both black and white filmmakers in the 1990s. If viewed in this light, Lee not only transformed African American city spaces and black filmmaking practices, he also changed American filmmaking as a whole.

Even before Lee introduced black Brooklyn into cinematic discourse, a number of hip-hop influenced films were released that bear the early traces of the urban look, sound, and themes that Lee developed in his films and the hood films of the 1990s would further refine. One of the characteristics of the hip-hop films is a focus on urban youth culture, particularly song and dance. Films such as *Wild Style* (Charlie Ahearn, 1982) and *Beat Street* (Stan Lathan, 1984) introduced the sights and sounds of the graffiti, rap, and break-dancing cultures, which had emerged from New York's South Bronx neighborhoods in the 1970s and which by the 1980s had migrated to downtown clubs and galleries. Another film, *Krush Groove* (Michael Schultz, 1985), focused on rappers in particular and suggested in addition that rap music, at least in the first half of the 1980s, was a subculture not only associated with an African American community but with an entire downtown "scene" that developed out of disco and other dance music. This is supported by the film's references to actual downtown venues such as the after-hours club Save the Robots, a space identified at the time with a multiplicity of musical genres.

The release of the early hip-hop films closely coincides with the launch of MTV in 1981, and the history of the musical form's relationship to the network bears striking similarities to the relationship between black-directed film and commercial cinema from the time. The music network, which quickly asserted an influence on American youth culture, is present in *Krush Groove*'s references to MTV's influence over the careers of emerging artists. In fact, it is the stated desire for the rappers in the film, particularly the members of Run-DMC, to secure an appearance on the network. But while MTV was responsible for bringing rap to mainstream attention with its 1981 broadcast of Debbie

Harry's "Rapture," the reality was that the network was reluctant to integrate hip-hop into its video rotation. Network executives argued that rap's audience was not "substantial" enough to warrant inclusion, thus echoing the film industry's fear over investing large budgets in African American film. It wasn't until they saw that "hip hop culture was . . . emerging as a crucial sphere of youth discourse, contouring not on the popular cultures of many black and Latino youth but the larger youth body politic" that rap was added to MTV's format—in a segregated manner—through "Yo! MTV Raps" and "Fade to Black."[10] Sharing the experience of African American film, it was not until rap had proven its crossover appeal that it became a legitimate—recognized by MTV and the music industry as a whole—musical form.

Krush Groove and *Wild Style* feature rappers playing themselves, a casting practice that was extended in many of the 1990s films. For example, *Krush Groove* stars Run-DMC, The Fat Boys, Kurtis Blow, and

Beat Street focused on hip-hop culture before Spike Lee (Orion Pictures, 1984). Courtesy of the Museum of Modern Art Film Stills Archive.

Sheila E., and includes appearances by LL Cool J and The Beastie Boys. While accused of being one long music video (echoing the critical dismissals of *Stormy Weather* from decades before), the film's utilization of rap celebrities was rooted in blaxploitation's blurring of sound track and narrative and diegetic and nondiegetic elements. The film also illustrates the rising importance of rap as a youth discourse, targeting an audience of both urban and suburban, black and white, youth viewers. Most important of all, however, was the assertion of the MC as a celebrity and community griot. Out of this we can see the progression to the role that Public Enemy would have four years later in Spike Lee's *Do The Right Thing* (1989). Even though Public Enemy does not appear in the narrative, the diegetic and nondiegetic use of their song "Fight the Power" effectively inserts them into the cinematic space by continually acknowledging their presence and by using their words to speak for the struggles faced by some facets of the African American community. Even earlier, Lee's films acknowledged hip-hop's force in black culture in their use of rap and references to b-boy fashion and, most literally, through his collaboration with Ernest Dickerson, a film-school friend and the cinematographer on *Krush Groove*.

As early as 1983 and the completion of his award-winning NYU Graduate School thesis film, *Joe's Bed-Stuy Barbershop: We Cut Heads*, Lee focused on core themes that, while adapted over time, still remain seminal to his work. Lee has addressed all of his films to an African American audience (even though many also draw in a substantial mixed audience), and his focus on the role of the city and history in shaping black life has engendered a vast amount of dialogue in the academic and popular presses. Lee's films have also been highly reflexive in form, and they often explicitly or implicitly evaluate and rearticulate African American cinematic representation. This reflexivity is present in *Joe's Bed-Stuy Barbershop*, which is Lee's variation of the gangster genre made for an African American context. Like Ralph Cooper's *Dark Manhattan*, the film focuses on the black-run numbers racket, and there are similarities between the earlier film's suggestion of the numbers banker as a race man and Nicholas Lovejoy (Tommy Hicks) in Lee's film. Both men, while criminals, are devoted to the community, and both feel as though they are serving neighborhood residents in a positive way by running black-owned and -operated businesses (echoing Lee's early establishment of the Brooklyn-based production company, 40 Acres & a Mule Filmworks, Inc.).

While *Joe's Bed-Stuy Barbershop* revisits and revises the black gangster film, its focus is on a young married couple and their struggles with living in Bed-Stuy, Brooklyn, earning a living, and maintaining their integrity and pride in the process. In its focus on Zachariah (Monty Ross) and Ruth (Donna Bailey) Homer, the film provided some of the first sympathetic and detailed glimpses of the borough's African American faces, personalities, and communities, from the customers who use Joe's barbershop both as a community center and as a numbers parlor to the children who play games in the streets. Additionally, the film emphasized community concerns, such as the governmental abandonment and the decay of New York's public housing, the inability of the city government to service the area effectively, the lure of criminal activities for African American youth, and the temptation of many middle-class black residents to abandon the area for "better" areas like Atlanta (acknowledging the existence of a trend in African American migration back to the South). While much of the film consists of interior settings, its exterior locations, especially the housing projects that Ruth visits as part of her job as a social worker, illustrate the area's poverty in gritty detail.

The film's emphasis on the realities of location, indicated in its grainy visuals, extends to its use of sound. Most characters speak in a combination of middle-class and contemporary urban speech idioms, making reference—for example, in a scene in which Zach offers a detailed analysis of the shapes of heads—to the specifics of African American urban culture in its cadences and concerns. Lee also uses music to set time and place, and the film's references to early rap suggest the prevailing presence of the musical form in black neighborhoods. This rap influence extends to *Joe's Bed-Stuy Barbershop*'s visuals as well. In one scene in particular, for example, Ruth is forced to wade through a group of breakdancers using the entrance to an apartment building as a performance space. Rather than using the performance simply to supply background, Lee's camera lingers on the dancers in the foreground, providing urban youth culture with a moment in the spotlight and quoting other films like *Beat Street* in the process.[11]

While *Joe's Bed-Stuy Barbershop* provides an important early example of Lee's thematic concerns, it is *She's Gotta Have It* (1986) that truly placed black Brooklyn onto the cinematic map and into the minds and imaginations of national and international audiences. This was due to the amazing critical response that Lee's first feature, made with $175,000 scraped together from grants and private donations, engendered in the filmmaking community. Debuting at the San Francisco Film Festival, *She's Gotta Have It* was an instant success on the festival and art film circuits, where it went on to win the *Prix de la Jeunesse* at the Cannes Film Festival, indicating the ways it was marketed and succeeded as a crossover vehicle aimed at both mixed art house and black middle-class audiences.[12] In fact, in many of the film's first reviews, the focus was on its status as an independent film rather than solely as a "black film."

She's Gotta Have It capitalized on the factors often missing from blaxploitation vehicles—more complex representations of African American life, a female lead, and crossover appeal—while enjoying similar large-scale returns ($11 million, including international receipts).[13] Unlike blaxploitation, however, the film introduced multilayered and contemporary African American characters, such as Nola Darling (Tracy Camilla Johns) and her three lovers and friends, Mars Blackmon (Spike Lee), Jamie Overstreet (Tommy Hicks), and Greer Childs (John Canada Terrell), and its narrative was set in the streets and interiors of what would soon become a recognizable Brooklyn cityscape. The film, ostensibly a *Rashomon*-like exploration of Nola's personality, desires, and sexual fetishes, provided a multifaceted glimpse of a black urbanscape that was different from any other African American space screened thus far, bringing to "commercial cinema a distinct style of discourse about the shifting contours of race in postindustrial American culture."[14] The film was located in a space comprised of intelligent, liberated, and middleclass women, sure of their independence and their sexual preferences. Also, Lee provided, in the guise of Nola's love interests, a rich variety of black male characters rather than one-dimensional variations on the sexually and physically empowered Sweetbacks and Shafts from the 1970s or the more recent "neo-minstrel" spook and coon characters resuscitated in mainstream cinema in the late 1970s and early 1980s in the roles often played by Richard Pryor and Eddie Murphy in their narrative films.[15]

In *She's Gotta Have It* Lee moved beyond one-dimensional characterizations and archetypes of the black male by suggesting a multiplicity of subject positions. For example, Jamie and Greer rearticulate representations of African American men in different, although related, ways. Jamie, who is the most emotionally intimate with Nola, is confident, comfortable with himself, and overwhelmingly middle-class. In some ways his characterization has its closest referents in the roles most often played by Sidney Poitier from decades before except that Jamie radiates a sexuality that is neither absent (like the majority of Poitier's characters) nor overblown (like 1970s characterizations from blaxploitation). In fact, Jamie's hope for a monogamous relationship is sincere and yet he is continually frustrated by Nola, who does not want to be contained by limitations on her sexual life. Through the couple's interactions the film offers an alternative to the demonized welfare mothers and absent fathers made into archetypes by the Moynihan report of the mid-1960s.

Greer, on the other hand, is young and upwardly mobile, a Buppie figure virtually absent from commercial cinematic representations of African American men from this time. Greer's aspirations, both personal and professional, remove him from everything in the surrounding community, except for Nola. This distance is geographically signified through his choice to live in Manhattan rather than Brooklyn. Greer also desires to have a monogamous relationship with Nola, and when he is frustrated in his endeavors, he threatens to leave her for a white woman. In both cases, Greer's preferences align him with the white community and indicate both his metaphorical and his real distance from the black community.

Spike Lee's Mars introduced the b-boy to art cinema in *She's Gotta Have It* (40 Acres and a Mule Filmworks, Inc., 1986). Courtesy of 40 Acres and a Mule Filmworks, Inc.

Finally, with Mars, Lee introduced a character modeled after those in films like *Krush Groove*. Young, unemployed, and seemingly irresponsible, Mars spoke to a generation of African American theatergoers with what Lee himself describes as "OFFICIAL B-BOY ATTIRE"[16] (gold jewelry and expensive sneakers), his expertise in the rhythms of contemporary urban speech idioms, and a rap-based musical motif accompanying him in his initial onscreen appearance. In short, Mars "symbolizes the Black urban underclass," or at least its male version.[17] Mars was such a popular figure that Lee had to resist following up this effort with additional films dedicated to the character's highjinks. Instead, Lee channeled Mars' popularity into a series of ads for Nike's Air Jordans sneaker line, ironically replicating the commodity fetishism at the heart of Mars' character and foreshadowing the focus on street fashion that would become one of the characteristics of hip-hop. This progression also suggests the way in which Lee dispersed much of the threat associated with a young, black, unemployed male through the use of comedy. Mars is a "fool" like the Pryor and Murphy characters that preceded and were contemporary with him. But Mars is also likable and sympathetic and, like Pryor and Murphy, a carnivalesque subversiveness characterizes many of his antics. Examples of this include his sarcastic disruptions of many of the more serious monologues given by Jamie and Greer or the way in which his comments on events act as a Greek chorus, shedding light on characters' motives. With some fine-tuning—a reduction in the comedy and an introduction of violence—Mars developed into the archetype for what followed in the 1990s, culminating in "America's nightmare": the narrator's description for O-Dog in *Menace II Society*. The difference between the two is that O-Dog's threat will not be mediated by comedic strategies.

The ways that the film's characters are incorporated into a specific urbanscape provide another signal that Lee took African American film in a new direction. The neighborhood is introduced in the film before any of the major characters by means of an establishing long shot of the Brooklyn Bridge photographed from the Brooklyn side and framed in a low angle with the camera placed on the ground. Rather than directed across the East River toward Manhattan, the perspective of nearly all establishing shots of the city in other films set in New York, this shot focuses solely on Brooklyn; Manhattan is nowhere to be seen. A view of Nola's loft building (later revealed to be her apartment windows) fills the frame and the top of the bridge appears only in the background. Because the diegesis is not concerned with the other side of the East River, but with Nola's life and surroundings, the film begins with a perspective that originates from within Brooklyn and does not leave the area.

Following this introduction, the film references the borough's streets, neighborhoods, and landmarks through location shooting and shots that acknowledge identifiable subway stops, the Fulton Mall, the Promenade along the East River, and Fort Greene Park in downtown Brooklyn. Like earlier representations of the black city, especially those set in Harlem, the film names certain key sites, but these sites are not nearly as recognizable to an uninitiated audience as 125th Street or the Apollo Theater. The effect is to introduce another, more realistic Brooklyn to the audience. Lee's rendering of the borough is a complicated subject considering the film's experimental style, which combines documentary and fiction conventions and provides a verité look in an experimental narrative. In his journal entries describing the process of making *She's Gotta Have It*, Lee lists many influences, most of which are drawn from European and U.S. art cinema. Additionally, Lee borrowed from documentary tradition, namely, cinema verité and direct cinema, in the characters' direct address, identifying title cards, black-and-white film stock, hand-held camerawork, and location shooting. While also a function of financial exigencies, the effect is to make the film look and sound like a documentary.

The film's reflexivity extends to its narrative experimentation, which provides a nonlinear, open-ended explication of events. It is perhaps, however, Lee's use of still photos and color stock that indicates the ways in which the film blurs the boundaries between presenting an actual space and a refraction or highly constructed version of that space. There are three separate occasions in which stills interrupt the narrative, two of which are nondiegetic and provide detailed shots of Brooklyn cityscapes during different seasons. These have no relation to events and yet they situate the narrative in fully explicated space and provide another lovingly rendered introduction to the area. Furthermore, they are an intertextual reference to *Superfly*'s inclusion of still photos documenting the trail of cocaine sale and use. Unlike *Superfly*, however, the stills in *She's Gotta Have It* celebrate the space. The film's already reflexive verité strategies are ruptured further by a six-minute color sequence shot in Fort Greene Park. Ostensibly Lee's homage to Vincente Minnelli and the Hollywood musical, the sequence also explicitly cites Victor Fleming's *The Wizard of Oz* (1939). In all these references, the sequence reflexively reminds the audience of the film's construction of fantasy, even in actual settings: the color sequence represents Jamie's fantasy—in the form of a birthday presentation of song and dance—of a monogamous relationship with Nola. Once the film shifts back to Nola's point of view, the black-and-white film stock is restored. In this context, Jamie's attempt to define Nola is presented in fantasy, while Fort Greene Park, shot in both black and white and color stock, is celebrated.

The cinematography indicates that this urban landscape is not a "ghetto space," defined by burned-out buildings and other outward signs of poverty and decay, like earlier representations of the black city. Instead, Lee places complex characters into a fully defined setting that is not easily readable as a ghetto, thus suggesting that the space itself requires a different narrative from those from the preceding decade. Furthermore, the heteroglot collection of characters suggests that the urbanscape is home to a highly complex and variegated community. By constructing an urban space defined outside the more common parameters of poverty, criminality, and drugs, Lee provides a view of a community that is more diverse than the majority of representations of black city space so far would have one believe, and in doing so, he changes representations of the inner city away from earlier spatiotemporal constructions of the ghetto. In fact, Lee might be responsible for the construction of a "Brooklyn chronotope," with himself the American filmmaker so consistently associated with the borough.

Bed-Stuy, Do or Die: *Do The Right Thing* and the Contested Terrain of the Cityscape

> You can't fully appreciate *Do The Right Thing* (1989) until you learn a thing or two about Brooklyn.
> —Nelson George (1991)[18]

In his subsequent films Lee continued to articulate and rearticulate different views of Brooklyn's various neighborhoods and people. While the heterogeneity of the black city would become central to all of his films, it is most fully realized in *Do The Right Thing*, his third feature. With this film Lee not only succeeds in emphasizing and examining the heteroglossia (racial, economic, generational, and gendered) at play in one block in Bed-Stuy, but his commercial success (as well that of Robert Townsend's *Hollywood Shuffle* in 1987) ushered in a whole new generation of young, African American filmmakers and a generation of independent filmmakers who had witnessed the disappearance of funding and studio interest in the wake of the move to bigger budget blockbusters.[19]

Do The Right Thing's narrative is disarmingly simple. Set in a single block in Brooklyn's Bedford-Stuyvesant area, it details twenty-four hours in the life of a neighborhood on the hottest day of the year. Rather than exploring the macrocosm of causes and effects leading to the conditions of this particular block, Lee lets the block, its residents, and the day's events reveal the conditions and pressures of the inner city. Salim Muwakkil observes that

> Lee doesn't avert his gaze from the pathologies in the community, but neither does he judge them. His depiction of life on a block in Brooklyn is empathetic and lovingly rendered. However, he's not concerned with the glaze of romanticism. Lee's flesh-toned portrayals of African-Americans in all their complexity and self-deceptive guises lend to his film an almost anthropological authenticity.[20]

Do The Right Thing is an exploration of racism, its many causes and effects, and how it all plays out in this small urbanscape. Its single-block setting embodies multiple signifiers of the extradiegetic conditions affecting the neighborhood.

As a film school graduate, Lee was familiar with the international history of cinematic movements, styles, and techniques. In *Do The Right Thing* he continued to employ many of the techniques introduced by the Italian Neorealists, the French New Wave, and Soviet filmmaking from the 1920s that had characterized his earlier films. From the Neorealists Lee adapted the use of moving camera, location shooting, and a focus on small-scale stories and ordinary characters—the concern, in other words, with an individual maneuvering through a world much larger than himself, much like the "thief's" experience in Vittorio DeSica's *Bicycle Thieves* (1941). For instance, Mookie (Spike Lee) learns that his concern with "just getting paid" doesn't absolve him from his responsibility to the neighborhood and this is what constructs the moral dilemma he faces near the end of the film. *Do The Right Thing* also bears the influence of the French New Wave, especially in the use of the Brechtian concepts of alienation and distanciation and their related formal and narrative techniques. Lee capitalizes on the techniques of

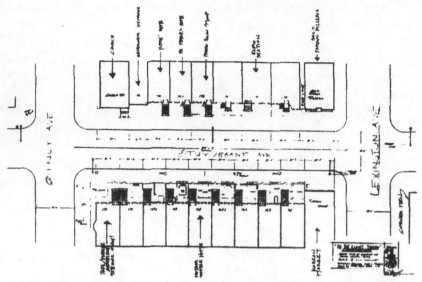

The importance of the space is indicated in Lee's rendering of the block. *Do The Right Thing* (40 Acres and a Mule Filmworks, Inc., 1989). Courtesy of 40 Acres and a Mule Filmworks, Inc.

dutch angles, visible editing strategies such as jump cuts, and direct address to explore the interactions between the cinematic apparatus and his subject matter. This is also apparent in the abundance of canted angles, wide-angle shots, and rapid-fire editing patterns during scenes of extreme tension. Additionally, a montage sequence in the middle of the film disrupts narrative suture by presenting a series of characters reciting racial slurs directly into the camera, first by starting with a medium shot before tracking forward into a close-up of their mouths.[21] Finally, from the Soviets Lee borrows Sergei Eisenstein's theories about montage and the dialectical nature of constructing cinematic meaning. By capitalizing on discontinuous editing strategies and combining them with more conventional analytical editing, Lee manipulates the meaning and the pacing of the scenes. Many of these techniques were already mobilized by African American filmmakers in the 1970s, in particular, Melvin Van Peebles, Haile Gerima, and other directors associated with the LA Rebellion, who also had similar international influences. In this way Lee was not really introducing anything new inasmuch as he was continuing a tradition.

In numerous articles and interviews Lee has discussed these and other influential movements, styles, and directors, including the urban, ethnic narratives of Martin Scorsese. In fact, Lee would later work with Scorsese on *Clockers* and even later he modeled his own version of an Italian-American neighborhood in *Summer of Sam* (1999) on Scorsese's works.[22] However, it is in Lee's appropriation of the methods of what he called "guerrilla filmmaking" that his links to Oscar Micheaux and especially Van Peebles are the strongest. The three filmmakers have much in common: their outspoken public presence, their refusal to compromise, and the controversies their films engendered in the press (the fear, for example, that the films would incite violence). However, their greatest commonality is the fact that they all managed to maintain some level of independence in the production, exhibition, and distribution of their films. Lee notes:

> Melvin Van Peebles is the man. We all know and read about pioneer filmmaker Oscar Micheaux. But Melvin did it in our lifetime, and he's alive to talk about what he did. His *Sweet Sweetback's Baadasssss Song* gave us the answers we needed. This was an example of how to make a film (a real movie), distribute it yourself, and most important, get *paid*. Without *Sweetback* who knows if there could have been a *Shaft* or *Superfly*? Or looking down the road a little further, would there have been a *She's Gotta Have It*, *Hollywood Shuffle*, or *House Party*?[23]

These earlier filmmakers also influenced Lee's marketing of film-related products, such as sound tracks and other merchandise, a method of profit-making that had its roots in Micheaux's door-to-door trips selling his novels and in Van Peebles' packaging *Sweetback*'s sound track and an accompanying book for promotional and profit making purposes. Lee perfected this technique, and pioneered the now ubiquitous practice of selling films with accompanying materials: sound tracks, "making-of" journals, T-shirts, baseball hats, and other clothing bearing the film's or the production company's insignia. Lee learned early in his career that word-of-mouth would sell as many tickets as advertising campaigns and that T-shirts and hats function as walking billboards. To expand on this aspect of film marketing, Lee opened a retail store, a "joint," in Fort Greene, in the process helping to revitalize the neighborhood. What is unusual about Lee's marketing is that he uses commercial strategies for what are often small, independent, specialty films.

In addition to the film's self-conscious combination of camera technique and montage, Lee constructs a no-less self-conscious mise-en-scène and narrative. Like the city-based films from the 1970s, Lee's film utilizes specific referents of contemporary urban black culture to provide the narrative with elements of realism and immediacy. *Do The Right Thing* references current events through the inclusion of graffiti ("Tawana Told the Truth"), signs (billboards of Mike Tyson), and fashion. The characters' clothing, in particular, functions almost like a Greek chorus, commenting on the environment and providing insight into characters' actions. For instance, homeboy Radio Raheem's (Bill Nunn) colorful T-shirt, reading simply "Bed-Stuy," encodes him as a part of the neighborhood similar to the way in which Mars was often shot in proximity to the Brooklyn Bridge in *She's Gotta Have It*. DJ Señor Love Daddy's (Samuel L. Jackson) hats change according to the situation and mood. Mookie's ambiguous and often compromised position is suggested more by his Jackie Robinson baseball shirt than through his words or actions. Buggin' Out's (Giancarlo Esposito) kente-patterned T-shirt and shorts signify his "Afro-Nationalist" political agenda. And the embodiment of neighborhood gentrification is Clifton (John Savage), the white owner of a brownstone, who is outfitted in a Larry Bird Celtics' shirt, iconography bespeaking the ultimate white boy's basketball hero. Clifton's presence directly communicates Lee's criticism of the fact that previously underdeveloped parts of the city were becoming a "new frontier" for upwardly mobile professionals tired of suburban living and looking to invest in inner-city areas with low property values.[24]

The aural signifiers of the contemporary African American political and cultural landscape, particularly the sound track's mixture of dialogue, dialect, and music, combine with this polyphony of visual signifiers.[25] *Do The Right Thing* overflows with the sounds of contemporary urban patois, which is most evident in Mookie's and Buggin' Out's speech patterns. But the film does not privilege their speech over that of other characters. For instance, Da Mayor (Ossie Davis) and Mother Sister (Ruby Dee) speak with the soft cadence of the South in their voices, a verbal reference to the history of African American migration during the twentieth century and an indication of intragenerational tensions that exist in the narratives and in many of Lee's other films. Furthermore, Davis and Dee extradiegetically reference the history of African American visual culture through their well-known professional histories, which include involvement in both stage and screen and in Davis' direction of *Cotton Comes to Harlem*. The history of the diaspora's migrations and displacements is further echoed in Coconut Sid's (one of the three "Cornermen") Caribbean accent, indicating Brooklyn's multitextured immigrant history reflective of all aspects of the African diaspora. Additionally, the sound track is filled with the cadences of other accents—English inflected with Puerto Rican "Spanglish," a middle-class "non"accent, a Bensonhurst "American-Italian" accent, and Korean—permeating the streets and shops and suggestive of even later migrations into the area. Through this orchestration of differing neighborhood discourses, Lee succeeds in communicating black Brooklyn's inherent heteroglossia, as well as diffusing the audience's identification with characters among a collection of individuals.

Another way in which the film's aural track references narrative events and the contemporary political environment is its incorporation of rap- and jazz-based musical motifs. For example, Public Enemy's "Fight the Power" fills the theater from the opening credits on. The song both introduces and defines Radio Raheem because he communicates through his music rather than his words. Raheem has been described as "big and silent. Sort of a quintessential stand-in for what is threatening about young black maleness. What you don't know you assume, erring in the direction of ugliness and danger."[26] Raheem's medium of communication concurrently symbolizes an African American male subculture and white middle-class fears of it. Raheem's "ghetto-blaster" is significant as

> an Ur-symbol of interracial animosity and class style wars . . . [a] perfect radiator for black anger and white noise (and vice versa). Next to semi-automatic weaponry, the ghetto blaster is the easiest way for the underclass to exact vengeance and aggression on an unwary bourgeoisie. In New York, Boston, Chicago—any metropolis with public transportation—a black youth strolling onto a subway car with his personal, multi-decibel sound track sends up red-alerts signals and draws out palpable racial vibes. An urban commonplace, it has become something of a mass-media leitmotif.[27]

Sal's (Danny Aiello) and Raheem's dispute over the music is a "war for position,"[28] in which those in control of the noise are in control of the space. Furthermore, through this musical motif, Lee expands on his earlier b-boy characterization of Mars in *She's Gotta Have It*. Raheem, like Mars, is unemployed and seemingly aimless, although in this characterization the comedy has been replaced by anger and tension. While Mars only suggested the potential threat posed by such a characterization, Raheem makes it literal. This is facilitated by the boom box's volume and Raheem's silence, his size, and Lee's choice to frame him with dutch angles and a wide-angle distorting lens, making him appear to loom over other characters and the audience.

The importance of music in the definition of identity, seen in Mars as well as characters from a number of other films (such as *Beat Street* and, especially, *Krush Groove*), and the rise in popularity of music videos are the film's historical markers; the music Radio Raheem listens to gives his personality more depth than his few spoken lines. In effect, the music begins articulating the characters, in part, because this is one of the few media of communication left open to them.[29] We also see a "new relationship between image and sound in a culture in which the encoded sounds of speech and music have held a specially privileged place."[30] These characterizations represent the results of the increased economic emasculation of the urbanscape. The song's nationalist call-to-arms foreshadows later events and acts as an unconscious rallying cry for Radio Raheem's, Buggin' Out's, and Smiley's attempt to boycott Sal's Famous Pizzeria. Mars raps in *She's Gotta Have It*, "fifty dollar sneakers and I got no job." With Radio Raheem and Buggin' Out, the stakes are higher. The new refrain could be: "hundred fifty dollar sneakers *and* a big radio, and I *still* got no job." In future films the borders between music and character become increasingly blurred, as rap stars appear in films set in the inner city and rap about the appeal of material goods such as designer clothing and expensive cars.

Raheem's anger resides at the heart of *Do The Right Thing* because the film's main concern is to examine the pressures coming to bear on the residents of the neighborhood.[31] One of the results of this combination of circumstances is the murder and riot that conclude the film. Lee pinpoints a number of factors that inexorably lead to this end; importantly, they all call attention to circumstances central to African American urban life of the time period, whether in Brooklyn or Los Angeles. Economic displacement and police surveillance and brutality were frequent themes in films from the 1970s, and they continue in *Do The Right Thing* and in a number of films to follow. Lee's articulation of Brooklyn's cityscape picks up from where Van Peebles and Gerima, among others, left off, and it becomes the seed for the cinematic construction of Watts and South Central Los Angeles in the 1990s.

The chronic economic displacement of young African American men is explored via the experiences of the film's characters. *Do The Right*

Thing reprises the b-boy culture first suggested by Lee's Mars in *She's Gotta Have It* and develops the characterizations of young men. The iconography of urban youth culture is embodied in Buggin' Out, Radio Raheem, and Mookie. Buggin' Out and Radio Raheem, in particular, manifest an identity infused with late 1980s African American popular culture in their clothing, haircuts, and dialogue as "shorthand material markers which are both representable to and understandable across a generalized social field."[32] In these characters the film details the results of the ghettoization and years of increasing unemployment rates in the postindustrial city, when flight of both the black and the white middle classes and the relocation of unskilled jobs outside the country left little economic growth in urban centers.[33]

In this environment, Mookie's almost mono-maniacal obsession with "gettin' paid" is all the more telling. In a hyper-materialist consumer culture in which income and clothing define individuals, Mookie derives much of his self-esteem from the money in his pocket and the clothes on his back. Unfortunately, the only job available is as a pizza delivery man for Sal's Famous, a job that for "two-hundred and fifty dollars a week plus tips" makes Mookie beholden to Sal and his sons, and also forces him to cross the variety of visible and invisible borders with which people stake their claims on the neighborhood. The most significant boundary Mookie traverses is the one between Sal's Famous Pizzeria and the rest of the block. Ostensibly just a job—one that he doesn't even do very well, according to Jade (Joie Lee) and Sal—Mookie's position becomes increasingly difficult to maintain as the tensions rise and what begins as a conflict over representation results in a conflagration.

Mookie's baseball shirt foreshadows the difficulties engendered by his position in the pizzeria. Mookie is the "Jackie Robinson of another American pastime, a pioneer with all the privilege and pressure that comes with crossing frontiers."[34] Just as Jackie Robinson was responsible for crossing baseball's color line, Mookie also challenges color lines. But whereas Robinson was successful in beginning the integration of major league baseball, Mookie brings together the distinct parts of the neighborhood in a complex and no less contentious manner. By working for the pizzeria, Mookie is part of a private world that is not seen by most residents of the neighborhood. This is clear not only in the animosity and verbal abuse he receives from Pino (John Turturro), Sal's oldest son and the most vehemently racist character in the film, but also in his friendship with Vito (Richard Edson), Sal's younger son. Because of this, Mookie is forced, on more than one occasion, to defend himself against accusations of aligning himself too closely with Sal. As Buggin' Out's reminder to "Stay Black" exemplifies, Mookie's position in the pizzeria endangers his relationships with the rest of the community. This line also echoes Deke O'Malley's question, "Is It Black Enough For You?" in *Cotton Comes to Harlem* two decades before. The difference is that in *Cotton Comes to Harlem* it was interrogatory and united the community. In *Do The Right Thing* it is a test of racial allegiance, indicating the ways in which the community is splintered.

The film's conclusion further explores the complexities of Mookie's mediated status when, after witnessing Raheem's murder, he throws a trashcan through the pizzeria's window and thus precipitates the looting and burning of the storefront by neighborhood residents. Sal views Mookie's actions as treasonous because they are the direct cause of the destruction of his livelihood. Mookie, however, is more pragmatic about his actions. As he explains, the damage is minimal because the pizzeria is insured. Mookie acknowledges the fact that Sal will get paid either way, with or without the pizzeria. But Mookie's words and actions indicate a more important facet of the film's conclusion, one not addressed by the number of critics and theorists who have examined the *Do The Right Thing*'s final scenes. To call Mookie's action simply violence, vengeance, or destruction misses a crucial point, because in deciding to throw the trashcan, Mookie reveals the links between economics and violence at the heart of the neighborhood's tensions and the film's examination of racism.[35] For Sal, money has always meant power; as he repeatedly states, as long as he owns the pizzeria, it will be run his way, including what celebrities he'll hang on his "Wall of Fame," how much cheese he'll put on slices, and whether music will be played inside. This is Sal's "inalienable right," and as such it is not to be questioned, especially not by Buggin' Out or Radio Raheem. This belief, and the force implicit at its roots, are why matters escalate to the point of Raheem's death.

The fact that Sal's walls exclude African Americans is an issue for Buggin' Out because the absence of African Americans on the private wall also "signifies [their] exclusion from the public sphere."[36] Mookie's act draws attention to the connections between public and private interests and illustrates that he is endowed with an insight that is more complex than that of his boss. In Radio Raheem's murder at the hands of the NYPD, Mookie is a firsthand witness to the way economics inflects racism, and how the tensions between the two, especially in a context of such disproportional differences, can lead to violence. Mookie's action is a device that attempts to express the tension, at the same time that it shifts the focus of the neighborhood's rage from individuals to institutions and it "resituates both violence and nonviolence as strategies within a struggle that is simply an ineradicable fact of American public life."[37] In effect, Mookie's recognition of the power and reality of money leads him to save Sal's, Pino's, and Vito's lives while affecting them where it hurts the most—their property.

The NYPD is a presence from the very beginning of the film. While certainly not as ubiquitous as in films set in Los Angeles' black neighborhoods in the 1990s—in part because the NYPD rarely uses helicopters as part of its neighborhood policing strategies—the police still present a significant threat to the neighborhood's residents. Radio Raheem's murder is instigated by the confrontation in the pizzeria, but it is also ultimately the culmination of the tensions between the community and the police, who both patrol and control it. In the opening scenes, the police define the block's residents through discourses of criminality as they urge an outsider to leave the area before his car is stripped. While it is not until the film's final scenes that the police again play a significant role in the narrative, their occupation of the space is constant; they patrol the streets in their cruisers and appear in the background of scenes in which they play no part. The animosity between the cops and the residents is more apparent in the few interactions they have prior to Raheem's murder. For example, in one scene, the patrol car swings by the three Cornermen. In a slow-motion and silent exchange of glances and mouthed insults, the scene communicates the general lack of respect the men have for each other. (Significantly, Lee supplies the point-of-view of the Cornermen, which at the time was a rare cinematic perspective.) It is this sort of interaction in the summer heat that lends the film a sense of foreboding because the residents are reminded of the NYPD's constant surveillance of their actions as potentially illegal. Additionally, the police are aligned with the more racist elements of the film, for instance, Pino, when they question Sal's desire to stay in Bed-Stuy, where to them he clearly doesn't belong.

Jacquie Jones has argued that what is ultimately at stake in *Do The Right Thing* is "a kind of person, a young black male kind, a kind who is not offered protection from the law, a kind instead whom others (read: white people) feel they need protection from."[38] In keeping with the

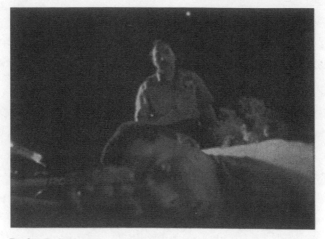

Radio Raheem, Murdered! (*Do the Right Thing*, 40 Acres
and a Mule Filmworks, Inc., 1989). Courtesy of 40 Acres
and a Mule Filmworks, Inc.

film's system of referents to the contemporary urban social and political landscape, Raheem's death specifically references the murders of
other African Americans who died under questionable circumstances at
the hands of the police. As the sound track finally falls silent and the
camera pans over the faces of the crowd, individual characters name
actual victims of police brutality, such as Eleanor Bumpers and Michael
Stewart. In this manner, Lee's construction of the contemporary city
follows Gerima's approach in *Bush Mama*, in which intertextual reference is also made to actual occurrences of police brutality—through real
events, reenactments, and newsprint—to underscore the realities of the
police state in the inner city.

  Do The Right Thing suggests that the neighborhood is a complex
community rather than a collection of purely disparate and antithetical
discourses. This construction of the African American city as community differs from more mainstream examples of the represented black
city spaces from the time period, such as *Colors* (Dennis Hopper, 1988),
which presented its African American and Mexican American communities through the eyes of white LAPD officers. It also differs from the
majority of 1970s representations of the cityscape, which focused on
one or two main characters to the exclusion of a collection of poorly
defined background players. But in Lee's careful orchestration of this
multiplicity of voices, there also resides an acknowledgment that the

neighborhood lacks a unity of vision. This discord is spread among three separate ideological and generational positions: an older generation, embodied by Mother Sister and Da Mayor; an intermediate generation (the bridge) personified by DJ Mister Señor Love Daddy and (to a lesser extent) the three Cornermen; and a youth generation represented by Mookie, Buggin' Out, Radio Raheem, and many of the neighborhood's younger residents. The musical motifs accompanying the characters indicate the tensions among the generations, especially their political and social outlooks, and "underscores . . . Lee's recurring concern with older and younger generations, their knowledge, histories, and differing responses to contemporary problems of race relations."[39]

Lee's orchestration of generational discourses stresses a point that will be crucial to our understanding of the formulation of the spatiotemporal construction of the hood in later films. The archetypes of Lee's characters can be found in the history of African American political engagement and constitute a national allegory: accommodationist/integrationist, post-civil rights/Black Power, and a contemporary nihilism born of the political and economic environment of the 1980s and 1990s. The separation among the generations and their politics is portentous if we understand the initial influence that Raheem's music exerts over the film. "Fight the Power" introduces the film, recurs throughout the narrative, and is the catalyst for the violence near the conclusion. Not only do Raheem and his music foreshadow the central position that a younger, post-civil rights generation will have in the majority of African American films that follow *Do The Right Thing*, they also indicate the tensions among generations that will surface most obviously in the form of anger at the absence of a political direction. Lee observes of his characters:

> Mookie and his sister love each other very much, but they go at it at times. She is bothered that Mookie—like many Black youths—has no vision. Mookie's sister constantly tells him he can't see beyond the next day, the end of his nose. It's the truth. The future might be too scary for kids like Mookie, so they don't think about it. They live for the present moment, because there is nothing they feel they can do about the future. What I'm really talking about is a feeling of helplessness, or powerlessness, that who you are and what effect you can have on things is absolutely nil, zero, jack shit, nada.[40]

While Lee's observation supports the view that the lives of young black men are what are centrally at stake in the film, it is important to focus on the generational tensions to determine what else is crucial to the narrative. Throughout the film Da Mayor and Mother Sister signify a past that is no longer relevant. In Lee's highly self-conscious iconography, Da Mayor's alcohol abuse, unemployment, and soiled clothing signify the ineffectiveness of his generation as a whole. In fact, a group of the younger men who live in the neighborhood more or less state this directly to Da Mayor at one point in the film. But as I mentioned in my discussion of speech patterns, both Da Mayor and Mother Sister are traces of a southern rural past, a past that has been inflected by segregation, migration, and changing political and aesthetic ideologies in the African American community and in American society at large. The young man's rejection of Da Mayor may be more of a rejection of the past Da Mayor represents than the individual he is.

From very early in his career Lee has made it a practice to reference African American history, especially in the city's ongoing links to its southern roots. The South has literally entered Lee's visions of contemporary life in films like *School Daze* (1988) and his documentary *4 Little Girls* (1997), set respectively in Atlanta and Birmingham, Alabama. In other films, like *Joe's Bed-Stuy Barbershop*, places like Atlanta are links to family and provide an escape from the city. It is no accident, therefore, that Lee includes Da Mayor and Mother Sister in some of the final minutes of the *Do The Right Thing*. The couple's presence in the film initiates a complex dialogue between urban youth and their elders that is sometimes based on tension and conflict and, at other times, on respect, which is evident in both Mookie's and Jade's interactions with Mother Sister in particular. Mother Sister's claim at the film's conclusion, "We're still standing," acknowledges the continuing influence of the past in the contemporary city. Her statement will resonate in opposite ways in the films that follow *Do The Right Thing*: in the insistence on an almost totalizing temporal immediacy in films from the 1990s, and Lee's rejoinder to the films with *Bamboozled* (2000), which takes its characters and its audience to task for their historical ignorance.

It is significant that what is excluded from *Do The Right Thing*, but included in most films to follow, is the presence and effects of drugs and ubiquitous crime on the community. This was to become, alongside criticisms directed at the film's concluding events, one of the most frequently voiced critiques of the *Do The Right Thing*—that in his construction of the block, Lee "whitewashed" its spaces of the more unsavory aspects of the neighborhood's existence. Lee repeatedly addressed these accusations by suggesting that it was his decision to concentrate on other details and tensions of the space.[41] The issue is more interesting in that it indicates the critics' and public's desire to see such images and the overall expectation that they should be included in any film dealing "realistically" with the African American city. What these responses do not seem to acknowledge, however, is that Lee's urbanscape has always been a self-consciously constructed terrain, whether shot on location or not. In *Do The Right Thing* Lee consistently foregrounds the selection of locations and the film's construction, whether in the theatrical nature of its mise-en-scène or in the obtrusive editing patterns and camera angles. The film's diegesis consists of a world made up of "highly realistic representations of the public *images* of blacks, the characters imposed on them and acted out by them," not realistic representations of actual people.[42] In the 1990s, city films will emerge with different intentions, to define the hood as it really "is," thus belying their own participation in a specific ideological and political moment.

In what is at first glance a film about the social and institutional pressures affecting a block in Bed-Stuy, *Do The Right Thing* addresses the racism informing the interactions among people in the community: those who reside there and those who economically control and police its terrain. In the process, the film also employs specific extradiegetic and cinematic tropes that will become the core features of a number of films in the 1990s, such as *Juice*, *Boyz N The Hood*, *Straight Out of Brooklyn*, *Above the Rim*, and *Menace II Society* (the culmination). These "New Jack" tropes include signs of the effects of economic shifts, such as rising rates of unemployment among African American men, an increasing association of criminality with black youth, the growing influence of rap music and its attendant signifiers and cultural referents, an escalating feeling of helplessness and lack of agency (often interpreted as nihilism), and the related rearticulation of and concern with specific urban spaces, most often Brooklyn and Los Angeles. *Do The Right Thing* points to the tensions and anger generated by these conditions, and its concluding riot touches upon the fear of racial violence repressed at the core of American culture throughout the twentieth century and suggested in the response to black-focused films as early as Oscar Micheaux's *Within Our Gates* in 1920 and reiterated in the critical responses to film like *Boyz N the Hood* in the 1990s.

5

Out of the Ghetto, into the Hood: Changes in the Construction of Black City Cinema

uring the early 1990s, a new group of African American city films appeared. Variously described as "ghettocentric," "New Jack," "New Black Realism," or hood films, films such as *New Jack City* (Mario Van Peebles, 1991), *Straight Out of Brooklyn* (Matty Rich, 1991), *Boyz N the Hood* (John Singleton, 1991), *Juice* (Ernest Dickerson, 1992), and *Menace II Society* (Allen and Albert Hughes, 1993) were directly influenced by black-focused films from the 1970s and the changing industrial, political, and economic environment that emerged in the 1980s around filmmakers like Spike Lee.[1] Hood films are characterized by identifiable urban settings and contemporary time frames. The films' location shooting and references to urban signs acknowledge actual city spaces such as New York and Los Angeles and, to a lesser extent, places like Oakland and New Jersey. Their construction of city space and city time is also meta-textual, and they focus, through quotation, allusion, and homage, on the plethora of images associated with African American urban youth culture in film, television, and music video.

Hood films share a number of characteristics with blaxploitation, and their subject matter, settings, and techniques have often been compared to the earlier genre. Like blaxploitation, hood films are shot with specific cinematic techniques that connote both temporal immediacy and documentary verisi-militude. Many of these techniques, such as sync-sound, location shoot-ing, hand-held camera (or Steadicam), and grainy film stock are influ-enced by cinema verité and lend many of the films, especially *Straight*, *Juice*, and *Menace*, a documentary-like realism. Both film genres also incorporate the music, clothing, speech idioms, and personalities from their respective cultural contexts, thus echoing through visual and aural signposts the audiences' lived experiences.

As with blaxploitation films from twenty years before, the verité style of hood films was partially (and initially) contingent upon budgetary limitations. For example Rich's *Straight* was made for approximately $100,000, and these financial constraints dictated the overall look of the film.[2] Both blaxploitation and hood films were relatively low-risk, low-cost genres and each appeared during periods of financial crises within the industry. Blaxploitation, with its minimal budgets and max-imum profit potential, provided studios with a much needed, influx of reliable cash. The industry experienced a similar slump in the early 1990s, and Hollywood again—spurred on by the financial successes of Spike Lee, Robert Townsend, and the Hudlin brothers (*House Party*)—turned its attention to African American film production and the black and crossover box office.[3] Underlying both "waves" of African Amer-ican film production, therefore, was the premise that "making cheap movies aimed at a core black audience can mean lucrative business" and subsequently fix the industry's financial woes.[4] The films' immediacy—and the core of their "realness"—is the ironic result of these industrial limitations.

Twenty years passed between the emergence of *Sweetback* and *Shaft* and the relative "boom" year of 1991, in which more than nineteen films directed by African American directors were released.[5] One of the fac-tors affecting the new filmmaking environment was the rise in the num-ber of film programs and, subsequently, in the number of film-literate directors being hired by studios right out of film school. The result of this can be seen in the films made by Lee and Singleton, both of whom self-consciously utilize a variety of cinematic techniques in order again to signify a realism in their work. The directors who did not attend film school also possess a remarkable knowledge of film style, technique, history, and genres, which is linked to the growing number of cable-movie channels, to the appearance of the VCR, and to the increased availability of cheap copies of older films on tape (and, increasingly,

DVD). For example, Allen and Albert Hughes cite the influence of the gangster genre (even including clips of gangster films in *Menace*) and the filmmaking of Martin Scorsese and Brian De Palma in their own work.[6] Like Scorsese's urban ethnic narratives, the Hugheses' focus is on tight-knit communities and their involvement in often highly organized forms of "alternative economies."

The fundamental differences between black-focused films from the 1970s and those from the 1990s are the result of industrial, political, and economic changes in the intervening decade. While the ghetto and the hood may appear to be the same places, representations of the latter are distinguished by a redefinition of the inner city during the Reagan and Bush (Sr.) years and a related and increasing conflation of African American popular culture (specifically film and music) with youth culture, especially as it relates to a rap and later to a gangsta' rap aesthetic. Therefore, I contend that what is at the foundation of the cinematic constructions of the hood in the 1990s is not only an understanding of the historical city and the effects of "successive displacements, migrations, movements, and journeys (forced and otherwise)"on its definition,[7] but also an understanding of the tropes of the inner city as shaped by a different set of sociological and political discourses.

The differences between hood films and blaxploitation tell us a number of things about the changing political and aesthetic environment between the 1970s and the 1990s. For example, the focal point of many blaxploitation films was an adult male, whereas hood films narrate the coming-of-age of a young male protagonist and the difficulties of such an undertaking in the dystopian environment of the inner city. The earlier films were concerned with their protagonists defining their adult masculinity against a white man's world, while the later films' protagonists define their masculinity against the constraints of the environment. While the hood may be a result of racist economic and political conditions, there is less concern with getting one over on "The Man" than in previous decades. This distinction identifies crucial generational and representational differences within the later films, especially as they relate to the incorporation of the signs and symbols of urban youth culture and the rage at the core of the films often directed not only at the system but at an absent ideological father. Coupled with this is a related nihilistic strain identified in many of the films as well as in the thematically linked media of gangsta' rap.

The economic and cultural transformations experienced in the city during the 1980s effectively redefined its borders from the ghetto to the hood. In what follows I contemplate some general factors affecting urban spaces at the time but I also focus on Los Angeles in particular because it is the setting of the two films with which I am most concerned, *Boyz N the Hood* and *Menace II Society*. Furthermore, I examine the direct correlation between the geographies explored in these films and in the lyrics of gangsta' rap, a musical form most specifically associated with Los Angeles, because "filmic representation of gangsta culture draws many of its influences from rap music, and in turn rap music assumes a great deal of identity with the work of Singleton and the Hughes brothers."[8] Ice Cube's participation in *Boyz* and the performances of rappers M. C. Eiht and Pooh Man in *Menace* illustrate rap's connection to hood films. Central to all of this is the city, specifically the postindustrial city of the late 1980s and 1990s. As Robin D. G. Kelley observes, the lyrics of gangsta rappers function as "an echo of the city" that "magnify what they describe."[9]

Most of the African American films set in Los Angeles construct an image of the contemporary city overrun with poverty, violence, and drugs, a likeness that stands in contradistinction to the tropical paradise manufactured both by the city's boosters and by the movie industry. If one were to believe the plethora of images produced by mainstream Hollywood releases, Los Angeles is exclusively composed of Beverly Hills, Bel Air, and Malibu. LA generates its own very particular images, and the city "broadcasts its self-imagery so widely that probably more people have seen this place—or at least fragments of it—than any other in the planet."[10] In order to promote this self-image (which is often mistaken for the reality of the city), entire neighborhoods have been excluded. But African American film and rap of the 1990s and, much to the booster's disdain, the images of Rodney King's beating and the footage from the riots following the verdicts acquitting the officers involved, show the extent to which these other spaces have become increasing hard to contain in geographic and aesthetic enclaves. Through their insistence on examining these spaces—the hoods of South Central, Compton, and Watts, for instance—contemporary African American films visualize the dynamics of power inherent in the city's self-imagery and in technologies of the visible as a whole. The films are self-reflexive discourses about the exclusions of representation and image manufacture. They expose African American identification and cinematic production as at once inside mainstream American experience and, at the same time, liminal and critical of that experience.

Nowhere is this complicated existence made clearer than in LA's history as an African American city. Both during and after World War II, California was a promised land for thousands of black and white migrants seeking work in the factories committed to the war effort. The defense industry, initially closed to African Americans, was forced to open its doors to black workers in 1941 with the passage of Executive Order 8802. Even with the resulting segregated work teams, union gangs, and unequal opportunities among workers, an ironic counterpoint to the industry's "Rosie the Riveter" image of inclusion, African American migrants flocked to California—especially Los Angeles— encouraged by the promise of wages that were much higher than what they could earn in the agricultural economies they left behind. As a result, between 1920 and 1950, the years of the highest migration to Los Angeles, the city's African American population rose from 2.7 to 8.7 percent of the total population, almost all of whom were "crowded into the traditionally Black neighborhoods."[11] An additional draw was the potential for future home ownership, for even though the city's black population was restricted to a few segregated enclaves, such as the area surrounding Central Avenue and Watts, they enjoyed a relatively high percentage of home ownership, certainly more than in the older northern industrialized cities whose inner-city residential culture was confined to apartment and tenement dwelling.[12]

In his discussion of the development of Los Angeles' gang culture, Mike Davis outlines the economic changes experienced by the city's African American population after the relative period of affluence in the 1940s and 1950s. As he explains, during the late 1950s to 1965, the year of the Watts Rebellion, "the Black version of the Southern California Dream, which had lured hundreds of thousands of hopeful immigrants from the Southwest, was collapsing. . . . Median incomes in South Central L.A. declined by almost a tenth, and Black unemployment skyrocketed from 12 per cent to 20 per cent (30 percent in Watts)."[13] The integrity of inner-city neighborhoods such as South Central and Watts, was often maintained by a sustained a sense of community, shored up in part by a mixture of households of varying incomes. With the gains made by the civil rights movement, however, previously segregated residential areas were opened up, primarily to the black middle class. The result was that areas like South Central and Watts lost a number of their middle- and working-class households to the suburbs. The increase in unemployment and the loss of the middle- and working-classes resulted in an inner city was populated by a rising number of the chronically poor and unemployed.[14]

While the Watts Rebellion had the effect of galvanizing a new stage in the civil rights movement, one that was more pro-active than in previous years, its most immediate physical effects on the area were devastating. By turning its rage inward, the African American community destroyed a number of black-owned businesses that had neither the capital nor the insurance to rebuild afterward. Additionally, many of the factories that had supplied the community with the manufacturing jobs that were its mainstay shifted out of the area. Part of this movement reflected a larger wave of industrial migration out of the cities in the 1970s; however, it also indicated the insurance companies' (and industries') increasing reluctance to take a risk on "troubled" urban areas.

The economic slowdown following the OPEC oil crisis in 1974 and the following recession worsened the situation. Davis notes: "The 1978–82 wave of factory closings in the wake of Japanese import penetration and recession, which shuttered ten of the largest non-aerospace plants in Southern California and displaced 75,000 blue-collar workers, erased the ephemeral gains won by blue-collar blacks between 1965 and 1975." These factors contributed to the "economic destruction in South Central neighborhoods," with unemployment rising almost 50 percent between the early 1970s and early 1980s.[15] Because the majority of the former jobs required little skill or education, many of the displaced workers were unable to move into other areas of employment. This was complicated as well by the types of jobs that became available in the postindustrial urban environment, which were concentrated in the low-wage service sector.[16] With a lack of access to adequate education to facilitate a change in employment, and with the ability to move to the suburbs with the factory jobs curtailed by economic constraints, the poorer segment of Los Angeles' African American community was cut out of the economy—and the sector of the community to bear the brunt of this situation was young men, as women were still able to find jobs in the more traditional and lower-paying sectors of domestic and service economies. As a result, between 1973 and 1986, black males between the ages of 18 and 29 experienced a 31 percent decrease in earnings.[17]

At the same time, the nation's black communities were experiencing a spike in the growth of their youth populations. For example, between

1970 and 1977, the number of urban blacks between the ages of 14 and 24 increased by 21 percent.[18] While this number slightly decreased in the following years, the proportion of the African American population made up of young people continued to grow through the 1980s, resulting in a significantly younger median population than that of either the white or Latino populations. Yet, while the proportion of African American youth expanded, the portion of it residing in the inner city was increasingly isolated from economic opportunity; for example, "unemployment for Black youth in Los Angeles County—despite unbroken regional growth and a new explosion of conspicuous consumption—remained at a staggering 45 percent through the late eighties."[19] It is thus no surprise that the majority of the young men in *Boyz* and *Menace* are unemployed. The only options that seem available are in the low-wage service industry, with Tre from *Boyz* the only one to accept this option when he works in a clothing store in the local mall. However, it is not so surprising that Tre is also subsidized by an upper-middle-class mother.

In an urban environment defined by an increasing number of young people and a decreasing availability of jobs, the appearance of crack cocaine had a significant impact. Introduced to the streets in the early to mid-1980s, crack changed the urbanscape.[20] First, it was a cheaper and more potent form of cocaine, enabling increased highs, addiction, and profits. Crack's money-making potential was especially appealing to a generation of young, urban residents, lacking hope for a "legitimate" job paying a livable wage. Crack became a way to make a profitable living, and this translated into an expansion of materialism and nihilism in black youth culture.[21]

Even before the introduction of crack, the lack of jobs and "growing immerization [sic] of black youth in L.A." had led to an increase in juvenile and young adult crimes.[22] With crack came a rise in youth crime rates. Kelley argues that "when the crack economy made its presence felt in inner-city black communities, violence intensified as various gangs and groups of peddlers battled for control over markets."[23] The result of this was a "juvenocracy," in which young black men held "economic rule and illegal tyranny" over the African American city.[24] In this way, crack further stigmatized a segment of the population that had already seen a rise in violent inner-city crime.

Additionally, the "war on drugs" initiatives supported by the Reagan and Bush (Sr.) administrations resulted in even higher rates of incarceration than those previously experienced with 35 percent of African American men alone arrested in 1989.[25] The result of the hysteria associated with crack was the demonization of African American and (increasingly) Latino inner-city youth. Most explicitly, these initiatives translated into the increased occupation of inner-city spaces by police departments that had been given the power to ignore its residents' civil rights and the decreased mobility of young, non-Anglo teens. These constraints on mobility (whether through incarceration or the policing of borders) and the resultant stripping away of agency are central themes in hood films. They also act as an ironic counterpoint to the car culture so associated with Los Angeles.

Besides changing the face of the black urbanscape, the increase in the youth population significantly impacted the tenor of both African American and American popular culture from the 1980s on, first in music and increasingly in film. Gangsta' rap and films such as *Boyz* and *Menace* (among others) are related in their focus on a particular place and worldview. Each uses the iconography of the inner city to "describe daily life in the 'ghetto'—an overcrowded world of deteriorating tenement apartments or tiny cellblock, prisonlike 'projects,' streets filthy from the lack of city services, liquor stores, and billboards selling malt liquor and cigarettes" and to "construct the 'ghetto' as a living nightmare and 'gangstas' as products of that nightmare."[26] In their construction of a specifically coded, young, male space, both media document the hood, and have increasingly transformed it into a space marked by a stylized nihilism removed from the black nationalist politics of the 1960s and 1970s.

Welcome to the Hood: Cinematic Inscriptions of Contemporary Los Angeles

The boom in African American filmmaking in the early 1990s emerged out of a complex tangle of political, social, aesthetic, and industrial circumstances. The industry's relaxation of its prior reluctance to invest in black-focused films contributed to the production of a number of African American directed features, culminating in the boom years of 1991–1992, during which more films were released than the total number of black-directed films released during all of the 1980s combined.[27] The films represented a wide range of genres, from the Hudlins' teenage comedies to Lee's political melodramas to Julie Dash's historical dramas. However, the genre of African American filmmaking that received the most attention—and which would be mistaken for black filmmaking as a whole in some quarters—was the hood film genre associated with young, first-time directors like John Singleton, Matty Rich, and Allen and Albert Hughes. Their films were coming-of-age tales of young African American men living in the inner city, what through rap lyrics had begun to be known as the hood. I have identified their cinematic construction of the contemporary African American city as a hood chronotope. This, in combination with a particular "rap aesthetic," which "draws its text directly from the lyrics of hip hoppers,"[28] is what makes these films so relevant to my discussion of the filmic representation of black urban space.

While cinematic constructions of the hood were not limited to Los Angeles, because of the films' close association with a rap aesthetic, South Central and Watts became archetypes of this particular city space. This was further emphasized by the release of Singleton's *Boyz N the Hood* in 1991. The film literally mapped out the terrain of the contemporary black city for white, mainstream audiences. One of my primary reasons for including the film in my present discussion is because it was seminal in constructing a crossover image of the hood. To complicate this discussion, I have also chosen *Menace II Society* as a counterpoint to *Boyz* because it was made, in part, as a response to its predecessor. As such, *Menace* self-consciously "ups the ante" regarding the construction of an African American urbanscape and its cinematic representations by dialoguing with *Boyz* in a similar manner as MC's often respond to each other in rap.

Boyz's opening shots introduce the major concerns of the film: mobility, entrapment, violence, and a concern with the role of space and time in the lives of young black men. The first image is a black screen, upon which appears text providing statistics regarding the high mortality rates of African American men as the result of violent crimes, the majority of which are black-on-black: "One out of every twenty-one Black American males will be murdered in their lifetime." The next shot continues the text: "Most will die at the hands of another Black male." From this, the film cuts to the image of a stop sign, shot from a slightly low angle, and with an airplane visible in the distance above and behind the sign. What soon follows is another title, this time identifying the film's spatial and temporal parameters ("South Central Los Angeles, 1984"). In the following narrative, the space remains the same;

however, the time changes. After the introductory vignette introduces the major characters, another title appears and projects the narrative forward seven years to 1991, the diegesis of the film coinciding with the extradiegetic present of the film's release.

By providing details about life-threatening conditions in the inner city, the film's titles position its subject—young black men—in a particular environment, one that will be best articulated by Mr. Butler in *Menace* when he observes, "The hunt is on and you [young black men] are the prey." These opening titles also provide the film with a sociological authority almost in keeping with "Moynihan-type scenario[s]" or with the work of more contemporary policymakers like William Julius Wilson.[29] However, *Boyz* shifts the agency from those on the outside who provide names and statistics for inner-city phenomena to those on the inside who are named. Both *Boyz* and *Menace* are struggles for control over the naming and the description of African American men and African American film, an inversion of "hierarchies of power . . . in which some decide and others are decided for."[30]

With the abrupt cut from the opening titles to the stop sign, however, the film announces the constraints placed upon power and agency. The stop sign also suggests that while the narrative's main emphasis may be in detailing the rites of passage for Tre (Cuba Gooding Jr.), the film's central protagonist, another important focus is the power relations inherent in space and geography. The stop sign is just one example of a system of signifiers that encodes the film's urban milieu and the limitations placed on characters' movements both within and across its boundaries. The film's "urban reference system" consists of the street names, the districts, and the boundaries that form an "urban texture or an urban text."[31] These signs are both real and symbolic, and can be interpreted in a number of ways. First, the juxtaposition of the stop sign with a plane flying overhead symbolizes the desire for mobility both inside and outside the ghetto. The urge to escape this dystopian space is one of the central themes of hood films, whether it is escape from the physical space or from the socioeconomic conditions associated with it.

This shot further suggests the system of institutional limits that stop or complicate movement.[32] Signs appear repeatedly throughout the film (for example, "One Way" and "Do Not Enter") and convey the message that free passage is not allowed. This indicates the ways in which the mythology of mobility promised by LA's car culture may be more illusory than real, at least for young black men in South Central Los Angeles. Charles Scruggs has argued, following Louis Wirth, that in an urban environment in which various and differentiated social sectors are geographically segregated, "the transition from one to the other is abrupt" and movement is discouraged.[33] Markers of specific terrain may ultimately may be nothing more than something like a stop sign on a designated street corner—if even that. The film illustrates that "boundary lines are dynamic; at the extreme case, as perhaps in Los Angeles, they may move from block to block, street to street, as one group moves in and another moves on or out, and only social or ethnic characteristics may separate one ethnic quarter from the other."[34] The city's segmentation is exemplified in Tre's and Ricky's (Morris Chestnutt) unease when Furious (Laurence Fishburne) takes them to Compton. At first glance this particular hood appears to be the same as their own block; however, the social dynamics have completely changed. The young men recognize this difference, but it is not as immediately recognizable to Furious, whose "blindness" is a result of generational difference.

The LAPD is identified with the constraints on mobility, and it is a presence that is at once more subtle but ultimately much more controlling than street signs. The film presents us with an alternative view of the LAPD to that provided by *Colors* (1988), an earlier film set in the area and focusing on the police, because it posits the LAPD as an occupying force, signified through the presence of visual and aural signs, rather than as a group of sympathetic individuals struggling to keep order in a chaotic world as it was in the earlier film. The LAPD is first introduced indirectly, a crime-scene cordon announcing "Police Line—Do Not Cross" preventing the movement through a murder scene and suggesting the relationship of the police with the community. After this, the police oppression of the area is constant and personified in the recurring appearance of two patrolmen who menace Tre, his family, and his friends at various times during the film. The fact that one of the cops—the more abusive of the two—is black echoes and expands upon Lee's exploration of police brutality in *Do The Right Thing*. While an African American police officer may not have been responsible for Raheem's death in the earlier film, at least one black officer was present. His indirect involvement in the murder—he makes no attempt to stop the abuse—is duly noted by Coconut Sid, who observes that "One of the cops was Black!" *Boyz* expands upon this complicity by indicating, in the black officer's words and actions, the self-hatred necessary for him to fulfill such a role and how that self-hatred is turned outward and onto the residents of the community.

The interactions between Tre and the LAPD indicate a sense of continuity at the same time that there is a subtle change in attitudes. Through the recurring appearance of the officers, even after several years, the film posits the continuation of the LAPD's brutal approach to policing the neighborhood. But while the cops' literal appearance may not have changed in the seven years, what has is the black officer's attitude toward Tre. As a young boy Tre is condescendingly referred to as a "little man," while the burglar who has escaped from his house is symbolically stripped of his masculinity and reduced to a "nigger." By the time that Tre has another interaction with the police, he has reached young adulthood. In this second encounter Tre is transformed linguistically by the black officer from being a man to being a suspected gang member and "nigga." Tre's response indicates how successful the cop's tactics are in stripping him of his self-respect (and masculinity). Upon being released, Tre's first action is to go to his girlfriend Brandi's (Nia Long) house, where he physically strikes out at real and imagined demons before dissolving into tears.

A proliferation of aural and visual cues also signify the ubiquity of the police, most notably through the repeated searchlights and offscreen sounds of surveillance helicopters. This method of policing was adopted by the LAPD prior to the Watts Rebellion as a means of patrolling the city's dispersed neighborhoods. Soon after the Rebellion, however, the helicopters became one of the most identifiable aspects of the department's policing strategies, illustrating its adoption of military technology and exemplifying its alienation from the communities it "protects and serves." In the diegesis the helicopters are the invisible although constant signs of the limitation of movement and the power relations inherent in that delimitation. Their pervasiveness "defines" the hood "as a ghetto by using surveillance from above and outside to take agency away from people in the community."[35] As with Foucault's panopticon, this method of control, dispersed over the urbanscape, facilitates efforts to keep the community in its place through the internalization of surveillance and the consciousness of perceived criminality.[36]

The success of these controls is evident when Tre and Ricky are caught driving in the wrong place at the wrong time. That the police see this as a suspicious act and as a legitimate cause to terrorize the pair underscores the forces working to isolate the residents of the hood. This scene, in combination with the sounds of gunfire, which puncture what little means of escape Brandi has when doing her schoolwork, as well as Ricky's death during a drive-by shooting, creates the central dilemma of the film for Tre. Should he give up a promising future and its potential for escape from the hood by taking part in a drive-by shooting to avenge Ricky's death, and thus fulfilling, if not the path laid out for him by those forces trying to define and contain him as an African American man living in the hood, then at least their premonitions of his behavior? Or should he resist being defined by others, and instead seek to define himself? This dilemma is based upon a paradigm of geography that "recognizes spatiality as simultaneously . . . a social product (or outcome) and a shaping force (or medium) in social life."[37]

Boyz references the signs of containment and control over the characters' ability to maneuver freely through the city's spatial parameters, and the film develops this project further by means of the incorporation of contemporary culture. *Boyz* is situated in specific times and places. The film is temporally, and unevenly, split between two time periods, 1984 and 1991, and it utilizes two different strategies to position itself within each time frame. The initial, shorter segment—the 1984 episode—introduces the central characters (Tre, Furious, Doughboy, Ricky) and sets up the plot points (why Tre is living with his father, his friends' fatherlessness) which will be relevant to the later story. Because it is set in the past, this opening section, "Tre's Childhood," utilizes specific signs in order to connote an early 1980s political and social environment. Singleton then uses these elements to set up the circumstances contributing to the conditions that will be foregrounded in the second part of the film.

The film's most obvious reference to the political context is the inclusion of political posters for Reagan's reelection campaign on the wall bordering a murder scene, which link—even momentarily—the conditions in South Central Los Angeles with the Reagan and Bush administrations' virtual abandonment of the inner cities.[38] The result, the film suggests, is a "south-central Los Angeles neighborhood which is booby-trapped everywhere by the corporate police state for the 'self-destruction' of its inhabitants—gun shops and liquor stores on every street corner, the omnipresence of searchlights from LAPD helicopters circling overhead."[39] This is certainly the terrain crossed by Reva (Angela Bassett), Tre's mother, as she shuttles him to Furious' house.[40] Her reasons? She doesn't want him to end up drunk or dead. Significantly,

Reva's explanation is offered as the camera pans over an urbanscape dotted with gunshops, pawn shops, and liquor stores.

As we will see in the second part of the film, music sets *Boyz* in a certain time period and provides it with cultural currency. This differs from the "Tre's Childhood" episode, in which music is employed in a much more conventional manner, as a nondiegetic complement to the onscreen images. In fact, the first forty minutes of the film comprising "Tre's Childhood" are marked more by their silences than by their noise. There are a few instances, however, when the silence is punctuated. The first occurs as an accompaniment to the opening titles, including the text regarding male mortality. At this moment, the sound track consists of the nondiegetic sounds of a verbal dispute, gunfire, sirens, and helicopters. After this, the image of the stop sign appears onscreen. Thus, even prior to any actual visual information, the violence and police presence, which characterize the space, already exist. This use of sound effects returns with the image of the Reagan poster. As the camera cuts to the poster, gunfire is the only noise. While this is suggestive of the cause of the murder, it also links Reagan to the deaths of young black men.

Throughout most of this first section, music is almost always employed nondiegetically—accompanying some scenes and commenting on others. Notably, most of these examples of music consist of barely audible, jazz-based, ambient tunes. This occurs most often in the scenes involving Furious and Tre, and it provides their interactions with a feeling of warmth. This pattern changes on three different occasions when music punctuates certain moments in the narrative. The first time this happens is when music, presumably on the radio, is in the background at Ricky and Doughboy's (Ice Cube) house. Here it provides atmosphere. More significant, however, are two later occasions. The first is when the boys view a dead body in an empty lot. As they approach the site, they have to walk past a group of young men hanging out, listening to music, and drinking malt liquor. Ironically, the juxtaposition of the dead body and the young men is what Reva was trying to take Tre away from, not deliver him to. The music they are listening to (Run-DMC's "Sucker MC's"), their threatening behavior toward the boys, and their lack of any visible means of employment embody in embryonic form later cinematic inscriptions of young black men, in both *Boyz*'s narrative and other films. Furthermore, the choice of Run-DMC is a reference to earlier rap films such as *Krush Groove*. But whereas earlier cinematic inscriptions of a rap culture focused on its more celebratory aspects, these young men have moved far away from the individuals in *Krush Groove* or Spike Lee's Mars from *She's Gotta Have It*.

The last example of music entering the diegesis is The Five Stairsteps' "Ooh Child," which is audible on Furious' car radio when he and Tre return from fishing. The song is acknowledged by Furious, who demands that Tre (and the audience) listen, and his mock-performance of the lyrics occurs as the music carries over from the diegetic space to the nondiegetic space, where it bridges the slow-motion images of Tre's friends being taken away by the police for shoplifting. While seemingly insignificant, the song identifies Furious with a different time (the 1970s), which has already been somewhat suggested by his "Nationalist" dialogue. The music crosses over with the sounds of police sirens before disappearing altogether (to be replaced by rap music). Furious may be an integral presence in *Boyz*, but as the narrative shifts to the 1990s, his discourse is silenced and the optimism suggested by the lyrics is undercut by the images of the police cruiser and the sounds of sirens before being overtaken by rap.[41]

With this transition, signified as well by a new title, the narrative is propelled seven years ahead to the same year as the film's release. The use of rap music to signify this change in time situates the film in a more immediate context, and involves a move from more conventional uses of sound. Singleton's choice to cast Ice Cube in the role of Doughboy not only allows Singleton "to seize symbolic capital from a real-life rap icon,"[42] but also contributes to the film's credibility, authenticity, and appeal for its young audiences. Many films use hip-hop culture to add to their realism: "the characters look *real* because they dress in the style of hip hop, talk the lingo of hip hop, practice its world view toward the police and women, and are played by rap stars such as Ice Cube,"[43] who not only performs in the film but also performs on the sound track. Consequently, the film conveys a sense of a "here and now" that its targeted audience perhaps might experience on a day-to-day level. But even if the audience did not share the experiences, *Boyz* brought to its audience an assumption of a familiarity with these images and sounds from MTV, VH1, The Box, BET, and the radio. This connection is not a new observation regarding the hood film. However, what I want to stress is how elements such as music and casting contribute to the genre's immediacy. It is not only the films' specificity of space, but also how that space utilizes a particular present.

The film's mimetic qualities are further enhanced by its heteroglossia via dialogue, clothing, and extradiegetic references. One of the appeals of the hood film, as with blaxploitation before it, is that it has the look and sound of contemporary urban experience. This is translated, in one respect, into a contemporary African American urban patois, first heard in rap music and in films like *She's Gotta Have It*, which introduced the b-boy dialect and look to mainstream and art house culture. Furthermore, *Boyz*'s use of specific costuming contributes to its cultural currency, especially in its referencing of LA's gang culture in the color-coding of the characters' clothing as either Bloods or Crips. By this point in the 1990s, such coding was easily recognizable because of films like *Colors* and the multiple television news broadcasts detailing gang culture.[44]

While the film employs gangsta' iconography throughout its narrative, and in the process draws on a similar vernacular tradition of the "Bad Nigger" that we saw in films like *Sweetback* and *Superfly*, it also references a dwindling black nationalism in Furious' words and actions. In his abstinence from pork and his lectures on African American economic self-determination, Furious is a cross between a Malcolm X and a Farrakhan, although the film stops short of identifying his links with the Nation of Islam. Instead, it is Doughboy who makes the connection in a discussion with Tre.

Finally, *Boyz* details other forces affecting the lives of its male protagonists—specifically, drugs, absent fathers, and a culture of violence. While there is little evidence that any of the main characters actually smoke crack, multiple allusions are made to the fact that Doughboy is dealing drugs: his numerous arrests, his expensive car, his lack of a job, and, at the film's conclusion, the onscreen exchange with a buyer. Here then, Ice Cube, as Doughboy, becomes the dealer he has already sung about in "A Bird in the Hand," in which a young man resorts to selling drugs because they "are the only people making decent money."[45] As with *Superfly*'s "Pusherman," the separation between the pro-filmic and the surrounding aural space is blurred. This will happen again in *Menace* when the song "Dopeman" accompanies images of crack preparation.[46]

Another aspect of contemporary urban life referenced by the film is the ongoing debate about the high rate of absent fathers in African American urban communities. In this regard, Mikhail Bakhtin's views about the relationship between the text and the real world are relevant. As explained by Robert Stam and Ella Shohat, "artistic discourse constitutes a refraction of a refraction . . . a mediated version of an already textualized and 'discursivized' socioideological world." The film's project is "an act of contextualized interlocution" with sociopolitical discourses that have sought to "explain" the black family.[47] However, *Boyz* strives to reinsert the black man into the domestic sphere on its own terms. In order to reinscribe a black masculinity into this dialogue, the film must first set it in opposition to the single mother, the symbol of what is (according to Wilson) and has been (according to Moynihan) wrong with the African American community. The film's construction of women pales in comparison to its more complex rendering of the male characters, especially Furious.

This circles back to the central dilemma faced by Tre: murder or college. It is no surprise that Tre chooses the latter option, for the narrative structure of the film prevents him from crossing the boundaries set up for him in what is in many respects a "very traditional Hollywood melodrama."[48] This is evident in the film's privileging of the father. While the narrative is structured around the challenges Tre faces while growing up in the hood, these challenges are mitigated by Furious' words and worldview. The film stresses the importance of strong father figures as enabling factors in the survival of young African American men in the hood. Nowhere is this more apparent than in the fates of Tre's two friends, Ricky and Doughboy, half brothers with different but equally absent fathers. The fact that they die and Tre survives *and* escapes is the film's not-so-subtle message of the healing power of the father to the virtual exclusion of the mother. However, the film also suggests that Furious' influence over Tre's life is tenuous. It achieves this first by distancing Furious from the immediate concerns of the young men surrounding his son and then by having Tre initially go with Doughboy and his friends during the drive-by before changing his mind. Furious' politics, therefore, just barely overcome the environment.

The film's unintentional irony is that even though Furious instills a sense of self-confidence, responsibility, and community in Tre, this influence ultimately equips Tre with the imagination he needs to escape the hood for college in Atlanta, a space defined and verbally signified as a utopia in comparison to LA's dystopia.[49] Thus, while *Boyz* explores the limits placed on residents of the hood, its solutions actually replicate the problems that first contributed to the conditions under investigation— the demonization of the black mother and the flight of the black middle classes from the inner city. This, however, would not be the case with

Menace II Society, which borrows from other genres, such as gangster films, to address and revamp *Boyz*'s cinematic strategies.

Realer Than Real: The Hood in *Menace II Society*

Right before the opening titles of the Hughes brothers' *Menace II Society*, a robbery occurs. Caine (Tyrin Turner), the film's main character, and his friend O-Dog (Larenz Tate) enter a store to buy something to drink. When the store's owners treat them as criminals, the pair acts as such, with O-Dog murdering the shop's Korean owners—a result of perceived criminality and an insult directed toward someone's mother. The robbery, following O-Dog's execution of the proprietors, takes place only as an afterthought, as a form of retribution for slights received rather than as a premeditated act. Significantly, the crime appears on a television screen because it has been recorded by a surveillance camera. These images recur throughout the film, played back for the amusement of Caine's and O-Dog's friends, the result of the latter's retrieval of the store's security tape.[50] Thus, even before the film "proper" begins, a central theme is introduced: violence and its televisual and cinematic representations, a link made by O-Dog's claim that he's "larger" than Steven Segal.

Following this opening scene, which is dramatically different from *Boyz*'s prologue, which only suggests violence, *Menace* follows a narrative comparable to that of the former film. *Menace* is set in contemporary South Central Los Angeles and it is also a coming-of-age tale. But, whereas *Boyz* ends on an uplifting note, *Menace* refuses to give its audience the satisfaction of a happy ending for Caine, its primary protagonist. Reportedly "outraged by the Hollywood sentimentality"[51] of Singleton's film, Allen and Albert Hughes set out to capture what they felt was the "real" situation in the hood—"sort of a docudrama . . . like a slice of life."[52] This characterization is telling because prior to directing *Menace*, the Hugheses were best known for their music videos and their segments of "America's Most Wanted," an early reality-based television series known for its reenactments of actual crimes. The final result is a text with both marked similarities to and differences from *Boyz*.

As with *Boyz*, *Menace* represents LA through the spatiotemporal characteristics of the hood chronotope. The film is replete with literal and figurative signs connoting its South Central geography, which first appears in the titles following the opening scene. After the present-day murder and robbery, the film cuts to a title, which situates the narrative in a particular place (Watts), at a particular time (1965), during a particular event (the Watts Rebellion). The film uses this strategy to introduce Caine and to provide an historical and personal context to the following events. In effect, Caine's story is introduced and framed by a mapping of the city space first, even before we see his face, suggesting that he is a product of the urbanscape and of a particular set of urban conditions. The city defines Caine; he doesn't define the city.

Following the title and the bird's-eye view of a burning Watts, the image changes to pixilated black-and-white footage of the Rebellion—thus exemplifying the represented space as a "refraction of a refraction." The images are accompanied by Caine's voice-over, explaining the transformation of the neighborhood following these events. Caine's monologue not only maps out the specific boundaries of the narrative, but it also acts as an informal history lesson (in documentary format) that provides background about the neighborhood. According to Allen Hughes,

> *Menace* was made with a historical perspective. That's how we did it, starting with the Watts riots. We're telling the audience that this is not our fault. That there's history here. The '65 riots, right. This is where this art came from. The despair, and the bloodshed, the whole thing.[53]

In this opening, the film references some of the historical circumstances affecting the area. Like *Sweet Sweetback's Baadasssss Song*, it uses media representations to provide historical context. In choosing this representational strategy, the Hugheses expanded upon the historical parameters first defined by Singleton in *Boyz* because *Menace* traces the roots of the contemporary African American city farther back than Reagan and Bush. Moreover, the scope of the narrative extends from Caine's experiences to the community's experiences. This is important because it enlarges the narrative scope from one that is personal to one that explicitly makes links to a larger political context.

In a film renowned for its sound design, this introductory segment offers an interesting aural mixture that defines specific aspects of the city space and which resembles Haile Gerima's use of sound in *Bush Mama*. In addition to Caine's voice-over, documentary-like aural footage of news reports explain the immediate causes and effects of what sounds like the 1965 Rebellion, but might actually be the 1992 riots. These voices are mixed with police radios and the chants of neighborhood residents. At the same time, images of police in riot gear clashing with civilians foreground the dissension. This aural and visual polyphony creates an environment in which the tensions of space—especially those caused by police oppression—are stressed through sensory stimuli. This section stands out all the more because of the previous episode's conventional use of diegetic sound strictly limited to sound effects and dialogue.

Following this historical exposition of the area, the film shifts to an explanation of Caine's personal history with a title reading "Watts Late 1970s" appearing over a color-saturated scene of a house party. Caine's voice-over introduces his parents, a drug dealer and a heroin addict, and recounts how they turned him on to the gangsta' life at an early age. There is a definite break with the verité look and sound of the previous section. Here, the Hugheses shot the film in over-saturated reds and blues—almost as a homage to its blaxploitation predecessors. In fact, the connection to blaxploitation is made by a character who accuses Caine's father of trying to act like Ron O'Neal (Priest in *Superfly*). It is only a matter of moments before Caine's dad (Samuel L. Jackson) meets this slight in a tell-tale "bad-ass" way by shooting his challenger.

Moreover, the aural design of this section differs from the earlier episode. Caine's voice-over offers more of a history here, albeit in a dispassionate tone. Caine provides information about his childhood and he outlines the hold that drugs had on the community. In fact, his assertion that "when the riots stopped, the drugs started" introduces the entire section when he recites it over the titles. Besides this, however, the sound track is a conventional mixture of sound effects (gunshots), dialogue, and contemporary musical selections by artists such as Marvin Gaye. As with *Boyz*'s introductory episodes, the music is diegetic, and along with specific costuming, makeup, and hair style choices, it situates the film in a specific cultural milieu.

The combination of sound and mise-en-scène contradicts Caine's words. Whereas Caine's voice-over discusses the demise of the neighborhood and his parents' role in it, the image and aural tracks fetishize this space and time. The presentation is not exactly nostalgic, but the Hugheses' stylistic choices indicate the particular appeal of blaxploitation films for filmmakers in the 1990s, celebrating aspects of the vernacular (for example, the bad-ass nigger and urban trickster figures) that were so integral to the earlier genre. This was part of a more widespread interest in popular culture from the 1970s, not only for African American youth culture but for youth culture as a whole. The Hugheses' interest in the trickster figure culminated years later in their documentary, *American Pimp* (2000), an unfettered celebration of the pimp whose subjects even appear to be from the 1970s rather than the 1990s.

After Caine's retelling of his father's act of murder and voice-over foreshadowing how his childhood experiences fed into his nascent gangsterism, the screen fades to black and a title announces "Watts 1993." This title is similar to the second title in *Boyz* because it propels the narrative into the present—not only the pro-filmic present, but the present experienced by the film's initial audiences (the film was released in 1993). The title then cuts to a bird's-eye view of Watts similar to that introducing the areas during the Rebellion of 1965. This shot, however, is punctuated by Simon Rodia's Watts Towers, and is accompanied by the sounds of rap on the sound track.[54] If the title were not enough, the music and image also signify the film's transition to a contemporary time and place.

Menace shares *Boyz*'s concern with the representation of an African American urbanscape, and the mise-en-scène the film utilizes as part of this project is replete with both literal and figurative signs connoting its geography. This project is introduced in the recurring calling out of Watts as the film's location, and it is developed through a bird's-eye view of the area. Whereas in *Boyz*, the themes of entrapment, mobility, and the desire for escape are conveyed in its first few frames, this opening shot suggests an anthropological concern ("sort of a docudrama"), a delving into the neighborhood rather than looking beyond it. The introductory shot also conforms with the Hugheses' project of showing the hood "as it really is," for it introduces the spatiotemporal parameters of the city in an almost ethnographic manner, with an invasive camera looking down on and documenting the neighborhood.[55]

Like Singleton's film, *Menace*'s narrative is a product of the tension between the realities of life in the hood and the contradictory relationship between the illusions of and the desire for mobility and escape. For Caine, the realities of his situation are poverty, life in the projects, the temptations of drugs and drug dealing, the economic and social lure of crime, the threat of death, and police oppression. But unlike Tre, who, with his father's influence, stays away from crime, Caine, with his father's influence, sees no other option, and the film exposes the psychological dynamics intrinsic to Caine's actions, primarily through his voice-overs. His unreliable voice-over, combined with his drug dealing and brutal activities, problematizes conventional narrative identification by refusing the audience access to a sympathetic protagonist—at least until the film's conclusion. Thus, Caine, and the even less sympathetic O-Dog, are the culmination of a long line of contemporary b-boy characterizations, from Lee's Mars and Radio Raheem through Singleton's Doughboy.[56] The difference is that with Caine and O-Dog, sympathy and insight are gone. They are not only victims of their circumstances, as was Ricky in *Boyz*; instead, they possess an unconventional agency that marks O-Dog as Caine describes him: "America's nightmare . . . young, black, and don't give a fuck." In the 1960s and 1970s, the American terrifying other was a generalized inner-city ghetto; in the 1990s, it became the young black man.

Significantly, the film highlights the ways in which Caine's actions result, in some part, from the internalization of the institutional boundaries placed on his existence (in a manner similar to the dilemma faced by Tre). Again, these pressures are signified by the LAPD. While there is a surprising absence of surveillance helicopters in the film, the police are still ubiquitous, patrolling the neighborhood in cars and making Caine and his friends scatter on sight. It is such patrolling that are the "booby traps" whose "most pernicious features . . . are as much their ubiquity as the ways in which they prohibit exit from the besieged black enclaves. Ringed by the LAPD from above and on the ground, Caine and O-Dog can only turn inward back into their depleted community."[57] Caine and his friends rarely leave the claustrophobic confines of their immediate neighborhood. They stay in the hood, as does the narrative as a whole, which seldom ventures out from the setting and its pattern of tightly-framed, medium and close upshots, which begin immediately after the initial bird's-eye view of the neighborhood.

The constraints placed on Caine and his friends by the LAPD are best exemplified in a scene of racial profiling similar to one in *Boyz*, in which Caine and his friend Sharif (Vonte Sweet) are stopped by the police simply for driving the wrong car in the wrong place. Whereas in *Boyz* the reasons for Tre and Ricky being stopped are never explained, here Caine's voice-over clearly articulates the factors behind why the two were pulled over: Caine is a black man driving a flashy car with expensive rims in Compton. The result of this encounter is much more brutal than in the earlier film. Caine and Sharif are beaten and dropped in a neighboring Mexican American barrio. This scene exposes the idea that the perceived criminality of young black men is based on geography, a concept given full rein during the 1980s and 1990s and the stepped-up war on drugs. Basically, Caine and Sharif are criminals by virtue of trespassing outside the economic and geographic boundaries of the hood. Furthermore, the police play a major part in enforcing borders between separate neighborhoods and anticipate (and encourage) violence to break out when they dump the pair outside of their own territory.

The cops' decision to drop Caine and Sharif outside their hood also illustrates how imaginary or invisible boundaries can become internalized and made real through outside measures of control. Caine knows, for instance, that he takes a chance whenever he leaves his neighborhood. When dumped outside their identifiable experiential parameters, both he and Sharif fear the worst. Similarly, Tre and Ricky express unease when Furious takes them to Compton. Both films illustrate the actual segregation that exists in the seemingly homogenous city of Los Angeles and suggest the means by which "artificially-imposed boundaries" maintain interracial antagonisms.[58] The city is no longer a unified urbanscape but an area criss-crossed by both visible and invisible boundaries marking smaller, sometimes violently heterogeneous areas.

In addition to the opening shots, titles, and voice-over, *Menace* includes a number of textual and intertextual references to a contemporary urban cartography. These references map specific areas and advance the film's overall discourse of containment. Like Singleton's film, *Menace* employs street signs to signify particular aspects of and locations within the cityscape. This strategy problematizes movement in the context of specific and identifiable locations in South Central. One example that occurs early in the film is the use of signs for Crenshaw Boulevard, which appear prior to and above a streetlight changing from yellow (caution) to red (stop). This light, like the stop sign in *Boyz*, suggests that travel is not permitted beyond a certain point. By showing the street sign and stop light prior to a scene in which Caine is shot and his cousin is fatally wounded in a car-jacking, the combination of narrative and iconography connotes not only the limitations on movement across borders but also within the hood. It also underscores the paradox inherent in the automobile: while it promises freedom and mobility, it also signifies death by drive-by shootings and car-jackings. Grant Farred notes that "with the ghetto cordoned off and 'no escape' possible, the most 'devastating' pathology that can follow is that its residents are destined to be its only victims."[59] Caine and his cousin are the graphic victims of the black-on-black crime like the statistics that introduce *Boyz*. The result of this crime will not only be the death of Caine's cousin, but also a chain of vengeance that leads to the eventual murder of the car-jackers by Caine, O-Dog, and Doc (Pooh Man).

This particular set of signs foreshadows the following events as the yellow light cautions Caine and his cousin prior to the car-jacking. Because the Hugheses set out with a specific agenda (to problematize the sentimentality of *Boyz*), there is no happy ending; Caine's hopes for escape are dashed by a fatal gunshot wound, and he never reaches Atlanta. Even the utopian vision of Atlanta is revealed to be a mirage through Caine's suggestion that it is yet another ghetto with a similar system of institutionalized racism. As Caine responds to Ronnie (Jada Pinkett), "You act like Atlanta ain't America. They don't give a fuck." Yet while the film questions Atlanta's utopian connotations, the film's references to places like Atlanta and Kansas deepens its historical context beyond the Watts Rebellion because it also acknowledges the history of African American migration at the roots of the contemporary city. While *Boyz* makes allusions to similar subject matter, the narratives are very different: Tre and Brandi follow a traditional middle-class trajectory of going away to college. Caine and Sharif aren't lured to Atlanta or Kansas for education but because of the potential for escape from their surroundings.

Caine's death is similar to Doughboy's and to a lesser extent Ricky's, for Caine becomes another statistic of black-on-black crime and the institutions that promote and propagate the violence. Yet whereas the earlier film presented us with "Moynihanized recapitulations of . . . 'family failure' in the ghetto, abetted by indulgent welfarism, the decline of paternal role models, and the flight of the Black middle class,"[60] *Menace* responds with the suggestion that this characterization is not enough. Caine, while without a living biological father, has a number of paternal figures (including his grandfather) who seek, at different times, to advise him. And Sharif, another victim of the drive-by that kills Caine, has a strong and persuasive father in Mr. Butler (Charles Dutton), who also reaches out to Caine. Finally, while the film concludes with its own form of melodrama—Caine is gunned down just as he is about to leave for Atlanta with Ronnie, but he manages to shield her son from the bullets as his last act—the Hugheses succeed in breaking away from Singleton's sentimentality. Whereas *Boyz* suggests that individual will and human emotions triumph over social conditions and economic realities, *Menace* makes no such claims.[61] More important, however, *Menace* draws specific links to a potentially disabling generation gap separating Caine's grandfather, Mr. Butler, and even Furious in *Boyz* from what has been increasingly referred to as a nihilistic streak pervading African American male youth culture.

"Don't Care If I Live or Die": Nihilism in the Hood

> Nihilism is to be understood here not as a philosophic doctrine that there
> are no rational grounds for legitimate standards or authority; it is, far more,
> the lived experience of coping with a life of horrifying meaninglessness,
> hopelessness, and (most important) lovelessness.
>
> —Cornel West (1991)[62]

The critical debates surrounding the representational strategies of films like *Menace* and the videos and lyrics of gangsta' rap (whether in the popular or academic press) often have focused on what has been identified as a nihilism pervading the texts. This nihilism, most often understood in the terms articulated above, has culminated in what has been called an "antisocial" attitude, which "refuses to give an ideological explanation for the violent culture that it represents. Instead it uses cinematic spectacle to depict this culture in all its blighted glory."[63] This antisocial, apolitical set of behaviors is most apparent in the actions of Caine and his friends, who resort to violence as their one means of agency and who all (except for Sharif) scoff at most political engagement unless it is involved in consumerism and its attendant pleasures. As Caine explains, they don't care whether they live or die.

In order, however, to understand the complexities of an increasingly overdetermined concept such as nihilism, especially in its role in a text like *Menace*, I would like to consider Paul Gilroy's concept of "vernacular nihilism." According to Gilroy, nihilism has its roots in black vernacular culture dating from slavery, in which the possibility of freedom was often premised on transgressions or the breaking of race-coded rules. "By breaking [the] rules," according to Gilroy, "it was possible to deface the clean edifice of white supremacy that fortified tainted and therefore inauthentic freedoms." Forms of "nihilistic" rule-breaking helped to express the complicated nature of hope experienced by African Americans at the same time that it pointed beyond forms of insubordination to the possibility of freedom.[64] While it may be that *Menace*'s violence and misogyny are difficult to interpret as a progressive political agenda, the film and some facets of gangsta' culture in general utilize a similar system of transgressions in which rule-breaking and insubordination are a response to social, economic, and political constraints. A nihilistic form of rebellion has developed, perhaps, because there appear to be no other options available. It is a refusal of the optimism of the American Dream, its "you can make it if you try" mentality, and the underlying middle-class values that this ethos evokes which seemed at the time so out of reach for many black inner-city youth. This positive contemporary nihilism is a result of the combination of this ideology of transgression with the characteristics of the urban trickster valorized in the vernacular.

What I would like to avoid is an inventory of the film's antisocial or apolitical aspects, which is often the tendency in discussions of *Menace*. Instead, I want to consider how this nihilistic attitude, expressed by the cinematic text and the Hugheses' relationship with gangsta' rap, points to the specific contours of a postindustrial city. In the contemporary environment of disappearing employment spurred on by governmental disinterest and identity formation based upon the cyclic premise of "masculinity-power-aggression-violence,"[65] the hood's young male residents have been stripped of agency and hope. It is important to remember here that while the film may not explicitly address the issue of unemployment, many of the rappers it utilizes on its sound track—and the gangsta' culture in general—rap about the relationship of joblessness and crime.[66]

Furthermore, this nihilism has to be situated generationally, because hood films and the gangsta' iconography they reference are specifically produced by a younger generation of artists than what we saw in the 1970s. Both *Menace* and (to a lesser extent) *Boyz* indicate that it is not solely economics that have played into this sense of hopelessness; it is also the experiential gap that has arisen between contemporary African American youth and the preceding generations, especially those who came of age during the civil rights movement or in its immediate aftermath. This doubt also stems from questions about the feasibility of collective struggle as a whole and to the general decline of leftist radicalism.[67] Therefore, nihilism is a form of anger directed not only at white power structures, but also at the facet of the black community that experienced the pre- and civil rights' periods (Caine's grandparents and Mr. Butler or Da Mayor in *Do The Right Thing*, for example).[68]

For young inner-city youth in the early 1990s, the advances of the 1960s remained in the distant past, and some of the behaviors valorized in gangsta' culture can be read as a response to a perceived emasculation of the older generations, including those from the civil rights movement. This focus on the "ineffectiveness" of earlier struggles became strikingly clear during the 1992 riots in Los Angeles. A link with the Watts Rebellion was made by a writer from *Newsweek*:

> Inevitably, the catastrophe summoned up memories of Watts, but the differences were more striking than the similarities. "All you had then was bottles and bricks," said one blood opening his trunk to show a stash of automatic weapons. "That ain't it now—this ain't gonna be like the 60's."[69]

This political point of view is in stark comparison to the more conventional discourses of the 1960s as a time of dramatic advances for African Americans. Here, the Blood not only critiques the 1960s but implies the failure of its political strategies. Furthermore, this failure, he suggests, came about not because of lack of vision but because of a lack of effective weapons (ironically echoing Priest's disdain for the militants in *Superfly*).[70]

While no one in *Menace* makes similar claims, it is worthwhile returning to the Hugheses' incorporation of history in order to position the film's images with regard to this generational distrust and anxiety. The choice to introduce the film's spatiotemporal parameters through footage from the Watts Rebellion contributes an historical dimension to *Menace* that was not necessarily lacking in *Boyz*, but which was far more short-sighted in the latter film. This footage has been critiqued by Todd Boyd, who argues that its inclusion is "simply to remind us that the event happened—a use of historical spectacle for the sake of spectacle."[71] Unfortunately, this reading overlooks the ways in which the historical context is specifically marked in the cinematic text in order to reference the history of collective action and also as an intertextual reference to the events of 1992, which may have been too fresh to include outright but which would have still been suggested by the sight of Los Angeles in flames. The Hugheses' inclusion of reports from the 1992 riots on the sound track makes a more literal link. Another way of viewing this, then, would be more aligned with the practice of sampling songs in contemporary music, in which "history is conscripted into the service of the present," a technique that may be understood "creatively," but not necessarily progressively.[72] In short, the Hugheses cite Watts, 1965, both to add dimension to their contemporary construction of the hood and to indicate the ways in which the events of the 1960s were detrimental to the area.

The hood as constructed by *Menace* in particular is the product of a post-civil rights, post-Reagan, post-Rodney King society. Seen in this historical context, residents of the inner city experienced the conditions in the urban landscape go from bad to worse, as politics have offered no viable solutions. In the process, freedoms (both real and perceived) have dramatically declined. In addition, African American leadership has become splintered and often overwhelmed by self-interest. In the light of this environment, there have been few effective options for any form of agency and self-determination. The nihilism so often seen in the films and rap songs is a political struggle in that it is a struggle for just these very things—as well as for access to the means of mobility (geographic, but also economic). This, itself, is a transgressive move.[73] Where it falls short is in its limited involvement with a larger social sphere. It is solely concerned with individual mobility and gives little, if anything, back to the community, a critique that can be leveled as much at Furious as it can be at Caine. In this manner, the film also belies that the protagonists develop a "politics of caring for the community."[74] The politics of caring might be there, but its reach beyond the individual and his immediate friends and family is limited.

It is possible to read *Menace* as stylistically transgressive as well, at least throughout most of the narrative. In fact, the film represents a "nihilistic style" that moves away from the more conventional renderings of the hood offered by Singleton, Dickerson, Rich, and Van Peebles. The film begins with a meta-discourse on the history of representation, especially of images of criminalized inner-city African American men seen most often on the network news. By referencing television news and, most directly, by using the stylistic conventions of Prime Time "journalism" shows like "America's Most Wanted," the film—especially in the repeated showings of the store surveillance tape—identifies Caine, O-Dog, and their friends as America's most wanted commodity, whether in the prison system or on the cinematic screen. But this meta-discourse extends beyond mass media referentiality to concentrate specifically on cinematic conventions. By giving Caine the privileged point-of-view through his voice-over, *Menace* forces the audience not only to identify with a drug-dealer and murderer, but it also undermines sympathetic identification by making Caine an unreliable narrator—he changes his mind, he misrepresents the truth, he states problematic positions. Ultimately, Caine is a protagonist who may not be likable in conventional Hollywood terms, but who is, even more important, visible.

Manthia Diawara observes that "space is related to power and powerlessness, insofar as those who occupy the center of the screen are usually more powerful than those situated in the background or completely absent from the screen."[75] This is a basic tenet of film theory and one that became a crucial focus for African American filmmakers in the late 1980s and early 1990s. It is also a central question for this discussion, for in a cityscape such as Los Angeles, in which "residential specialization and enclosure keep[s] everyone in their place,"[76] the signifying system of the hood chronotope works on multiple levels, dialoguing with and refracting the world around it. The fact that hood films even exist indicates a literal move out of the ghetto for black filmmakers and points to an important movement of African American film onto the commercial screen. Furthermore, in choosing to place in the center of the screen narratives based on and about a disenfranchised part of the African American diaspora, young urban men, filmmakers such as Singleton and the Hugheses deliberately link representation to power by calling into question the images that have been reified by mainstream Hollywood. Instead, they offer images and narratives that are more contested, but extend a dialogue about representation and the black urbanscape.

Finally, while with *Menace* the Hugheses succeeded in making complex the narrative issues and signifying practices introduced in *Boyz*, *Menace* would and could not have been the film it was without relying on the very significations that it seeks to redefine more realistically—or nihilistically. In this manner, *Boyz* lays the groundwork and traces the spatiotemporal parameters of the narrative and signifying systems that the Hugheses then used in a shorthand manner, especially the construction of a contemporary urbanscape. For the Hugheses, the hood had already been mapped out as a recognizable space and time, and thus an exploration of its general terrain was not necessary. If considered in this manner, *Menace* is interesting not for the reality or authenticity it claims, but for its dialogue with conventions of representation, especially with regard to previous cinematic constructions of the contemporary African American city.

While films like *Boyz* and *Menace* explore the black cityscape as a metonym of African American experience, they are markedly different from their literary and filmic predecessors in that they explicitly create a space and discourse concerned with representation and the Hollywood power structure. In doing so, the films and filmmakers succeed in visualizing previously unexplored spaces of the contemporary hood, South Central Los Angeles in particular, and do so for black and white audiences.[77] In addition, they also cross boundaries within filmic discourse by drawing on the history of African American film production and by extending the boundaries of the cinematic black city and the history of Hollywood film production as a whole.

6

Taking the A-Train: The City, the Train, and Migration in Spike Lee's *Clockers*

Welcome to the cinema, you're standing on sacred grounds,
observe us recording the debris of fallen empires, the last spasm
of dying cultures and the drunken madness of disembodied
nations in wide angle. Nomads, migrants, wandering spirits,
philosophers from another time, life and space, hold up the
mirrors in which you may glimpse your fate in hues of blues,
yellows and reds.
—Reece Auguiste (1998)[1]

While British filmmaker Reece Auguiste refers specifically to
the sociopolitical and the historical circumstances influenc
ing the members of the London-based Black Audio Film
Collective, in the epigraph above he stresses movement as
one of the defining thematic concerns of black diasporan
peoples. In fact, the very reference to a diaspora underscores
the influence that movement, especially that which has been
coerced, has had on persons of African descent.[2] As I have
emphasized throughout this work, the themes of movement
and mobility—migration in particular—are prime forces in
the history of African American filmmaking and its construction of cinematic metropolises. In this chapter I focus on the
years that follow the hood films of the early 1990s. In the
later 1990s, black films moved out of contemporary urban

spaecs and distanced themselves from the cinematic conventions of the hood film. Instead of the city presented with a concentrated immediacy, filmmakers increasingly turned away from the hood by means of revisions, parodies, appropriations, and the production of other genre films. Some of these, like *Posse* (Mario Van Peebles 1993), retained traces of the hood film while dialoguing with the history of the black Western. Other films, like Spike Lee's *Clockers* (1995), remained in the contemporary city both to self-consciously examine hood film conventions and to explore the history of black migration.

The Generic Dissemination of the Hood Film

African American film production went through a resurgence in the late 1980s and early 1990s as more black directors released a greater number of black-themed films than in previous years. A notable proportion of these films, especially those released in 1991 and 1992, were part of the hood, or "ghettocentric,"[3] genre and utilized what I have described as the spatiotemporal dynamics of the hood chronotope: identifiable urban settings and cinematic techniques connoting temporal immediacy. By 1993 and the release of the Hughes brothers' *Menace II Society*, this subject matter and mise-en-scène were familiar to audiences. At the same time, however, the production of films utilizing the conventions of the hood genre paradoxically began to decrease. In fact, *Menace*, a film considered by many to be the apex of the genre, actually appeared at its tail end; in the years following its release, fewer films relied solely on the contemporary city for story and setting. Hood films continued to be released on a much smaller scale, for example with *Set It Off* (F. Gary Gray, 1996), *Caught Up* (Darin Scott, 1998), and most recently *Baby Boy* (John Singleton, 2001). Moreover, the hood continued as a referent—mostly of African American contemporaneity—in many of the films directed by African American and white filmmakers in the years following 1993; for example, Warren Beatty's *Bulworth* (1998) adapts hood conventions for a political comedy/drama.[4]

The decreasing visibility of the hood as a primary trope in contemporary black film is related to two phenomena. First, while hood films never actually were the majority of African American releases during the early 1990s, they were the films—and the filmmakers (Singleton, Rich, Van Peebles, the Hugheses)—which received the most media attention. This concentration of focus was the partial result of the overwhelming financial success of films like *Boyz N the Hood, Straight Out of Brooklyn, New Jack City,* and *Menace II Society.*[5] The films' inner-city tales about young black men appealed to an African American and white youth audience that formed the bulk of their box office and who were attracted by the films' incorporation of the visual and aural referents of rap, hip-hop, and gangsta' rap. The disproportionate amount of attention paid to hood films also was a result of the controversy they engendered both because of their violence and purported nihilism and for the mythology circulating around them regarding the sometimes violent nature of their audiences—the result of a few much publicized incidences at screenings. Finally, the films inspired sometimes rigorous critical inquiry within universities as scores of articles were published and panels were organized around the subject of a "New Jack Aesthetic" and its consequences for black filmmaking.[6] The end result of this attention was that black-focused film from the time was disproportionately marked in both African American and American cultural memory as the domain of the hood—a phenomenon amplified by the critical and intellectual focus on the related media of gangsta' rap and music video. For a few years black film was equated with the hood almost to the exclusion of any other stories, genres, or settings.

One of the problems critics of hood films (especially more cynical cultural critics and journalists) often raised was the fear that "New Jack Cinema" would suffer the same fate as blaxploitation, its most famous predecessor, because the two genres shared aesthetic and industrial similarities (contemporary urban themes, hip and hip-hop subject matter, low budget, low risk, high return). It is not my intention to engage in a detailed comparative analysis of blaxploitation and the hood genres here, as some of this has already been done.[7] Yet the contrasts between the two time periods are important. A significant difference is that most of the hood films appeared between 1991 and 1993, indicating that the hood genre had an even shorter life-span than blaxploitation's three to four years. But as the later films by Van Peebles, Singleton, Rich, and the Hugheses attest, the directors who debuted in hood film production didn't experience the same fate as blaxploitation's African American filmmakers. Rather than continue making hood films, these and other directors pursued a diverse collection of projects, making deals with the studios and subsequently gaining more power within the industry (for example, John Singleton's initial three-picture deal with Columbia).

Additionally, young filmmakers were often schooled, film-literate, and aware of the history of African American film movements like blaxploitation. By diversifying genres and themes, contemporary filmmakers built names and reputations for themselves outside a particular genre, thus providing a modicum of assurance for a future in the industry and, in the process, expanding the cinematic and narrative possibilities for both already established directors like Bill Duke and Carl Franklin and newcomers such as F. Gary Gray, Rusty Cundieff, and Doug McHenry. The young directors' self-conscious awareness of their often tenuous position in the industry was noted by Mario Van Peebles, who said of *Posse*'s release, that it was "important that [black filmmakers] diversify a little bit. It is important that we don't get trapped into the repetitious sequel business of the '70s—*Shaft Goes to 7–11* and *Superfly Comes Back Twice*."[8] This combination of business-savvy and historical hindsight has contributed to the longevity of this generation of filmmakers in ways previously unavailable to their predecessors.

While the attention surrounding hood films has made it tempting to think that they wholly defined African American filmmaking during the early 1990s, a quick look at some of the releases, especially those by directors of hood films, reveals a different scenario. First, all of the directors cited followed their debut films with other films within two to three years—a remarkable return rate for young black filmmakers working within the industry. Second, each director shifted away from the genre (and sometimes style) of filmmaking that initially brought him fame.[9] The most notable example of this is Mario Van Peebles' *Posse*, a revisionist Western set in an all-black town at the turn of the century. John Singleton followed *Boyz* with *Poetic Justice* (1993) which, while sharing similarities with the former film, changes both its setting and point-of-view by concentrating on a young couple's romance (with primacy given to the female point-of-view) and their experiences on a trip from Los Angeles to Oakland. Matty Rich released *The Inkwell*, his second feature (and his debut to big-budget filmmaking), in 1994. This film, like *Posse*, was set in a different historical time frame—the 1970s—and focuses on a young city boy's experiences during a summer vacation spent with extended family at a beach resort.[10] Even Allen and Albert Hughes, whose *Menace* put them on the map precisely because it self-consciously capitalized on so many hood conventions, made *Dead Presidents* in 1995. Still maintaining their earlier focus on young black men in the city, the Hugheses moved the film's time frame back twenty-five years and included a subplot involving the Vietnam War. Van Peebles and Singleton continued their expansion of subject matter and setting in their following films: *Panther* (1995) and *Gang in Blue* (TVF, 1996) by the former and *Higher Learning* (1995) and *Rosewood* (1997) by the latter.[11] Most recently, the Hugheses broke with their former focus on African American subject matter with the release of *From Hell* (2001), a loose adaptation of the story of Jack the Ripper.

My interest in this departure from the hood lies in the transformation of the spatiotemporal parameters of the black urbanscape. This is not only exemplified by a change in settings from South Central Los Angeles and New York City to suburban or rural areas, but more so by a redefinition of the temporal framework privileging immediacy, the technique that was previously utilized by hood films. In short, in many of the black-focused and black-directed films released in 1993 and thereafter, the "here and now" which defined the temporal immediacy of hood films is no longer a driving force of their narratives. Nor is this temporality reflected in the look or the sound of the films in quite the same way or through the same means as we saw in the hood films in the previous chapter. The most obvious example of this trend is the rise in the number of films exploring and revising historical events and settings: *Posse, Panther, The Inkwell, Dead Presidents, Devil in a Blue Dress, Rosewood, Hoodlum,* and *Eve's Bayou.* Additionally, while not black-directed, *Amistad* and *Beloved* also fall in this category.

This is not to suggest that historical themes, subject matter, and settings did not exist prior to *New Jack City* and *Boyz N the Hood,* as films like *Mo' Better Blues, Harlem Nights,* and *A Rage in Harlem* indicate. It does, however, introduce the second phenomenon related to the hood's recession as a primary trope: its continuation as a motif in films from other genres. What we start to see is an end of the hood existing in and of itself, and a shift toward its engagement with other genres—as a sort of hood diaspora. The notion of multiple chronotopes existing in a text was first discussed by Mikhail Bakhtin, who noted that they are "mutually inclusive, they co-exist, they may be interwoven with, replace or oppose one another, contradict one another, or find themselves in ever more complex interrelationships."[12] For example, in my discussion of *Sweetback,* I identified the ways in which the antebellum idyll and the black ghetto coexist with each other in a heteroglot relationship in the film. That film was characterized primarily by the spatiotemporal dynamics of the contemporary black ghetto, the defining chronotope of black-focused films in the 1970s. However, *Sweetback* also contained connections to the antebellum idyll in the scenes in which Sweetback, dressed in the tattered rags of a slave, escapes through the California desert to Mexico. This interrelationship among different times and spaces forms "relations of a different order . . . relations of agreement or disagreement, of parody or polemic" that are "*dialogic* in nature."[13] There are two ways in which this is relevant to my discussion, first in the appearance of parodies of the hood genre, but more important in the moments in which traces of the hood dialogue with other genres, enhancing and structuring the films' narratives.

Don't Be a Menace: Parodies and Other Appropriations of the Hood

There is no denying that some of the elements of the hood had been exhausted by the early 1990s, a fact exemplified by the rapid appearance of films parodying the genre. As early as 1993, Tamra Davis' *CB-4* suggested the direction that parodies of the hood would take in their lampooning of rap music. Rusty Cundieff furthered Davis' efforts in *Fear of a Black Hat* (1994), a *Spinal Tap*-like "mockumentary" of the rap music business and its attendant codes and images in particular, the referents similar to those employed by hood films. *Fear* openly burlesques hood conventions by referencing thug culture and the inner-city authenticity associated with rappers and gangsta' rappers. Furthermore, the film acknowledges the link between rap and African American filmmaking in its interview with a young black director, "Jike Spingleton," who is directing rap-star "Ice Cold" in the film "*New Mack Village*." In a scene that self-consciously addresses both itself and the hood film, Spingleton addresses "John, Spike, and Matty":

> Jike: I got something to say to John, and to Spike, and to Matty. You stole my shit! I had the hat before you did; I had the glasses before you did; and I was short before you were! Wasn't I?
>
> Ice: This mutha fucka was short, near-sighted, and angry long before y'all mutha fuckas!
>
> Jike: I'm pissed!

Spingleton's words are indicative of the ways in which Lee's, Singleton's, and Rich's names and chosen subject matter stood for contemporary black filmmaking to the detriment of other filmmakers and narratives working in and outside of the industry (such as Cundieff himself). More important, it also indicts many directors for both the homogeneity of their personalities and for the homogeneity of their films.[14]

A more direct parody is the Wayans' *Don't Be a Menace to South Central While Drinking Your Juice in the Hood* (directed by Paris Barclay). This film, its title a pastiche of a variety of films (including *Boyz*, *Menace*, *Poetic Justice*, *Higher Learning*, *Dead Presidents*, and *Juice*), signaled that by 1995 the conventions of the genre were so familiar that they, and the films that helped in their manufacture, could be parodied. While the film never deviates from straightforward mimicry of the earlier texts, it undermines both the allegorical didacticism of *Boyz* and the alleged gangsta'ism of *Menace*. *Don't* also announces the death of the hood film while concurrently utilizing many of its narrative codes and conventions and relying heavily on audience identification with its referents. Yet the film's production stopped short of building its parody into its marketing strategies. Whereas many aspects of hood films were parodied, the incorporation and marketing of the film's sound track was not. Instead the music is a collection of straightforward and serious rap songs by artists such as The Lost Boyz, Lil' Kim, Ghostface Killer, and Mobb Deep, undermining its irreverent project. This is not the case, however, with *Fear of a Black Hat*, which lampooned rap's lyrics as much as it did its posturing. Cundieff was responsible for co-writing the majority of the songs performed by "NWH" (Negroes With Hats), as well as performing (as Ice Cool) a number of them.

The number of hood films released by white directors following Singleton's *Boyz* was another indication that the genre may have reached critical mass, a trend that struck at the heart of cultural critics' fears that Hollywood could appropriate the hood genre like blaxploitation before it. As Jesse Algeron Rhines opines in his epilogue to *Black Film/White Money*, "the pattern of white director/Black cast is returning. *White Men Can't Jump*, *Who's The Man?*, and *Fresh* are obvious examples."[15] While Rhines may not have been specifically discussing the hood film, there are films from the hood genre, for example, *Zebrahead* (Anthony Drazan, 1992), *South Central* (Steve Anderson, 1992), *Above the Rim* (Jeff Pollack, 1994), *New Jersey Drive* (Nick Gomez, 1995, with Spike Lee as executive producer), the aforementioned *CB-4* (Tamra Davis, 1993), and *Fresh* (Boaz Yakim, 1995) that support his thesis. Other white-directed features, like *Trespass* (Walter Hill, 1992), *Candyman* (Bernard Rose, 1992), and *Bulworth* (Warren Beatty, 1998) capitalized on particular aspects of hood films, such as Ice Cube's performance in the former and the rendering of specific urbanscapes, such as Chicago's South Side and South Central Los Angeles in the latter two films. Without overlooking the problematics of appropriation, what is more interesting is the extent to which the conventions of the genre were codified and therefore so recognizable that they could be easily and skillfully copied.

While a variety of hood and gangsta' signifiers had entered the stages of parody and appropriation, many of the themes that the hood film first introduced into mainstream (Hollywood) discourse continued in other unrelated genres. This is especially the case with the exploration of black male masculinity, its confrontations with racism, and the ways in which these tensions often transpire in an urban setting. The significant difference between the existence of these traces of the hood chronotope and hood films themselves is that the hood formed neither the primary genre nor the central spatiotemporal relationship of the narratives in the later films. The films were working within the aesthetic and narrative constraints of genres and (sometimes) time periods far removed from the spatiotemporal borders of the hood, even though traces of the contemporary city existed in them. With these other films, we see the hood functioning more as a motif and less as the central organizational trope of the narrative: the hood thus *crosses over* into other genres, and dialogues with other times and spaces.[16]

Gangstas Ride the Range: Traces of the Hood in *Posse*

One of the most interesting uses of hood conventions in a seemingly unrelated genre appears in Mario Van Peebles' *Posse*. Ostensibly a Western, *Posse* uses revisionist strategies to deconstruct and destabilize generic conventions in a way similar to Mel Brooks' *Blazing Saddles*. Van Peebles accomplishes this first by inserting African American cowboys and a contemporary multicultural discourse into the mythic West, a strategy that had not been seen since the black Westerns from the 1930s. The traces of the hood and, to a lesser extent, the black ghetto from blaxploitation in the film enhance this approach, both of which self-referentially rupture the spatiotemporal parameters of the narrative. This is evident in *Posse*'s casting, sound track, dialogue, and other references to present-day spaces and times. Rather than working against each other, the references dialogue with one another, creating "relations of a different order," and linking the time and space of the late-nineteenth-century Western frontier to contemporary Los Angeles and early African American filmmaking to the present.

Other than the use of a contemporary framing device, the film's narrative is embedded in the past—1898—and shifts locales from Cuba and New Orleans to Freemanville, an African American town located in an unspecified part of the West. The film narrates the travails of Jessie Lee (Mario Van Peebles) and the "Outlaw Posse," a group of soldiers who flee the army after an illegal mission in Cuba goes wrong. Besides its African American cast and the film's revisionist allusions to political injustices mythologized by traditional Westerns, *Posse*'s mise-en-scène and cinematography are closely aligned with the generic conventions of the Western. In fact, the text is self-consciously filled with archetypal Western iconography and homages to well-known directors of the genre, including Peckinpah, Mann, and Ford.[17] Woody Strode's role as the narrator further exemplifies this acknowledgment of both a classical and revisionist Western tradition by directly citing an African American cultural figure associated with the genre. This link is even further expanded at the end of the film, when scenes from early black Westerns, such as *Two Gun Man From Harlem*, or white Westerns with an African American presence, play under the credits.

In the story of Jessie Lee and the Outlaw Posse the film fulfills the narrative conventions of both traditional and revisionist Westerns—it is focused on an outcast with a past, which includes witnessing the lynching of his integrationist father. However, it is in *Posse*'s references to African American popular culture—especially those associated with rap—that we can identify contemporary urban influences. One of the hood film's strategies of integrating extradiegetic cultural material into the texts was the practice of routinely casting performers from rap music.[18] Not only did this strategy increase the marketing potential of the films, as the rappers' talents appeared on the sound track as well, but their presence also provided cultural cachet among a black (and white) youth audience—in the process, increasing box office profits. *Posse* adopts a similar strategy, Van Peebles continuing his own tradition begun with *New Jack City*. In *Posse*, he casts Big Daddy Kane and Tone Loc in supporting roles and uses their voices on the sound track. On a more subtle level, Van Peebles' decision to cast himself as the lead and other factors allude to his earlier appearance in *New Jack City*. For example, in both films his character wears a long and distinct overcoat, although one is black and associated with the romantic figure of the outlaw cowboy and the other is beige and equated with the more nondescript clothing of a police detective, private detective, or FBI agent.

Van Peebles also references black film of the 1970s. By casting his father, Melvin, as well as Pam Grier, Nipsy Russell, and Isaac Hayes, Van Peebles constructs a complex signifying system that not only pays homage to African American film history (especially blaxploitation) and to his father's role in that history, but which also acknowledges the performers' contemporary status as pop culture icons. Such personalities function as a two-tiered signifying system: first as they relate directly to black films from the 1970s, and second in the position of such performers in more contemporary discourse, which repeatedly places them in the space and time they inhabited two decades before. In other words, it is impossible to see Melvin Van Peebles in the film without remembering *Sweetback*, and then also without the knowledge of how contemporary filmmakers, such as Spike Lee, cite his work from the 1970s as inspiration for their own filmmaking.

The second way that *Posse* engages with the hood's spatiotemporal dimensions is in its incorporation of diegetic and nondiegetic sound, specifically music and dialogue. The casting of Tone Loc and Big Daddy Kane is not, in and of itself, a direct link to the contemporary hood film. While it alludes to the hood film practice of casting contemporary rappers, the narrative in no way calls out this fact—at least not diegetically because the rappers are strictly cowboys and members of the Outlaw Posse. Yet the moments of diegetic performance, in New Orleans and in The Promised Land, Freemanville's saloon, are examples of contemporary R&B music and therefore form a temporal disjuncture.[19] The a cappella quartet and the saloon's torch-song balladeer, while not a form of music normally associated with the hood, allude to twentieth-century African American musical forms, especially in the context of the film's nineteenth-century setting.

Posse acknowledges the presence of the rappers in its nondiegetic sound because the rhythms and rhymes of Tone Loc and other performers contribute to the sound track. Rap makes few appearances during the film; however, its manifestations in conjunction with both the opening titles and the closing credits act as a set of brackets, destabilizing the generic conventions and providing a specific contemporary mood as an entrance into and exit from the film. The use of rappers and rap music guarantees a modicum of appeal with a youth market, the same market that made *New Jack City* successful. But their use in a film set in such a vastly different space and time is more than just a form of marketing and pastiche because they connect the experiences of Jessie Lee, the Outlaw Posse, and the citizens of Freemanville with the experiences of the film's contemporary audience, especially a young, black male audience living in the hood. Furthermore, they draw together *Posse*'s contemporary project with the history of African American filmmaking because their rhythms accompany images from such films as *Two Gun Man From Harlem*, *Harlem on the Prairie*, *Harlem Rides the Range*, and *The Bronze Buckaroo*. *Posse*, like the earlier Westerns, references the present-day city through music.

Two related examples will support my point. First, like the music, *Posse*'s dialogue combines speech patterns from different genres and time periods. For example, many characters speak in nineteenth-century slang, a speechidiom associated with the Western genre. This dialogue adjoins the inner-city speech patterns associated with characters in the hood. The combination of distinct dialects is most apparent in the members of the Outlaw Posse, especially Weezie (Charles Lane) and Angel (Tone Loc). (Jessie Lee speaks in an upper-middle-class intonation, which separates him, as their leader, from the rest of the Posse.) An example of this occurs early in the film, when a number of characters use contemporary slang, such as "mutha fucka," while they are fighting Spanish troops in Cuba. Furthermore, this mixture of contemporary hood slang and Western dialect is present in the Outlaw Posse's name and in the film's title. Traditionally, a posse was convened for a common cause, usually to track down and capture an outlaw or outlaws. In the film the "outlaws" become the posse and their common foes are the individuals normally associated with the law: an officer in the U.S. Army and a sheriff.[20] But the term "posse" also has contemporary cultural currency and is commonly used in rap and hip-hop culture as a moniker for a group of "home boys" (again, men with a common cause). In this way, the title links the contemporary space with the past.

The interconnections of time and space are explicit in a scene from near the film's conclusion. The town of Freemanville is under attack by the joint forces of the Ku Klux Klan and Lieutenant Carver's (Billy Zane) soldiers. In a frequently discussed moment, Snopes (Nipsey Russell) quotes Rodney King, asking, "Can't we all get along?" while shielding himself from the violence and watching the town burn. While heavy-handed, the reference links the events in Freemanville in 1898 and those in Los Angeles in 1992. Additionally, Snopes' utterance underscores how such motifs are "congealed events . . . [or] reminders of the time and space that typically functions there."[21] Thus, this line of dialogue sets up a chain of associations that inserts the space and time of contemporary Los Angeles into the past of the film, linking current racialized violence with the West's frontier past.

Posse's polyphony is coherent in the context of the film's overarching project as a revisionist Western. In this sense, it is not just that the quotation of King's words injects the contemporary moment into the past. The reverse is also true because the film posits that the past is an important factor in contemporary popular culture and American mythology as a whole. This strategy is clearest in the stress placed on revising the history of Western expansion to include not only African American cowboys, but more important, the black settlers who built Freemanville or perished trying to either reach it or protect it. Thus the film's fetishization of the cowboy (especially Van Peebles' narcissistic attraction to Jessie Lee) and its pyrotechnics (in keeping with the most violent hood film) distracts from one of its central themes—settlement of the West and its direct relationship to contemporary urban conditions.

The very first few frames of *Posse* announce the theme of Western expansion when the voice-over narration explains that history has overlooked African American involvement in the settlement of the West. To make his point, the narrator offers the statistic that "one half of the original settlers in Los Angeles were black." From here the film switches to Jessie Lee's and the Outlaw Posse's story. However, while the narrative focus is on Jessie Lee's revenge, a subplot engages with the question of black settlement, particularly as it relates to the tensions between integration (Jessie Lee's father's desire) and segregation (what Freemanville seemingly is). Consequently, what starts out as a conventional outlaw narrative expands to include twentieth-century civil rights discourses (and even earlier references to figures like Marcus Garvey and W.E.B. DuBois) and the role of migration in African American urban and cinematic history. Many references to migration are contained within Van Peebles' revisionist project, and these references, in combination with traces of the hood film, explicitly link late-nineteenth-century migration with the contemporary city. This is first accomplished by blurring the distinctions between Los Angeles and Freemanville through allusions to African American settlement in Los Angeles, references to Rodney King and the 1992 riots, and the iconography of hood films, a spatiotemporal configuration specifically associated with contemporary Los Angeles. The allusions are then placed in dialogue with the whole of the Western genre. The second way that the film links migration to the city is in its repeated references to modes of transportation, especially ships and trains.

It is revealed near the end of the film that the reason for much of the white violence directed at the town is not so much racism as it is greed; Jessie Lee and the town's residents learn that Freemanville is located on the site of a future railway line. The railway is in the process of being built, a fact we know through a number of shots showing its construction (complete with African American and Chinese labor), and will soon reach the town. Prior to this revelation, the railroad has already maintained an important position in the narrative. In fact, the Western portion of the story is introduced with the shot of a moving train passing over the camera (quoting a multiplicity of Westerns, as well as Dziga Vertov). Initially, the train is foreboding as it transports Lieutenant Carver and his soldiers toward Jessie Lee and the Outlaw Posse. However, they disembark early in the narrative and long before the Posse has reached Freemanville. The train does not reappear until the end when it becomes, concurrently, a threat to the town's existence (as the residents of Carter, a neighboring all-white town, want to destroy Freemanville and relocate there in order to be on the train line) and a symbol of its prosperous future.

The train is much more than a mode of transportation, especially since Jessie Lee and the Outlaw Posse never utilize its services. It symbolizes the burdens and promises of settlement and migration, a link made clear by the troubled history of Freemanville as signified by The Promised Land saloon. The train's role "is twofold; it is both an agent of social integration and a device of social and individual disintegration."[22] Ironically, the train also becomes a "congealed event" itself because it signifies a multiplicity of African American migrations and settlements from the late nineteenth century to the late twentieth century. In this way, *Posse*'s examination of movement and settlement actually becomes a relation of disagreement in its dialogue with the hood film. While both *Posse* and the hood films examine movement and migration, they approach it from different directions. *Posse*'s signifying system triggers associations with the history of African American migrations in order to foreground an expansion of borders and the exploration of new territories. Hood films, on the other hand, focused on entrapment and the containment of characters within the physical, cultural, and psychic borders of the city—and the limits that this places both on geographic exploration and self-exploration. However, both *Posse* and the earlier hood films are speaking about the same thing: movement.

Spike Lee's *Clockers* focuses on precisely this nexus of ideas and amplifies the complex issues raised by the dialogue between hood conventions and *Posse*. While an undeniable influence on the genre, Lee had remained distant from the hood film, instead directing and producing a cross-section of films and genres, from the biography of Malcolm X to the serial-killer drama *Summer of Sam* (1999). While his films are consistently anchored in New York, Brooklyn in particular, his films are also resolutely historical. Even when set in the contemporary city, they are filled with referents to African American history: the illustrations of the cargo hold of the slave ship in the opening shots of *School Daze* (1988); the characters of Da Mayor and Mother Sister in *Do The Right Thing*; and his latest treatise on the history of African American representation in *Bamboozled* (2000).[23] Of all the African American directors working in the 1990s, Lee consistently referenced the links between northern urban spaces and their southern pasts. Therefore, *Clockers'* reconsideration of the hood chronotope and the trope of migration provides the key opportunity to examine what happens to hood film conventions after *Boyz N the Hood* and *Menace II Society*.

Revisioning the Hood: *Clockers* and the Legacy of Black City Cinema

> Nothing is experienced by itself, but always in relation to its surroundings, the sequences of events leading up to it, the memory of past experiences. . . . Every citizen has had long associations with some part of his city, and his image is soaked in memories and meanings.
>
> —Kevin Lynch (1960)[24]

In a variety of press releases and published interviews, Spike Lee publicly announced his intentions for *Clockers* (1995). Lee stated that he wanted the film to be more than just another hood film, what he referred to as the "black gangster, hip-hop shoot-'em-up . . . drug genre."[25] One of Lee's primary concerns was to differentiate *Clockers* from films such as *Boyz N the Hood* and *Menace II Society*. As Lee stated after the film's release, "It was always our intention that if we succeeded with this film, that this might be the final nail in the coffin and African-American film-makers would try telling new stories."[26] While *Clockers*' system of references is reliant upon the films immediately preceding it, the film's appropriation and revision of many of the conventions of the hood film problematizes a clear-cut alignment of it with earlier examples of the genre. Its use of hood conventions is too consciously self-referential, which is apparent in the film's narrative, style, and shifting character identification. As I've discussed, *Menace* is also a self-referential text, especially in its conscious appropriation of many of the narrative elements of *Boyz*. Yet where *Menace*'s self-consciousness both accepts and expands upon hood conventions, *Clockers* deconstructs and problematizes them.

It is not my intention to examine all the ways in which *Clockers* either succeeds or fails to fulfill generic requirements. Instead, I want to start from the understanding that *Clockers* utilizes iconography similar to that of a number of other films set in African American urban spaces in the 1990s. However, I want to expand this observation and suggest that Lee broadens this urban sign system in discrete ways. In fact, like *Posse*, Lee's film fuses the hood with the traces of another time and space by linking contemporary Brooklyn to an African American past, and this is accomplished through some specific changes in the novel's original story. The remainder of this chapter focuses on the ways in which *Clockers* reconsiders and revisions the hood film in particular and cinematic representations of the black city as a whole. In the process, I examine how the film's spatiotemporal parameters dialogue with the traces of another time and space through the motif of the train. My argument is that the presence of the train in *Clockers*, like *Posse* before it, inserts the tropes of migration, mobility, and settlement in the narrative in order to suggest a dialogue between African American history and contemporary African American filmmaking. The difference between it and more identifiably "historical" films like *Posse* is that *Clockers* accomplishes this in a contemporary setting and uses the conventions of a contemporary genre.

A knowledge of the circumstances involved in the film's production is crucial for understanding the significance of Lee's role in the final product. The film was adapted from Richard Price's novel of the same name. Price's original story focused on the experiences of two very different characters, Strike, a small-time drug dealer, and Rocco Klein, a

New Jersey homicide detective. The men are brought together when Rocco is assigned to investigate the murder of a local drug-dealer. The original story was optioned by Martin Scorsese, with Robert DeNiro slated to star as Rocco. Price, already well-known for other scripts based on his novels, adapted the screenplay. When Scorsese and DeNiro left the project to work on Scorsese's *Casino*, Lee was hired to direct, with Scorsese continuing his involvement as a co-producer. Lee, also a co-producer, rewrote the script, significantly altering the original story. The most telling links to the hood film and to the historical foundations of the cinematic urbanscape are located in these alterations. We can see this in three of the most important modifications made to the original story: main character, setting, and conclusion.

First, in reconceptualizing the narrative, Lee focused on Strike (Mekhi Phifer), a young drug dealer, or clocker. This was a change from both the novel and the original screenplay. The novel alternates point-of-view between Strike and Rocco (Harvey Keitel). This approach develops the psyches of both characters and provides background information for the tension informing the pair's interactions when Rocco first investigates Victor (Strike's brother) but then changes his focus to Strike. In his screenplay, Price changed the novel's original structure by shifting primary point-of-view to Rocco alone. The effect was to provide Rocco with a more fully developed psychology, at the expense of Strike's characterization, a decision most likely influenced by DeNiro's casting. Lee took Price's screenplay and changed the focus to Strike. This alteration expanded audience identification with (and thus sympathy for) a character traditionally lacking psychological development in most of the films focusing on similar protagonists, with the possible exceptions of Tre in *Boyz* and Caine in *Menace*.[27] Like Caine, Strike is often an unsympathetic character. Unlike the Hughes brothers however, Lee wanted to more thoroughly explore the trials and tribulations, the pressures and the motives, behind Strike's choice to clock rather than starting from the presumption that such a decision is made inevitably or comes naturally.[28] Furthermore, Lee's film more fully acknowledges the effects of Strike's and his crew's presence on the surrounding community, in particular, his family and his neighbors.

While Lee focused on the same subject matter as many hood films, Strike's characterization—as a young black man coming of age in the inner city—is more three-dimensional than the majority of related characterizations in the sense that he possesses a well-defined psychology.

This approach makes Strike more sympathetic because he's not only charismatic, but he is plagued by enough of a conscience that he's literally eaten up from the inside by ulcers over the stress of his daily activities. Also, in an interesting expansion and explication of street morality, Strike is made even more sympathetic when he has trouble carrying out orders to murder another dealer.[29] This shift reframes the more cold-blooded characterizations of Caine, Doughboy, or Bishop from *Juice*, who elicit no remorse over similar murderous acts. In fact, Caine's voice-over in *Menace* explicitly states that he feels nothing after participating in a drive-by shooting that results in the deaths of two young men.

Unlike earlier cinematic renderings of gangsta' characters and more like *Fear of a Black Hat*, *Clockers* problematizes the thug exterior associated with both their cinematic and musical personae.[30] Strike is relatively soft—he drinks a Yoo Hoo-like soft drink called Moo Moo rather than the ubiquitous "forties" malt liquor, he collects and plays with model trains, and he's often emasculated in the face of authority. In almost all of his interactions with authority figures, such as the police and his boss Rodney Little (Delroy Lindo), Strike is inarticulate (in the novel he even stutters when tense), ineffectual, and childlike, behaviors suggestive of his youth and inexperience. An interesting correlative to this is the fact that all the authority figures complicating Strike's life are distanced from him by generational factors (with Andre the housing cop coming the closest in age) as well as the more obvious structural and ideological factors. Generational miscommunication and disappointment resides at the core of many of the hood films' tensions, with agency and neighborhood control often ceded to a younger generation and elders characterized as ineffectual. *Clockers* inverts this relationship, not necessarily as a critique of Strike as much as it is to reinsert the influence of elders back into contemporary African American popular culture.

Living in the City: Brooklyn's Many-Storied Pasts

The second change Lee made was to shift the novel's setting from the Roosevelt Houses in Dempsy—a fictional New Jersey location roughly based on Jersey City—to the "Nelson Mandela Houses" of Brooklyn (in actuality the Gowanus Houses, located in the Boerum Hill section of Brooklyn). The effect of this move is quite significant, despite Lee's claim that "projects are projects."[31] First, by relocating to Brooklyn, Lee situated the film in the already storied and familiar spatial parameters of the hood. While the majority of hood films were set in Los Angeles, a few significant examples, such as *Straight Out of Brooklyn* and *Juice*, were located in New York City, and only one *New Jersey Drive*, was set in New Jersey. This move contributes to the film's already complex interweaving of references and temporalities. On the one hand, the film's identifiable urban location, frenetic camera techniques, rap-based sound track, current fashions, and references to contemporary African American popular culture announce its similarities with hood films, especially *Menace*. But this shift in location must also be viewed in the context of Lee's entire cinematic oeuvre, which, from almost its beginnings, has both acknowledged and explored the past in the context of the present—symbolized most often by references to particular character's and the city's southern roots. This feature appears in Lee's work as early as *Joe's Bed-Stuy Barbershop: We Cut Heads*, and has continued throughout his career, most notably in *School Daze*, *Do The Right Thing*, *Malcolm X*, and *Crooklyn*.[32] Thus, the move to Brooklyn locates *Clockers* in a particular urban history and acknowledges the effects of migration and ghettoization.

In order to see how the past functions in this film, it is important to understand Brooklyn's history as an African American community, a history that is often overlooked in most studies of urban black migration to metropolitan areas such as Los Angeles, Chicago, Detroit, and even New York City, where discussion is often limited to Harlem. During the Great Migration, Harlem played a crucial role as a black city within a city—a "promised land"—for many rural migrants. However, Brooklyn also has its own concurrent history as a home for a substantial African American population, a result of the same demographic shifts that helped constitute Harlem. As early as the turn of the century, Brooklyn—specifically the areas of Bedford and Stuyvesant—was home to an established black, predominantly middle-class population. In addition, through the 1920s many Harlem blacks also migrated the short distance to Brooklyn, "seeking social mobility and escape" from the factors that had already begun to turn their area into a ghetto.[33] The expansion of the New York City subway system (specifically the A-train) to the borough in 1936 facilitated the migration of Harlemites to Brooklyn, resulting in an increase in both the number of migrants and the area's African American population.[34] This local migration combined with the continuing addition of new arrivals from the rural South and the Caribbean, all of which expanded the neighborhood's black population. The area's demographic growth continued through the mid-century (especially with the employment offered by the Brooklyn naval yards) and into the 1980s. At the time, Bed-Stuy became synonymous with black.[35] Not coincidentally, this last development also corresponds with Lee's career, so much so that in the 1980s, cinematic representations of black Brooklyn became synonymous with Spike Lee.[36]

With the expansion of Brooklyn's African American population, the Bed-Stuy, Brownsville, and Boerum Hill sections of Brooklyn, among others, transformed from being relatively integrated to increasingly isolated and marginalized as other ethnic groups emigrated to different parts of the borough (Bensonhurst), to other New York City boroughs (Queens, Staten Island), or to the suburbs (Long Island, Westchester County, New Jersey). Property speculation, absentee landlords, and governmental disinterest in the 1960s and 1970s resulted in the area's lower property values and the increasing segregation and concurrent ghettoization of the black community—a ghettoization concurrently experienced in Los Angeles, Detroit, Chicago, and other major metropolitan areas. The situation was complicated by the construction and subsequent abandonment (through decreases in funding and governmental interest) of low-income housing projects, of which the Gowanus (Nelson Mandela) Houses are a prime example.[37] A similar view of projects in general has been expounded by Price, a product of them himself, who observes, "What was amazing to me was how the projects went from launching pads for working-class families to just terminals where generations are stacked up in the same apartment because there's no place to go."[38] Both observations echo the concerns of many contemporary African American filmmakers who use similar metaphors of entrapment in depicting discrete city spaces.

All of these factors complexify Lee's seemingly simple choice to relocate *Clockers* to Brooklyn, especially the area's significance as a terminal point of sorts. While it may have been that it was cheaper and easier to shoot in Brooklyn, or that Lee was more comfortable working in a familiar location, neither factor diminishes the importance of the choice of Brooklyn for the film's setting. On the one hand, the borough is the final destination of the majority of New York's subway lines running southeast. Brooklyn is where you get off, unless you want to head all the way back to Queens through Manhattan, and characters in *Clockers*, except for Victor (Isaiah Washington), never head in that direction.[39] Brooklyn was also the end point for many who had experienced multiple dislocations and migrations—the Middle Passage, the South, Harlem. In this history, Brooklyn is more than just a stopover or transitional point, as places such as Memphis were for many migrants. Brooklyn is the literal end of the line after multiple journeys. And, as Price's observation regarding the transformation of housing projects suggests, Brooklyn became a metaphorical terminal point as well when what was once the hope of moving from the poverty of the rural South, or the urban decay of Harlem, became the stagnation of the projects and economic displacement. Ironically, the end result of all this movement is entrapment, the core theme of hood films like Matty Rich's *Straight Out of Brooklyn*.

The architectonics of *Clockers* clearly makes this point. Most of the film is shot in the projects' central courtyard, a tree- and bench-lined circular plaza with a raised concrete platform that the community has ceded to Strike, his crew, and the crack business. According to Amy Taubin, this area, "is both stage and prison—an inversion of Foucault's panopticon. Trapped within it, Strike is under constant surveillance, vulnerable to aggressors who enter from all sides."[40] This facet of the projects is also noted in the novel:

> Strike scanned the canyon walls of the Roosevelt Houses. There were thirteen high rises, twelve hundred families over two square blocks, and the housing office gave the Fury [Housing Police] access to any vacant apartment for surveillance, so Strike never knew when or where they might be scoping him out.[41]

The projects are a carceral city, where the surrounding buildings act as sentries, looking down on the activities taking place below, guarding the boundaries of the projects, and barring movement from within their perimeter.[42]

As a socially constituted space, the Mandela Houses both reflect and refract the neighboring communities, societies, and histories. In its focus on boundaries, *Clockers* indicates that the projects (and most of their residents) may abut the surrounding communities, but they are not necessarily "of" the community. True, they contain social relations that mirror the society constituting them, and therefore act as a form of heterotopia, but the projects are roped off from the community with most pro-filmic events occurring there.[43] What lies beyond the Mandela Houses is an urban frontier not freely accessible to the characters imprisoned within the projects' visible and historic barricades. Most of

Foucault's panopticon in Brooklyn (*Clockers*, 40 Acres and a Mule Filmworks, Inc., 1995). Courtesy of 40 Acres and a Mule Filmworks, Inc.

the characters show little inclination or desire to leave their immediate surroundings. In fact, the majority of characters have been stripped of the ability to even envision an alternative existence. Strike and his brother Victor differ from the other characters because they, especially Victor, can see outside the projects. Victor works two demeaning and underpaid jobs in order to save enough money to move his family out of the projects, a desire based on the possibility of a literal move out of their present environment and on a more figurative desire for social (and economic) mobility from the underclass to the working or middle class. Strike's flight, on the other hand, is mostly imaginary, as his fantasies about trains carry him from his surroundings only in his mind. Strike doesn't experience real movement until the end of the film, although it is foreshadowed by these earlier scenes. The paradox of this situation is frustratedly articulated by Andre (Keith David) to Strike: "There's more than just these projects out there, you know. Don't you want to go someplace you've never been before? . . . you love trains but you've only ridden the subway." Here, the stasis of the projects is clearly contrasted with the mobility of subways and trains. By this time, however, subways offer no real exit—a clear reversal of their role from earlier in the century. It may be that Strike's knowledge of trains and the fact that he has already moved out of the projects will be his ticket out.

Before moving on to a discussion of Lee's third divergence from the novel, I want to consider the ways he reframes the film's city spaces in relation to the conventions of the hood film. On the one hand, the alteration of setting brings the narrative into a closer relationship to the familiar boundaries of the hood as seen in films like *Juice*, *Straight Out of Brooklyn*, *Just Another Girl on the IRT*, and *New Jack City*. The mise-en-scène resembles the spatial integrity of many of its predecessors, especially in the way that it calls attention to its location through prominently placed signage—the Nelson Mandela Houses and the references to Brooklyn and "Crooklyn" being the most obvious. Yet the film reworks the hood films' emphasis on "real" space (real streets and street signs, and the calling out of specific urban areas, for example) by constructing a space that is concurrently real (shot on location) and manufactured (announced by the self-referentiality of cinematic technique). In its reworking of these conventions, *Clockers* transforms the hood chronotope into traces that dialogue with other generic and historical traces or motifs—the most central of which is the train.

It cannot be disputed that the film's locations may be familiar to its targeted audience. However, it is in the ways that the film breaks down this a priori generic spatial integrity that indicates the way that the hood gradually diminishes in importance in black-directed films released after *Clockers*. Almost all of the action takes place within the boundaries of the projects, even though the two main characters, Rocco and Strike, are not themselves residents (although Strike was raised there). Most of the scenes are exterior shots, filmed on location in the projects' central plaza. The film rarely contains interior shots, instead focusing on the activity in this park-like area. In Lee's articulation of the space, especially in the establishing shots, the plaza differs from more conventional renderings of inner-city space. It is green, lush, and infused with a rich light that calls attention to the colors found in both the space's vegetation and the clothing worn by the clockers. Furthermore, the lively comings and goings of the community form a pleasant and ironic backdrop for crack entrepreneurs. Yet even in this change from the more dystopian and desolate urbanscape of the hood film, the plaza maintains a certain integrity as the Gowanus Houses. It appears to be authentic, a realism that the use of shaky camera movements and zoom lenses, resembling the style of reality-based television or a surveillance camera, emphasizes.[44]

The film foregrounds its own processes of manufacture, especially in its camera movement, editing, mise-en-scène, and cinematography.

In particular, the variety of film stock and lighting techniques calls attention to the tactile nature of the film's images. Lee's experimentation with filmic form is well known, and *Clockers* is no exception. It continues the development of certain of his signature techniques, such as the effect of placing characters and camera on a moving dolly while taking care to keep the changing background in focus. Lee's experimentation is also apparent in the film's mise-en-scène. Lee has always been known for constructing specific sets to meet his diegetic needs, a fact that provoked criticism for *Do The Right Thing* because it changed the look and nature of an existing city block in Bed-Stuy. In *Clockers*, the projects remain virtually untouched. The surrounding spaces—Ahab's (a fast food place), the bar, Strike's apartment, the train—are differentiated from the Mandela Houses.

Changes in setting and lighting distinguish the bar and Ahab's from Strike's apartment and the train. Violence characterizes the Kool Breeze and Ahab's: they are the sites in which violence is first planned and then performed. Moreover, they enable the narrative in that the actions that take place in these spaces set off the remaining chain of events. Both sites, which we only see at night, have brightly lit and colorful signage—Ahab's complete with a revolving whale that blows steam out its airhole. The spaces are also the sites of some of the film's most aggressive cinematography. First, Strike confronts Darryl (Steve White) before presumably murdering him. The scene is introduced with a close-up of a tabloid headline showing "Crooklyn" before the camera tracks back to reveal Strike in the foreground (from a low angle) and the billboard announcing "No More Packing" above his head. Significantly, Ahab's—and this scene in particular—will be revisited in various characters' flashbacks, with a gritty image quality diluting the hypersaturated colors of the original.

The Kool Breeze is also introduced by its brightly lit sign, which appears in an establishing shot prior to a cut, first to television images of a rap video and finally into the interior of the bar. Once inside, the editing and cinematography is conventional, with Victor and Strike framed in a two-shot as they discuss Darryl. Similar editing and cinematography are maintained when Rocco and his partner (John Turturro) enter the bar to question its patrons. In both of these examples time occurs in the narrative present and rap images on television introduce the Kool Breeze. These images link the activities presented in the videos and advertisements for malt liquor with those taking place in the bar. Later in the film, flashbacks of the bar and Ahab's appear with gritty cinematography and diluted colors, and the rap images have disappeared.

These spaces, always sites of violence, differ from those that are more closely associated with Strike—his apartment and the train. Strike's apartment is a run-of-the-mill tenement space, characterized by aged woodwork and wall and nondescript furniture. As such, the apartment is indistinguishable from other spaces of lesser narrative importance, such as Victor's Mandela House apartment. Yet it is the way the space is shot that makes it so interesting. As in the later scenes with the train, a golden, glowing light streaming through two windows in the background provides everything in the middle and foreground of the apartment with a slight halo. There's no narrative reason for this use of lighting. In fact, the activities that take place in these scenes undercut this visual treatment; one time Strike is teaching Tyrone (Peewee Love), a neighborhood kid, how to cut and weigh crack cocaine, and the second time Strike is packing his bags. In both examples, however, a narrative link is made with the trains, foreshadowed in these scenes but not realized until the film's conclusion. First, prior to teaching Tyrone about the drug business, Strike shows him his collection of model trains and teaches Tyrone their history, a history that will be reiterated by Tyrone to his mother at the film's conclusion. Second, when Strike is packing his bags, he pauses long enough to write a note to his landlord, leaving his trains to Tyrone.

Prior spatiotemporal constructions of the hood clearly influence the film's cinematography in *Clockers'* cinematic articulation of the Mandela Houses and a few other scenes (mostly street scenes, especially around Rodney's store and the police station). These scenes define the urbanscape, a space already identified in earlier films as the hood. Yet the scenes outside the boundaries of the projects indicate that *Clockers* is more than an appropriation of hood film conventions. Its manufacture of these other spaces indicates a self-conscious attempt to point to the possibility that the cinematic city might be more manufactured than it first appears. In fact, it might be, as in Ahab's, the Kool Breeze, and Strike's apartment, an entirely constructed terrain. This, in and of itself, already distinguishes *Clockers* from the "hip hop . . . drug genre." But it is where the traces of the hood film and Lee's self-conscious image manufacturing start to dialogue with the train that the text's polyphony expands to acknowledge history fully, especially the links between the city and African American migration.

Take the A(mtrak) Train: Trains, Sites, and Chronotopes

In classical narrative cinema the train was generally given the role of
integration and linkage, of stabilization, especially in terms of American
national identity: the mythology of assimilation to a "universal" American
identity.

—Lynne Kirby (1997)[45]

The significance of the change in setting and its relationship to what
Paul Gilroy refers to, in another context, as "movement, relocation,
displacement, and restlessness"[46] is evidenced in Lee's third and most
crucial change from the novel—Strike's fascination with trains. In the
novel, Strike has few interests outside of making money and dealing
drugs. He "had never really liked music. He had never cared about
sports, even girls that much if he thought about it."[47] Strike's world
revolves around his relationship with Rodney and the other clockers.
This conforms with the novel's strategy of splitting point-of-view between Strike and Rocco, and accords with its less sympathetic approach
to Strike's character. In the film, however, Strike's collection of model
trains humanizes his character—for who would expect a drug dealer to
have any interests outside of the criminality that defines and limits him
(the same criminality that defined and limited him in the novel, and that
wholly limits Caine in *Menace*)? Kirby suggests that between 1880 and
World War I the "cult" of toy trains "firmly linked masculinity with
railroading." However, African American boys "were barred" from fulfilling dreams of "glamorous railroad careers as engineers because of
skin color." The most that they could hope for was to become Pullman
porters, a position of "esteem," but still a position of servitude.[48] Ironically, in *Clockers* Strike's hobby, rather than his drug dealing or gun,
defines his masculinity. Yet Strike's interest in and knowledge of the
history of trains was viewed as insignificant by most viewers and critics,
if it was mentioned at all. For the more cynical viewers, the trains were
nothing more than the enabling metaphor for the film's "rapturous"
finale, or, worse, as just another detail of the mise-en-scène, simply an
excuse for Strike's outfit of overalls at the beginning of the film.[49]

While the trains humanize Strike, they also alter the novel's conclusion. Rather than leaving town on a bus from the Port Authority
bus terminal as in the novel, the cinematic Strike flees on a train from

Penn Station. The significance of the change is powerfully communicated in the way Lee shot the final scene, which is filtered with golden light and soft-focus lenses, a marked difference from the gritty cinematography constituting most of the film. The combination of Strike's hobby and *Clockers'* conclusion enables Lee to further historicize contemporary cinematic representations of the black city. Like *Posse, Clockers'* metonymic use of trains thus points to the interconnected histories of African American migration, the rise of inner-city ghettoes, and the subsequent demise of a black middle class. Furthermore, the train references the related tropes of mobility and entrapment, two of the most recurrent themes in African American cultural production in the twentieth century and in African American films from this time period, and a central theme of hood films.

To understand all this we must remain aware of the complex historical role that migration has played as a central trope in African American cultural production in particular and the African diaspora as a whole. For Gilroy, among others, an understanding of the construction of identity, and a politics of identity, is directly related to the concepts of location and dislocation. As he states, "It would appear that there are large questions raised about the direction and character of black culture and art if we take the powerful effects of even temporary experiences of exile, relocation, and displacement into account."[50] While in this context Gilroy is discussing the influence of freely chosen travel experiences on particular individuals, W.E.B. DuBois and Richard Wright, for example, his observations regarding the significance of movement are relevant to the experiences of African Americans in general. The question thus becomes not only how does travel affect an individual's sense of self, but also, how does massive migration affect or transform cultural production and reception and how is this further shaped by limitations on movement and agency? In short, how have "successive displacements, migrations, and journeys (forced and otherwise) . . . come to constitute . . . black cultures' special conditions of existence?"[51]

Keeping in mind the history of migration and how it relates to the film's Brooklyn location, Strike's fascination with trains is a particularly telling addition, especially if we understand the train as a chronotopic motif. In *Clockers'* narrative, the train forms a sort of spatiotemporal unity which fuses the history of twentieth-century African American migration, the growth of an identifiable black city space, the ghettoization of the black city, and the demonization of black youth together in

Strike leaving town for better places in *Clockers* (40 Acres and a Mule Filmworks, Inc., 1995). Courtesy of 40 Acres and a Mule Filmworks, Inc.

one sign. Therefore, the train symbolizes the contestations of African American mobility by signifying a past, a present, and—in the case of the film's conclusion—a possible future that is immeasurably intertwined with the city.

Border Crossing: Spike, Strike, and the Legacy of the Porter

It is no accident that Lee's additions to *Clockers* include a train because it links the film's urban present with both its urban and rural pasts. The train also raises important questions regarding African American mobility, both literal movement from place to place and in the figurative sense as a symbol of African American social mobility. Mobility and entrapment have been central themes in black films from their very inception and increasingly became a central thematic concern (in both film and literature) as the nation's black population's association with the city increased, and the city became equated with a dystopian economic and social prison. In short, the focus on mobility becomes more pressing as the urbanscape goes from promised land to dystopia.

Clockers is no different in this respect, as it, like the hood films it quotes, focuses on the sense of entrapment and lack of agency that the project's prison-like spaces engenders in its characters. Most characters are content to remain in the hood, living (and often) dying in the same limited spaces. In fact, they cannot envision any other existence. But some of the characters—Victor and Strike in particular—look beyond the hood, and desire (Strike belatedly) an escape from their surroundings. Victor and Strike thus provide the link with the second aspect of the film's concern with mobility, that which is concurrently related to the literal mobility of escape, and to a more figurative social mobility and agency. This expands the role of the train in the film. Not only does it represent Strike's escape, but the train also references social mobility, especially in the connections it makes to African American history and the Pullman porter, links that expand on Kirby's earlier words.

In this regard, I'd like to return to Gilroy, his discussion of trains, and their relationship to Pullman porters. According to Gilroy, "porters worked in ways that both continued patterns of exploitation established during slavery and anticipated the novel forms of debasement and humiliation associated with contemporary service work." Paradoxically, the porter's movement illustrates the curiously constructed and conscripted terms of progress as experienced by African Americans—and, by extension, black diasporic peoples—in what Gilroy defines as early modernism. In this moment of massive industrialization (of which the train and film are by-products), and its attendant opening of new frontiers, some boundaries—however much they gave the illusion of breaking down—ultimately remained the same. The history of the train thus presents a significant mediation of the contradictions and limitations of African American mobility, specifically as related to the experiences of the Jim Crow car and the Pullman porter, "an important symbol of the new opportunities and the new constraints that fell upon blacks in the 19th century."[52] In a similar way, the city symbolized both new opportunities and constraints: "the city as a symbol of community, of home" and "the city of brute fact in which blacks in the 20th century have had to live."[53] Porters "enjoyed" increased mobility, both physical and economic, but this was always mediated by their positions as servants. If not porters, then African American passengers were segregated to the Jim Crow cars.

The porter's job equipped him with the often problematic ability to move between worlds—to cross borders. While serving the train's white passengers, the porter also possessed the "freedom" to move into (although never to occupy) cars where other African American passengers were not allowed. In this situation, porters mediated the tension between two segregated poles. Strike's position in the narrative, because it is so closely aligned with trains and the concurrent references to migration and mobility, is similar to that of the porter, but it is a similarity that is not unproblematic. At the beginning of the film, there is little to differentiate Strike from his clocker counterparts. The murder of a local dealer linked with his boss, Rodney, and Victor's subsequent confession mark Strike for the unwanted attention of the homicide detectives. As Rocco and his partner increasingly pressure Strike, his safety within his community and with Rodney drastically decreases because he is increasingly forced out of this world. The detectives, Rocco in particular, purposely pursue Strike and their most effective weapon is to "out" him by interacting with him in full view of the community. In effect, Strike is forced to become an unwilling and literal border-crosser, rather than just an imaginary one with his trains. But, the more he becomes associated with the detectives, the more his life is endangered. Ultimately, Strike's movement between the two worlds becomes the threat—he is imagined to have crossed a line—that forces Rodney to order his execution. The end result is that Strike is compelled to leave town, rejected by his family, the community, the police, and Rodney.

Strike's experiences are indicative of the danger inherent in African American border-crossing, a danger, however, that is more fully exemplified in Victor's experiences. In a discussion focusing on Chester Himes' *A Rage in Harlem*, Manthia Diawara notes that

> the train's power . . . coincides with the devaluation of Black life. The train is also powerful because of its mobility; nothing hinders its traversing of Harlem, and its movements into the white world which connotes power, economic prosperity, and freedom. Mobility empowers the train . . . and the lack of mobility constitutes a check on the freedom of Black people.[54]

Nowhere are these contradictions more apparent than in Victor's struggles to break free from his immediate situation.

Everyone, especially Strike, is surprised when Victor confesses to Darryl's murder. In the course of his investigation, Rocco is convinced that Strike committed the murder, not Victor, because, in Rocco's words, "Victor's a good kid; not the murdering type." Victor is presented sympathetically throughout the narrative: he's a family man who is supporting a wife, two kids, and his mother with the income from two jobs. In addition, he's trying to save enough money to buy a house and move his family outside the projects. By all accounts, Rocco is correct to look to Strike for the murder—Strike is the homeboy, the clocker, the criminal with a record.

Cracks start appearing in Victor's near-perfect facade, cracks that are directly linked to his ambitions. In the course of Rocco's investigation, he hears nothing but praises for Victor. But Rocco also learns of incidents in which Victor had disputes with different young men from the neighborhood, all of whom flashed large piles of cash at Victor and verbally demeaned him. By the film's conclusion, we learn that Victor was responsible for Darryl's death and that the motive was his rage at the realization of his own ineffectualness. In his mother's flashback version of events, Victor succumbs momentarily to this frustration, which is then directed at Darryl, a representative of every limit preventing Victor's dreams from coming to fruition, of every situation stripping him of his agency. While Darryl is the target, the cause of his death is related more to Victor's realization that his dreams for mobility are undervalued, even in his own community. Strike, on the other hand, shifts between two worlds; however, unlike the porter, Strike is eventually forced to choose a new world since he no longer fits into either. Thus, the contradictions inherent in the role of the porter indicate the cultural context from which the trains in *Clockers* emerge, and identify the train as a primal site of African American geographic and social mobility, geographic and social restraint.

The film concludes with aureate shots of Strike riding on a train, heading into the sunset. This scene is intercut with images of Scientific (Sticky Fingaz), one of Strike's clockers, lying dead in a pool of blood while Tyrone plays with Strike's trains and passes on their history—learned from Strike—to his mother. It would be easy to read this ending, as many critics did, as overly optimistic, "rapturous," or moral. Or, one could conclude that the film lapses into a nostalgia or a pessimism "which views the city as bad."[55] But to do so would be to miss the point. While Strike's train ride might lead out of the city, it signifies the themes of mobility and escape at the core of many African American cinematic narratives in the 1990s. To leave the city is perhaps in the final analysis not an act of nostalgia or a form of anti-urbanism, for there is neither the suggestion that Strike is returning to his rural roots nor that he is fleeing from urban life in general. It might be that in this ending Lee is illustrating Gilroy's idea of "the association of self-exploration with the exploration of new territories," at least for Strike.[56]

In relocating his version of events to Brooklyn and by utilizing the train in a metonymical manner, Lee constructs a version of the contemporary African American city that concurrently acknowledges its history of migrations while avoiding the nihilism of many contemporary hood films set in similar locations. In the process he provides at least one of his protagonists with a significant and rupturing agency as well as opening up contemporary African American cinema to an alternative vision of the black city.

Epilogue: New Millennium Minstrel Shows? African American Cinema in the Late 1990s

n Spike Lee's *Bamboozled* (2000), television writer Pierre "Peerless" Delacroix (Damon Wayans) attempts to get himself fired from his job at a fledgling television network by writing what he believes to be the most offensive show possible, *Mantan: The New Millennium Minstrel Show*, a variety show based upon American minstrel shows from the nineteenth and early twentieth centuries. It features "Mantan" (Savion Glover) and "Sleep 'N' Eat" (Tommy Davidson), a duo who wear blackface, dance, shuffle, shuck, and jive, all on a set that resembles a southern plantation very much like the idyllic settings from early vaudeville or from the black-cast musicals, such as Vincente Minnelli's *Cabin in the Sky*, produced by Hollywood between 1929 and 1943. To Pierre's surprise and (initial) dismay, the show is optioned by the Continental Network System (CNS), where it becomes an instant hit, subsequently sparking a vogue for African American memorabilia and blackface makeup.

Because this study is focused on the visualization of African American urban experiences in film at different periods in American history, *Bamboozled* might not seem relevant. The film is set in the predominantly white world of American television broadcasting at the turn of the twentieth century, and little of its narrative defines or explores any new or existing African American urban terrain. Yet in a brief moment in *Bamboozled*, all the elements discussed in the preceding chapters coalesce. This moment comments upon the state of contemporary African American popular culture while concurrently acknowledging the history of African American films set in the city.

During an early meeting, Pierre, his boss Dunwitty (Michael Rappaport), Pierre's assistant Sloan (Jada Pinkett Smith), and the two performers discuss the show's details. As they mull over possible settings, Pierre suggests that *The New Millennium Minstrel Show* should be set in "the projects." This engenders a negative response from Dunwitty, who feels he is "more black" than Harvard-educated, middle-class Pierre both because Dunwitty is a white man married to an African American woman and because he is more familiar with African American pop culture and sports icons (signified by the photos adorning the walls of his office). As Dunwitty claims, the problem with contemporary African American culture—television, music, film—is that "it all takes place in the hood. . . . Everyone wants to bust a cap." Pierre proposes, instead, that the show be set in a watermelon patch, to which Dunwitty excitedly concurs, adding that it should be a watermelon patch on an Alabama plantation. This setting, Dunwitty believes, will present a fresh (and profitable) perspective on African American life for the CNS viewers. Ironically, the antidote to the hood's ubiquity is a southern rural idyll.

In *Bamboozled* Lee's main point is to argue, through satire and irony, that what might appear to be innovative in urban popular culture actually has deep roots in the long and perhaps forgotten history of American cinematic, televisual, and theatrical representations. Pierre's choice of, and Dunwitty's enthusiasm about, the watermelon patch setting, combined with the performers' rag costumes, their blackface makeup, and their use of dialect suggest what is at stake when we either forget or are ignorant of this history. *Bamboozled* reminds audiences of the static boundaries of the antebellum idyll of black-cast musicals beginning in the late 1920s and showcasing performances by Mantan Moreland, Amos 'N' Andy, and Step 'N' Fetchit, all of whom made their living through various forms of minstrelsy, and some of whom appeared in black-cast musicals, race films, or both. These Hollywood black-cast musicals began my discussion of the cinematic visualizations of African American city spaces over the years and to the present. A somewhat similar connection between past and present is made clear in Sleep 'N'

Eat's claims that in the "New Millennium . . . it's the same old bullshit. We've come full circle."

Even more relevant to this work, however, is Lee's harsh indictment of the facets of African American visual culture influenced by hood films, gangsta' rap, and their reciprocal relationship with consumer culture. This critique is a clear continuation of the thematic explorations that Lee began in *Clockers*, except in *Bamboozled* Lee links contemporary forms of black culture with minstrelsy, if not in fact, then by association because advertisements for malt liquor and designer clothing ("Tommy Hillnigger"), products that are equated with the emasculation of the black community, are the show's sponsors. As African American filmmaking enters a new century, questions that need to be considered include whether the hood, as Dunwitty states, has become a problematic, potentially self-parodying, repository of stereotypes or whether a rejection of urban signifying and a return to rural settings and themes necessarily repeats an older form of minstrelsy. The remainder of this chapter briefly examines contemporary African American filmmaking in the latter half of the 1990s in order to answer these questions about the city and, by extension, the country as well. In particular, given Hollywood's history of placing African American stories in idyllic rural spaces, I want to address the latter question by returning to the appearance of films set in the South to determine how novel this "New South" is. Finally, I briefly examine the present-day return of blaxploitation, a genre associated with urban spaces of the 1970s, to determine the city's present role in black film.

The Here and Now: Or What's Up with Black Film?

Migration is an enduring and crucial influence on African American cultural production, urban film in particular. The Great Migration and subsequent waves of African American movement significantly affected the visualizations of urban areas such as New York and Los Angeles at different times during the twentieth century. This study has attempted to identify the shifting signifying systems and chronotopes used to both describe and explain these cinematic cities. The preceding chapters have shown how African American film presents the city in many different forms; it appears as often threatening traces in the antebellum idyll of black-cast musicals, as a symbolic promised land in race films from the early sound era, and as enabling different narratives in African American blaxploitation and independent films in the 1970s and hood films in the 1990s. By the end of the 1990s, African American cinematic subject matter expanded to include both a rearticulation of black urban spaces and the genres associated with them to a more complete move away from the city in historical dramas like *Eve's Bayou* (Kasi Lemmons, 1997) and love stories like *The Best Man* (Malcolm D. Lee, 1999) and *Love and Basketball* (Gina Prince-Bythewood, 2000).[1] Additionally, African American crossover comedy broadened with Eddie Murphy's remakes of Disney films like *The Nutty Professor* (Tom Shadyac, 1996) and Chris Rock's performances in a variety of films, such as *Dogma* (Kevin Smith, 1999), *Nurse Betty* (Neil LaBute, 2000), and *Down to Earth* (Chris and Paul Weitz, 2001).[2] These changes materialized almost immediately after the appearance of the first hood films in the early 1990s and were partially enabled by the filmmakers most associated with them as well as by changes in the film industry as a whole. Hood films did not completely disappear; nonetheless, their production has diminished. In the late 1990s, for example, "the hood" appeared more as traces in other genres rather than as a fully defined space and time, a fact most painfully proven by one of the latest generic hybrids to capitalize on the genre, *Leprechaun 5: In the Hood* (Rob Spera, 2000).[3]

As discussed previously, one of the characteristics of young African American filmmakers from the early 1990s that differentiated them from their blaxploitation predecessors was that many broke away from the production of hood films very soon after their debuts: Mario Van Peebles followed *New Jack City* with *Posse*; Matty Rich, *Straight Out of Brooklyn* with *The Inkwell*; John Singleton, *Boyz N The Hood* with *Poetic Justice* and then *Higher Learning*; and the Hughes Brothers, *Menace II Society* with *Dead Presidents*. Each filmmaker diverged from the conventions associated with hood films, including, in the cases of *Posse*, *The Inkwell*, and *Dead Presidents*, shifting away from the spatiotemporal borders of the hood by setting the films in the past and (often) outside of any recognizable city space. Singleton was a bit slower in these developments; his films often include traces of the hood film in casting choice and, sometimes, location, especially *Baby Boy* (2001), an attempted return to the genre. This is a clear indication of the way in which contemporary African American film has expanded from previously confined generic distinctions. (An inability to do so was the downfall of blaxploitation in the 1970s.)

Furthermore, at the turn of the twenty-first century, the same directors no longer dominated African American film as the decade before. Indeed, the latter half of the 1990s witnessed an increased diversity of both films and filmmakers. Even though minority filmmakers continue to be severely underrepresented in the industry, there is evidence of a very slight expansion of the number of African American filmmakers working in Hollywood, the result of which is linked to the box office appeal of the hood films in the early 1990s.[4] It is key that this most recent generation of filmmakers, Malcolm D. Lee, Theodore Witcher, Kasi Lemmons, George Tillman, and Gina Prince-Bythewood, for example, did not debut with films that were set in the hood, instead moving into a variety of genres and styles, many of which do not focus on the city at all and some of which do not focus solely on African American subject matter (see, for example, Tillman's *Men of Honor*). This diversity of talent is also the result of the increased production of films by cable networks like HBO, ShowTime, BET, TBS, and USA, where more inexperienced directors are often hired.[5]

When urban spaces appear in films from the late 1990s, they take a variety of forms, many of which, like in Theodore Witcher's *love jones* (Chicago) or Prince-Bythewood's *Love and Basketball* (Los Angeles), have little to do with the narrative or share little resemblance to the cityscape from hood films, primarily because of their focus on middle- and upper-middle-class characters and settings. The most significant development, however, as is evidenced by Lee's *Bamboozled*, is a cinematic reaction to some of the conventions associated with the hood genre. The best example of this sort of reaction is not *Bamboozled* (as I mentioned, the city has little to do with the film), but rather Maya Angelou's *Down in the Delta* (1998). Angelou's film not only considers and rejects certain inner-city tropes such as drugs, crime, and violence; it also advocates a migration out of the city and a return to the rural South, a location that is posited as the only site that can ensure the survival of African American families. The strategy Angelou adopted for making this suggestion is to refer to elements of the hood from film and rap in order to systematically reject them.

Down in the Delta reflects many of the industrial changes in African American filmmaking occurring in the 1990s. The film, originally commissioned by ShowTime Networks, was also the filmmaking debut of dancer-actor-writer-teacher Maya Angelou. Angelou is an interesting example of a debut director. At 70, she already had many different careers, and had even had film experience, primarily with acting and screenwriting (although she did not write the screenplay for *Down in the Delta*). With *Down in the Delta* Angelou joined a growing number of African American women directors who have made fiction films for either television or theatrical release since the beginning of the 1990s. Others include Julie Dash, Darnell Martin, Leslie Harris, Kasi Lemmons, Gina Price-Blythewood, Cauleen Smith, and Zeinabu irene Davis. For Angelou, and many other woman directors, television in particular appears to be more supportive of women's filmmaking than Hollywood. Angelou's film, while made for television, was released in the theaters, where it earned approximately $5 million in its first few months, off-setting its $3.5 million production costs.

Down in the Delta is about the Sinclair family—a grandmother, her daughter, and her two children—who lives in one of the vast high-rise housing projects located on Chicago's South Side. The film's urban setting and contemporary time frame draw upon conventions of the hood film in order to contrast the dystopian northern city with an idyllic rural South. The specifics of the film's urbanscape are consciously called out, with establishing shots of an easily recognizable Chicago skyline followed by long shots of the projects (although the projects are not named as they were in films such as *Menace II Society*, *Straight Out of Brooklyn*, and *Clockers*). The surrounding streets are composed of burned-out, boarded-up, and graffiti-covered buildings, empty lots, and litter, an urbanscape resembling the city spaces in hood films and which is also reminiscent of blaxploitation films from the 1970s. In short, South Side Chicago looks and sounds—gunfire fills the sound track during many night scenes—like a war zone.[6]

One of the film's main plot lines is about Tommy Sinclair (Mpho Koalo), and the pressures he faces as a young man coming of age in these inner-city surroundings. But the film quickly moves away from a strict adherence to this subject matter by expanding its attention to the entire family unit. The true focus of the film is Tommy's mother, Loretta (Alfre Woodard), a woman struggling with alcohol addiction and with her difficulties in caring for her two children, one of whom is autistic. The family elder, Rosa Lynn (Mary Alice), decides that the only way for the family to survive is to send Loretta and the two children to spend the summer with their Uncle Earl (Al Freeman Jr.) and Aunt Annie (Esther Rolle) in the Mississippi Delta. Unlike *Clockers*, *Down in the Delta* dispenses with any reference to the train as an important facet of migration, substituting a more contemporary form of transportation, the bus, for one that has become less associated with migration. Rosa Lynn pawns a family heirloom, a silver candelabra curiously named "Nathan," for bus fare. Therefore, the narrative spends only a short time in the city before the family travels down to Mississippi, a move that has already been foreshadowed in the film's opening shots of dirt roads and cornfields that precede the long shots of the Chicago cityscape. Once the shift out of the city has been made, the narrative—and the family—remains in Mississippi, the site of possible regeneration for individual family members and for the extended family as a whole.

The opposition between northern city and southern idyll structures the narrative in the film's assertion that something has been lost during decades of city living. *Down in the Delta*'s narrative suggests that many of the family's problems are rooted in the legacy of earlier migrations that resulted in their relocation to the city. First, the decision of Rosa Lynn and her now-deceased husband to leave the Delta for Chicago in the early 1950s was and continues to be viewed by the remaining family, especially Earl, as an act that caused the dissolution of their extended family. Earl takes a similar point of view toward his own son's, Will's (Wesley Snipes), move to Atlanta a generation later. Second, Rosa Lynn is the only Chicago Sinclair to remain uncorrupted by the city—perhaps because of her strong spiritual and geographic roots in the Delta. Third, the inner-city environment is presented as nothing more than a threat to the family unit: Loretta is tempted by the street, the women fear for what they believe is Tommy's inevitable entry into a life of violence (they believe that he will, for example, eventually have to get a gun for protection), and the entire family is surrounded by crime, exemplified by their multiple interactions with a local drug dealer and the repeated sounds of gunfire on the sound track.[7] *Down in the Delta* presents urban space as having no redeeming qualities, and while no character explicitly states a desire to leave the city, the running theme of the film is that the survival of future generations of Sinclairs is dependent upon escape from its borders.

Rosa Lynn's decision to pawn the candelabra, the significance of which is unknown in the early parts of the film, is an act of desperation, her last attempt to preserve the family. What this means is that Loretta and her children will return to the South, to kinfolk, and, by extension, to their roots. They become acquainted with the "ways" of the South, which includes a familiarity with nature, wide-open spaces, hard work, and religion. (Since the film creates a world in which whites do not exist, racism is not presented as a factor.) Their move south also means becoming better acquainted with the Sinclair family history, especially the story of their ancestor Jesse and the silver candelabra. Numerous flashbacks scattered throughout the film reveal that Jesse's father Nathan was sold by the "white Sinclairs" in exchange for a silver candelabra. Shortly after the Civil War, Jesse returned to the plantation and took the candelabra from the Sinclair house, naming it "Nathan" in honor of his father. Jesse remained on the Sinclair land as a sharecropper, and "Nathan" became a family heirloom, passed from oldest Sinclair child to oldest Sinclair child. In this process, "Nathan" is transformed into the symbol for family unity, enabling "a continuum of tradition and of family."[8] In all of this, Uncle Earl functions as the family *griot*, passing on crucial family history to Tommy and Loretta and providing Loretta with a chance to work and earn money to buy back the candelabra.

The only time that the narrative returns to the city is near the film's conclusion, when Loretta travels back to Chicago to visit Rosa Lynn and to retrieve the candelabra from the pawn shop. Once "Nathan" is liberated, both women make the trip back to Mississippi, carrying the candelabra with them in order to return it to the mantel in Earl's house, the old "big house," which he bought from the white Sinclairs in the 1970s. Closure is achieved once the extended family is finally gathered together again, and this is symbolically reinforced once "Nathan" is back in the ancestral home. At the film's conclusion, Loretta and her children remain in the Delta rather than return north with Rosa Lynn because the South proves to be the healthiest environment for them all: in Mississippi Loretta's addiction disappears, she finds gainful work (after learning to count), Tommy responds to nature, and Tracy's (Kulani Hassen) autism is tempered by her newly acquired ability to communicate.

In its emphasis on emigrating from the city and returning to one's roots, *Down in the Delta*, like many of the films discussed in this study, stages a dialogue with African American migration. Unlike *Clockers*, however, which acknowledges a similar history of migration, *Down in the Delta* makes more literal reference to the history of movement and its relationship to the city. In *Clockers* the dialogue with mobility was primarily symbolic and accomplished through the motif of the train and through the characters' psychological entrapment in their circumstances. *Down in the Delta* takes a more severe tone against the consequences of migration on African American life. The city is a dystopian environment of little redeeming value, the place that stripped southern migrants of family and roots.[9] *Clockers* focuses on specific representations of the city, not the city itself (a continuing source of inspiration for Lee). In comparison, *Down in the Delta* adopts a reactionary position in its claim that African American urban culture is solely associated with gangsta' motifs and is therefore bad, and that the only answer to this is to leave the city.

In this view of the city, *Down in the Delta* consciously refracts three specific aspects of its extradiegetic context. One of these emerges from the increasing backlash directed toward hip-hop culture in general, of which the critiques of hood films were just a part.[10] This was articulated by Angelou herself, who spoke against the negative effects of such imagery: "It's bad enough that the larger society believes that's the authentic way [black] people live . . . . But young men and young women take their lessons, too, from those caricatures."[11] Traces of this sentiment exist in *Down in the Delta*'s rejection of the city and the tropes related to the hood film and gangsta' rap. In this way *Down in the Delta* uses the city as a sign in a similar though inverted manner as race films referenced Harlem in the 1930s. For race film producers, Harlem was the sign of hope and urbanity. For Angelou, the city is a sign of loss and arrested development.

The film also dialogues with its historical context via its indirect reference to a rise in the level of African American reverse migration to the South, a movement that has been documented since the 1970s in texts like August Meier's and Elliott Rudwick's *From Plantation to Ghetto*. In the 1990s, a new wave of reverse migration was being discussed in the academic press in books like Carol Stack's *Call to Home: African Americans Reclaim the Rural South*. This trend also was noted by the popular press. In July 1997, for example, *Newsweek* featured an article entitled "South Toward Home," detailing the return of many migrants from northern industrial areas to rural southern homes. Basing their numbers on a study by sociologist William H. Frey, authors Vern E. Smith and Daniel Pederson argue that between 1990 and 1995 approximately 369,000 African American migrants moved back to the South.[12] Scholars in the 1970s noted that reverse migration was a result of civil rights legislation and the decline of northern industrial centers. The figures for the 1990s represent a significant increase over migration during the preceding decades and an important change in the causes for movement. The reasons for this migration were identified as enhanced economic opportunities in sun-belt communities such as metro-Atlanta and an increased desire to move away from inner-city problems such as youth crime.[13]

For the Sinclairs, like many of the recent migrants in the Smith and Pederson piece, "the peaceable rural South offers more to black families than the hard-edged urban North."[14] The Delta is also the site of a unifying family history, much of which is rooted in the antebellum period: "Nathan's" existence and the family living in the "big house," now the home of Earl and Annie Sinclair. "Nathan's" return to the house is ironic in that the family, which was originally broken apart by the slave trade, is only unified once a symbol of the trade is returned to its original (slave) home. Therefore, the film's rejection of the city argues for a return to family roots as the means of surviving the urban dystopia. More symbolically, it links the present with the past in an attempt, whether reactionary or not, to provide a future for the youngest generation of Sinclairs.

While *Down in the Delta*'s contemporary time frame would preclude it from consideration as an historical drama, it includes flashbacks to Jesse in slavery, as a soldier in the Civil War, and as a sharecropper, indicating a concern with writing personal history as part of a larger national history. In this way, the film is adjunct to a larger tendency in contemporary African American film, which returns to the past to create a relationship with the present. It also relates *Down in the Delta* to a number of films made in the 1990s, *Sankofa* (Haile Gerima, 1993), *Jefferson in Paris* (James Ivory, 1995), *Nightjohn* (Charles Burnett, 1996, TVF), *Amistad* (Steven Spielberg, 1997), *Beloved* (Jonathan Demme, 1998), and *A House Divided* (John Kent Harrison, 2000, TVF), which depict various aspects of slaves and slavery.

With this tendency and *Down in the Delta*'s reconstruction of an idyllic South, we appear to have indeed "come full circle," back to the antebellum idyll of the earliest films, even to the extent that Angelou's film is set in the very same delta (although in different states) as *The Green Pastures*. This reintroduction of slaves and slavery in American film has resuscitated Ed Guerrero's plantation genre, a group of films that disappeared in the 1970s and that forced us to

> confront a number of issues about the creation and ideological function of these representations, narratives, and images, persistent so long after the abolition of slavery itself and the collapse of the antebellum South. Central

to this discussion of looking at "Old South" epics are questions about the evolution and nature of the basic slave stereotypes in dominant cinema.[15]

The answer to Guerrero's challenge lies in the ways in which the films, *Down in the Delta* included, revise some of the old cinematic myths surrounding slavery and how they speak to the present moment. In addition to *Down in the Delta*, all the films mentioned above depict slavery in two basic ways. First, it is pictured as a system of labor that dehumanized its laborers. And yet the slaves are not helpless victims, but instead fight back through education, via the legal system, or through escape. Second, these films, as with *Roots* decades before, suggest that even in the face of extreme odds, the integrity of the African American family unit continued during and after slavery. Even more important, many of the films initially suggest a transcendence of time when they link the past to the present. *Sankofa*, for example, is set in the present, but it projects its main character into history, to a slaveholding sugar plantation in the West Indies, to encourage her to remember the past. *Beloved*, like the Toni Morrison novel upon which it is based, suggests that the trauma of slavery extends beyond a specific space and time so that past events are repeatedly replayed in the present in different settings. In *Down in the Delta*, slavery's legacy is made corporeal in the presence of "Nathan," the candelabra transcending time and space.

Earlier in this study I identified the antebellum idyll as one of the defining space-time continuums found in black-cast musicals. The antebellum idyll is characterized by a specific spatiotemporal dimension, a seemingly static plantation-like space. In it characters and narratives exist outside of history and have no relationship to a contemporary context unless the city appears as a motif or symbol of modernity within its borders. There are important differences between how the idyll functions in *Down in the Delta* and how it works in Hollywood-produced black-cast musicals. The main difference is in the idyll's construction of time. As I mentioned before, *Down in the Delta* is set in a contemporary time frame. The only moments that are set in the past are the flashback sequences. Unlike time in the antebellum idyll, however, these flashbacks are not ahistorical because they maintain a chronology that is not only connected to individual history (Jesse's experiences) but to national history (the antebellum period, the Civil War, and Reconstruction). Furthermore, they provide a direct link to other historical moments, in the fact that "Nathan" is carried north during the Sinclairs' migration and that the candelabra stays in the city from the 1950s to the 1990s.

Finally, "Nathan's" return home is a link to the South, which is now a contemporary industrialized site, the "New South." A subplot involves the dissolution of the town's main industry, a chicken factory. Loretta spearheads a movement, with Will's legal and Earl's financial aid, to start a mail-order business selling specialty chicken products, thereby ensuring the future of the town. The hope is that the business will result in franchises throughout the country. Therefore, the New South offers economic opportunities neither available in the postindustrial city nor present in the Old South.

While I maintain that *Down in the Delta* exhibits what I believe is a reactionary strain in its oversimplified assertion that the city is solely aligned with gangsta' culture and is therefore rife with negative imagery, in its return to the South the film avoids advocating a return to the static spatiotemporal borders of the antebellum idyll from decades ago. What the film advocates is a reconsideration of the South as a site that is dynamic and filled with possibility rather than a space that is static and unchanging. In this way, it is not the return to minstrelsy feared by Lee and expressed in *Bamboozled* because the Sinclair homestead is a far cry from a watermelon patch.[16] In *Down in the Delta* the South, a primary symbolic site of the past, is refigured for the future. How realistic this South will be and how much African American and American films might register the negative as well as the imaginatively celebrated aspects of slavery's legacy remains to be seen.[17]

Still the Man: Shaft in the 21st Century (Can You Dig It?)

While *Down in the Delta* and other African American films departed from contemporary depictions of black city spaces, the new millennium also has been marked by the return of old icons, many of which—unlike *Bamboozled*'s return to the plantation—celebrate certain aspects of the city film from the blaxploitation era. This tendency was evident as early as 1988 in Keenan Ivory Wayans' *I'm Gonna Git You Sucka*, a parody of the blaxploitation genre. By the 1990s, blaxploitation evolved away from parody and became fashionable once again as filmmakers such as Quentin Tarantino appropriated the narrative style, the character types, and (sometimes) the performers from 1970s films in a nostalgic celebration of urban—and not uncoincidentally black—cool. The results were *Pulp Fiction* (1994) and *Jackie Brown* (1997), which revived Pam

Grier's long dormant career. Additionally, Sig Shore reprised the myth of Youngblood Priest in his *The Return of Superfly* in 1990.

This tendency has continued in the twenty-first century, with the release of two films in the summer of 2000 that link directly back to blaxploitation; Allen and Albert Hugheses' *American Pimp* and John Singleton's *Shaft*. The former film is a documentary that is connected to blaxploitation in its choice of subject matter: a focus on a variety of pimps, many of whom in their clothing, dialect, and lifestyle resemble the Sweetbacks and the Dolemites of decades before even though they were interviewed in the late 1990s. *American Pimp*'s paean to the African American pimp is also a celebration of the tradition of the "bad-ass nigger" so prominent in African American folklore and blaxploitation film, a connection that is made with the aid of numerous clips from blaxploitation films. While *American Pimp* glorifies the trickster, Singleton's *Shaft* most interests me here because it revises blaxploitation and combines its conventions with those of the hood film and the action genre.

While blaxploitation and hood films have many differences, one of the suggestions I've made is that the two groups of film share common elements, many of which were introduced by films like *Sweet Sweetback's Baadasssss Song* and *Shaft*. These include a temporal immediacy—the films are of the here and now—enabled by location shooting in recognizable city spaces, a musical sound track that is marketed along with the films and that features heavily in the film's appeal (later, in hood films rappers become part of the cast), and the use of urban fashions and idioms derived from the immediate moment. In each genre there is a celebration of black urban culture that is also mitigated by a concern with the effects of poverty, violence, crime, and drugs on African American residents living in the city. The nature of this dystopian outlook differs in the two groups of film, marking the changes in sociopolitical context and the film industry over the two decades. Underlying both groups of film, however, is a concern with mobility; first, with the freedom to move around within the city, and then with hood films, the freedom to leave the city's borders.

Shaft references blaxploitation conventions by resuscitating one of the characters most associated with the genre, John Shaft. And yet the film is neither a remake nor a sequel to the Shaft series from the 1970s because it introduces a new John Shaft (Samuel L. Jackson), the nephew of the original Shaft. The nephew is a police officer, while the original Shaft remains a private investigator. Like *I'm Gonna Get You Sucka* and Larry Cohen's *Original Gangstas* (1996), another film that revises blaxploitation, *Shaft* relies on cameos for some of its self-referential cachet, with appearances by Richard Roundtree, reprising his role as John Shaft, and other personalities associated with the original series, such as Gordon Parks Sr. and Isaac Hayes. But the relationship between Singleton's film and the earlier films in the series is never clarified, especially since Singleton blurs the distinctions between the two Shafts. First, the film was originally entitled *Shaft Returns* (echoing *The Return of Superfly*). Second, the film's tag-line is "Still the Man, Any Questions?" The question remains, who is still the man, Uncle Shaft or his nephew?

Since the film is so expressly aligned with blaxploitation, the elements of the hood film are a little more difficult to trace. The most obvious connection is John Singleton, who co-wrote the screenplay with Richard Price (author of *Clockers*) and directed the film. While Singleton moved away from the hood film following *Boyz N The Hood*, many of his films, such as *Poetic Justice*, *Higher Learning*, and *Baby Boy*, have continued exploring or using characteristics of the genre. These elements include the casting of rappers and references to, at least at times, contemporary African American urban culture in the form of music, fashion, and dialogue even when the films, like *Higher Learning*, were not set in the city.[18] *Shaft* continues with some of these conventions, which is perhaps most evident in Singleton's choice to cast rapper Busta Rhymes as Rasaan, Shaft's right-hand man, his driver, and the source of comic relief throughout much of the film. One of the big changes for Singleton, however, is that *Shaft* is set in New York City, rather than the West Coast, the location of most of his films. While this breaks with the conventions most associated with Singleton in particular—he is responsible for mapping South Central Los Angeles as the hood—it is in keeping with the conventions of the *Shaft* series.

But the film truly blurs the distinctions between genres in its treatment of the city. The cityscape has symbolic resonance in African American film, and has changed according to time, place, and genre. What has not changed in the past few decades is the importance of the city as a site authorizing the production of African American popular culture through its signifying power as the location and home of African American people. In blaxploitation film parts of Los Angeles and New York enabled the films' narratives and provided them with both a temporal immediacy and their popular appeal for urban audiences. In hood films the city fulfilled a similar role. One of the strategies for calling out the city—more important, certain parts of the city, like Harlem or Brooklyn in New York or South Central in Los Angeles—was to reference particular areas with the use of dialogue and street signs. For example, many blaxploitation films set in New York, such as *Shaft* itself, included shots of 125th Street as a means of identifying Shaft with Harlem and its symbolic significance as an African American neighborhood. Furthermore, the ability to move around the city, even more than the oft-mentioned sexual prowess, was the sign of many blaxploitation heroes' agency.[19] The original Shaft went where he wanted, and this provided him with true agency.

Like the earlier films, *Shaft* is set in New York City. But the city is not nearly as important as it was in blaxploitation or hood films. Instead, it is more a backdrop than an integral part of the narrative. It is rare in *Shaft*, for example, for specific sites to be named, and even rarer that any of the locations are recognizable. There are a few exceptions to this, the most noticeable being when Shaft visits Uncle Shaft at the Lenox Lounge in Harlem. During this scene, which is mostly interior shots, the location is introduced by a long shot of the bar's lighted sign (similar to the way in which the Apollo was shot in the 1970s). This is a significant self-referential moment because the Lenox Lounge is the place where all the personalities associated with blaxploitation are gathered. Through the signage, Shaft is momentarily within the older world of blaxploitation, thereby providing him with a generic legitimacy. But this strategy also results in associating Harlem with the past rather than the present, because the only people who are identified with this particular site are figures from a bygone era and genre.

Other than the Lenox Lounge, the film rarely references identifiable urban sites, and none are marked visually through signage. We learn that Rasaan lives in Brooklyn through dialogue, not through any recognizable visuals. There's also a suggestion that Diane Palmieri (Toni Collette), a witness to the racially motivated murder that opens the film, is hiding out in Marine Park in Brooklyn, but again this is a passing verbal reference and the actual space is never confirmed as such. When on screen, the area appears to be more suburban and coastal than urban. Furthermore, there is some indication that Peoples Hernandez (Jeffrey Wright), the Dominican "drug-lord," lives in the South Bronx, but this is never confirmed, and like Rasaan's apartment building, Peoples' residence is a nondescript tenement. Characters who approach the apartment are shown climbing up the steps of a subway exit (a shot that occurs repeatedly). Each time the subway station's sign is obstructed so that the location remains unclear. Finally, the only other place that is mentioned in the film and then shown (again without any recognizable signage) is the Metronome Restaurant, the site of the murder in the film. The Metronome is an actual place located in Manhattan's Flatiron district, and yet neither the restaurant nor the area possesses symbolic resonance in African American film, or in films set in New York City as a whole.

The only time that the city has any symbolic significance, linked especially to the issues raised by hood films, comes in a brief exchange between Peoples and Walter Wade Jr. (Christian Bale). Wade, a wealthy son of an influential businessman, is on trial for the murder of a young black man named Trey (Mekhi Phifer). Palmieri, the only witness to the act, is in hiding. Wade meets Peoples in jail and later seeks his assistance in finding and eliminating her. Peoples is reluctant to accept Wade's offer unless Wade makes a deal; in exchange for Palmieri's life, Wade must introduce Peoples to people and places "downtown" (and pay him $40,000).[20] According to Peoples, he is a king when he is uptown, but when he is downtown, he feels insignificant and as if he does not belong.

Peoples is actually asking Wade to help him sell drugs. And yet the pair's exchange indicates the limits on mobility experienced by many African American and Latino residents of the city, limits that were self-consciously explored in many hood films set on both coasts in the early 1990s. Peoples' desire to "border cross" is viewed as a transgression by Wade, who refuses to take Peoples into his life. Importantly, one of Wade's reasons for killing the young man, Trey, at the beginning of the film was because Trey was guilty of both geographic and sexual trespass by being in an all-white downtown bar with a white woman. Like Tre in *Boyz N the Hood* and Caine in *Menace II Society*, Trey oversteps prescribed roles by being in the wrong place (there's never a right time). This is also one of the ways in which the film most breaks with blaxploitation: Roundtree's Shaft could go anywhere in the city, Priest in *Superfly* could sell his drugs downtown, and both could be with white women.

But what are we to make of the city's diminished role in the film? Some of it can be accounted for in generic terms. While *Shaft* returns to blaxploitation and is inflected by the hood film, it is also affected by three decades of action films. The focus of the action genre is not the city, but on one or two personalities. The action figure often works outside of the law even while representing it, the action film often responding to reactionary audience fantasies through the guise of rebellion. Often the hero is a cop who is at odds with his morally corrupt or simply inept superiors. Jackson's Shaft is no exception to this; the narrative tension is fueled just as much by his problems with the legal and justice systems as it is with his desire to capture and convict Wade. But Singleton has to perform a dangerous balancing act here because Shaft is an African American member of the NYPD (at least in the first half of the film). Furthermore, Shaft is also part of a squad that is similar in appearance to the NYPD's Street Crimes Unit, a specially trained squad now infamous for their murder of Amadou Diallo, an unarmed man, in the Bronx in 1999 and for scores of human rights violations directed toward "minority" populations in Brooklyn and the Bronx. The film in fact acknowledges this sociopolitical context by repeatedly suggesting the racism and criminality of many cops. In one key scene, the film's self-consciousness about the continuing tension between the law and African American communities is verbalized when Shaft, on his way to arrest everyone, refers to Mayor Rudolph Guiliani, the man behind the Street Crimes Unit and one of its biggest public supporters, by name.

Shaft disassociates himself from the NYPD when he quits in disgust over the racism and injustice of the system because wealthy, white Wade is repeatedly released. In *Shaft* the diminished role of urban spaces and a move away from a concern with the positives or negatives of the city, which was central to both blaxploitation and the hood film, signals a different focus on the legal system. The film's resolution is also distinct in that it argues that the community needs to take the law into its own hands in order to eliminate crime. The first example of this occurs when Shaft, seeking information from a woman who was at the Metronome the night of Trey's murder, beats a local dealer in order to protect her son from the dealer's recruiting. During the beating, a NYPD squad car passes by, and there is a momentary exchange of glances between Shaft and the white patrolman suggestive of some sort of solidarity between the two (unlike a similar exhange in Lee's *Do The Right Thing*, which indicates the vast chasm existing between the police and the black residents of the neighborhood). Given the context of police violence in New York City at the time of the film's release and the film's overall cynicism about institutional remedies for racially motivated crimes, this tenuous link between Shaft and the NYPD suggests a strange bond and ratifies individual action. In this way it is similar to *Down in the Delta*, which also encourages individual action over faith in the system because Loretta overcomes her addiction through hard work. The difference is that *Shaft* does not advocate an exit from the city, but a form of lone heroism. The focus on individual acts of crime-fighting is supported at the end of the film when Trey's mother, fearing that Wade will be acquitted of her son's murder, shoots Wade on the courthouse steps. Like the exchange of glances that occurred earlier in the film, Shaft and the shooter trade ambiguous, though almost approving, looks before she is led away.

Shaft's engagement with contemporary police brutality continues a theme that has been prevalent in African American film in the second half of the twentieth century, and which was also evident in city-based literature dating back even farther. In the films discussed in this study, this topic has surfaced repeatedly, from the extradiegetic refractions of Haile Gerima's *Bush Mama* to the Foucauldian police surveillance techniques in *Clockers*, both of which suggest that this is a continuing issue in African American film, especially those films set in the city. Singleton's examination of police tactics, however, is less explicit than in either *Bush Mama* or in Lee's *Do The Right Thing*, two highly self-conscious films that openly dialogue with their contexts. Gerima's focus is on Watts in the 1970s. The film references the police state in post-rebellion Watts through the inclusion of footage of his crew being arrested by the LAPD and in numerous cutaways to a poster of a black man who was gunned down by police. Lee's references to victims of police brutality are verbal and visual in *Do The Right Thing*: first, in the NYPD's choke-hold murder of Radio Raheem and then, following the murder, when characters state the names of actual victims of police brutality. Lee's *Clockers* is also partially focused on police tactics to fight crime in the projects and includes a similar scene as in *Shaft*, in which an African American housing cop, Andre, beats Strike for his involvement with a neighborhood boy. The difference is that in *Shaft*, point-of-view has shifted from the victims to the police (even if John Shaft sometimes works outside the law) and the film awkwardly invites audiences to sympathize with the fantasy.

While in the past the city fueled many cinematic narratives, enabling their story lines, at the beginning of the twenty-first century the city assumes a variety of functions, central to some narratives, the backdrop for others, and absent from many films in which rural or (increasingly) suburban locations figure. When it does appear as central, which is increasingly rare, it continues as traces of the hood chronotope from a decade before. More often, it is a backdrop or absent altogether, and either suburban or rural spaces have replaced it. Unlike decades before, however, these rural spaces in particular signify a contemporaneity rather than a static ahistoricity. They are set in the present, not the unchanged past of *Bamboozled*'s watermelon patch. What this means, contrary to the claims made by *Bamboozled*, is that we haven't really come full circle.

Notes

The epigraph to the book is from Charles Scruggs, *Sweet Home: Invisible Cities in the Afro-American Novel* (Baltimore: Johns Hopkins University Press, 1993), 212.

Introduction

1. Anthony Vidler, *The Architectural Uncanny: Essays in the Modern Unhomely* (Cambridge, Mass.: The MIT Press, 1992), 167.

2. Lynne Kirby, *Parallel Tracks: The Railroad and Silent Cinema* (Durham: Duke University Press, 1997), 184.

3. M. M. Bakhtin, *The Dialogic Imagination*, ed. Michael Holquist, trans. Caryl Emerson and Michael Holquist (Austin: University of Texas Press, 1981), 425.

4. Ibid., 247.

5. Robert Stam states that the chronotope is "even more appropriate to film than literature, for whereas literature plays itself out within a virtual, lexical space, the cinematic chronotope is quite literal, splayed out concretely across a screen with specific dimensions and unfolding in literal time . . . quite apart from the fictive time/space specific films might construct." Robert Stam, *Subversive Pleasures: Bakhtin, Cultural Criticism, and Film* (Baltimore: Johns Hopkins University Press, 1989), 11.

6. Ibid.

7. Bakhtin, *The Dialogic Imagination*, 253, author's emphasis.

8. Wahneema Lubiano offers a challenging deconstruction of Spike Lee's intermittent insistence on authenticity in "But Compared to What?: Reading Realism, Representation, and Essentialism in *School Daze*, *Do the Right Thing*, and the Spike Lee Discourse," in *Representing Blackness: Issues in Film and Video*, ed. Valerie Smith (New Brunswick: Rutgers University Press, 1997), 97–122. While not Bakhtinian in methodology, Lubiano's discussion points to the problematics of Lee's assertion of truth claims, what Kobena Mercer has referred to in another context as a "reality effect," in his cinematic and media discourses. See Kobena Mercer and Isaac Julien, "Race, Sexual Politics, and Black Masculinity: A Dossier," in *Male Order: Unrapping Masculinity*, ed. Rowena Chapman and Jonathan Rutherford (London: Lawrence and Wishart, 1988), 104.

9. According to Bakhtin, "We must never confuse—as has been done up to now and as is still often done—the *represented* world with the world outside the text (naive realism); nor must we confuse the author-creator of a world with the author as a human being (naive biographism); nor confuse the listener or reader of multiple and varied periods, recreating and renewing the text, with the passive listener or reader of one's own time (which leads to dogmatism in interpretation and evaluation)." Bakhtin, *The Dialogic Imagination*, 253.

10. Ella Shohat and Robert Stam, *Unthinking Eurocentrism: Multiculturalism and the Media* (New York: Routledge, 1994), 180.

11. Ibid., 80.

12. Stam, *Subversive Pleasures*, 11.

13. Bakhtin, *The Dialogic Imagination*, 252.

14. Gary Saul Morson and Caryl Emerson, *Mikhail Bakhtin: Creation of a Prosaics* (Stanford: Stanford University Press, 1990), 416–17.

15. James De Jongh, *Vicious Modernism: Black Harlem and the Literary Imagination* (New York: Cambridge University Press, 1990), 15.

Chapter 1

1. Rudolph Fisher, "City of Refuge," in *The New Negro: Voices of the Harlem Renaissance*, ed. Alain Locke (New York: Atheneum, 1992), 57–58.

2. "According to the census of 1910, blacks were overwhelmingly rural and Southern; approximately three out of four lived in rural areas and nine out of ten lived in the South. A half century later Negroes were mainly an urban population, almost three fourths of them being city dwellers. About half lived outside of the old slave states." August Meier and Elliott Rudwick, *From Plantation to Ghetto*, 3rd ed. (New York: Hill & Wang, 1976), 232.

3. Ann Douglas, *Terrible Honesty: Mongrel Manhattan in the 1920s* (New York: Noonday, 1995), 73.

4. Charles S. Johnson, "The New Frontage on American Life," in *The New Negro: Voices of the Harlem Renaissance*, ed. Alain Locke (New York: Atheneum, 1992), 279.

5. Sidney H. Bremer, *Urban Intersections: Meetings of Life and Literature in United States Cities* (Urbana: University of Illinois Press, 1992), 132.

6. James De Jongh, *Vicious Modernism: Black Harlem and the Literary Imagination* (New York: Cambridge University Press, 1990), 6.

7. Shirley Ann Moore, "Getting There, Being There: African-American Migration to Richmond, California, 1910–1945," in *The Great Migration in Historical Perspective: New Dimensions of Race, Class, and Gender*, ed. Joe William Trotter Jr. (Bloomington: Indiana University Press, 1991), 117.

8. Langston Hughes, *The Big Sea* (New York: Hill & Wang, 1998), 81–82.

9. Fisher, "City of Refuge," 59.

10. Ibid., 74.

11. Ibid., 61.

12. M. M. Bakhtin, *The Dialogic Imagination*, ed. Michael Holquist, trans. Caryl Emerson and Michael Holquist (Austin: University of Texas Press, 1981), 225.

13. After *Carmen Jones*, Hollywood adopted a more "assimilationist" policy toward African American stories, performers, and personnel; however, what this meant was that African American subject matter was placed in "problem pictures." For mainstream cinema, black subjects changed from a segregated to a social problem, at least until the appearance of blaxploitation films in the early 1970s.

14. James Snead, *White Screens/Black Images: Hollywood from the Dark Side*, ed. Colin MacCabe and Cornel West (New York: Routledge, 1994), 3.

15. While *Hearts in Dixie*, the first black-cast musical produced by Hollywood, also could be discussed in this context, it focuses on North-South tensions rather than an urban-rural dichotomy, and it makes no direct reference to a city space. *Hallelujah* shares common features with, but bears even more marked differences from, the earlier film. Both musicals are set in the rural South and both focus on the education of a young man. More significantly, both share very similar establishing shots, as *Hallelujah* opens with a high-angle long shot looking over black workers picking cotton. From this initial moment, it is clear that the space being explored in *Hallelujah* conforms to the spatiotemporal characteristics of the antebellum idyll. It is unclear if this is an ante- or postbellum time frame, although it appears to be pre–Civil War. It is equally unclear where the film is set, outside of the fact that it is somewhere in the rural South, as the African Americans onscreen are associated with the plantation economy, cotton picking in particular.

16. Gary Saul Morson and Caryl Emerson, *Mikhail Bakhtin: Creation of a Prosaics* (Stanford: Stanford University Press, 1990), 374.

17. Thomas Cripps, *Slow Fade to Black: The Negro in American Film, 1900–1942* (New York: Oxford University Press, 1993), 243.

18. From "Another Negro Film: King Vidor Realizes Ambition by Making 'Hallelujah,' an Audible Picture," an unattributed article from the *New York Times*, dated June, 2, 1929. Clippings file, Billy Rose Theater Collection, New York Public Library for the Performing Arts.

19. Thomas Cripps, *Black Film as Genre* (Bloomington: Indiana University Press, 1978), 78

20. Bakhtin, *The Dialogic Imagination*, 225.

21. Rick Altman, *The American Film Musical* (Bloomington: Indiana University Press, 1987), 292.

22. The play was adapted from Roark Bradford's *Ol' Man Adam an' His Chillun*. Cripps contends that Connelly may also have been influenced by the 1926 stage production of DuBose and Dorothy Heyward's *Porgy*. Thomas Cripps, *The Green Pastures* (Madison: University of Wisconsin Press, 1979), 15.

23. Cripps argues that "Most changes from script to screenplay, even those that heightened its visual quality, were strategic decisions in favor of theatrical, as opposed to cinematic, effects" (ibid., 27–28).

24. Altman, *The American Film Musical*, 274.

25. Donald Bogle, *Toms, Coons, Mulattoes, Mammies, & Bucks: An Interpretive History of Blacks in American Films*, 3rd ed. (New York: Continuum, 1995), 131.

26. Cripps, *Pastures*, 45.

27. Ed Guerrero, "The Slavery Motif in Recent Popular Cinema," *Jump Cut* 33 (1988): 56.

28. The image of De Lawd as an overseer is even clearer in Bradford's original story, "which depicted God not as black but 'as a stereotype southern planter with black fedora had, goatee, and cane'" (Cripps, *Pastures*, 17). Maybe a more appropriate analogy would be with Simon Legree from *Uncle Tom's Cabin*.

29. Moore, "Getting There," 111–12.

30. The one exception to this might be *The Green Pastures*, which, backed by the play's success, was conceived of by Warner Brothers as a "prestige film" (Cripps, *Pastures*, 27). The film was made for slightly under $800,000, an amount substantially higher than *Cabin*'s $700,000. In fact, the latter film's budget was the lowest for the Freed unit up to that time. See James Naremore, *The Films of Vincente Minnelli* (New York: Cambridge University Press, 1993), 57.

31. Georgia's name is much more contradictory. On the one hand, the character represents the urban (and thus evil) pull on Little Joe. On the other hand, her name signifies the South. This might be nothing more than the residue of the original play's Georgian location. Even so, it further indicates the film's ambiguous mixing of city and country.

32. Naremore, *Films of Vincente Minnelli*, 66.

33. Ibid., 54–59.

34. Bogle, *Toms, Coons, Mulattoes, Mammies, and Bucks*, 131; Daniel J. Leab, *From Sambo to Superspade: The Black Experience in Motion Pictures* (Boston: Houghton Mifflin, 1976), 122. These criticisms were also leveled at the film at the time of its release. For instance, a reviewer in the *New York Times* observed, "Fox . . . decided to bury a very thin and trite storyline with an abundance of the show world's leading colored talent . . . 'Stormy Weather' has more the appearance of a super-vaudeville bill than a motion picture" (15). Responses were also mixed for more political reasons, stemming from the studio's agreements with the NAACP to change their treatment of black subject matter. For more on this, see Cripps, *Slow Fade to Black*, 377–78.

35. Altman, *The American Film Musical*, 200.

36. Ibid., 231.

Chapter 2

1. Alain Locke, "The New Negro," in *The New Negro: Voices of the Harlem Renaissance*, ed. Alain Locke (New York: Atheneum, 1992), 4.

2. See also *The Edison Minstrels* (1897–1900), *Minstrels Battling in a Room* (1897–1900), and *Sambo and Aunt Jemima: Comedians* (1897–1900). Edison's company was not the only one to pursue this content. See also the Selig, Lubin, and Biograph company catalogues.

3. See Dan Streible, "The Harlem Theater: Black Film Exhibition in Austin, TX: 1920–1973," in *Black American Cinema*, ed. Manthia Diawara (New York: Routledge, 1993), 221–36; Gregory Waller, "Another Audience: Black Moviegoing,

1907–1916," *Cinema Journal* 31 (Winter 1992): 3–25; Waller, "Black Nickelodeon," *Black Film Review* 7.4 (1993): 28–31; and Mary Carbine, " 'The Finest Outside the Loop': Motion Picture Exhibition in Chicago's Black Metropolis, 1905–1928," *Camera Obscura* 23 (1991): 9–42.

4. Charles S. Johnson, "The New Frontage on American Life," in *The New Negro: Voices of the Harlem Renaissance* ed. Alain Locke (New York: Atheneum, 1992), 285.

5. Jane Gaines, "*The Scar of Shame*: Skin Color and Caste in Black Silent Melodrama," in *Representing Blackness: Issues in Film and Video*, ed. Valerie Smith (New Brunswick: Rutgers University Press, 1997), 62.

6. Cited in Henry T. Sampson, *Blacks in Black and White: A Sourcebook on Black Films*, 2nd ed. (Metuchen, N.J.: Scarecrow Press, 1995), 155. Walton's comments first appeared on September 11, 1920.

7. Cited in Thomas Cripps, *Slow Fade to Black: The Negro in American Film, 1900–1942* (New York: Oxford University Press, 1993), 184.

8. Thomas Cripps, *Black Film as Genre* (Bloomington: Indiana University Press, 1978), 17.

9. Micheaux's biography replicates many of the experiences of early African American migrants. Born in Illinois, Micheaux worked as a Pullman porter before heading west to South Dakota in 1905, where he was a homesteader, a rancher, and a novelist. It was his novels that led the Johnsons, from the Lincoln Motion Picture Company, to approach Micheaux about film. It was also the novels that financed Micheaux's early films. Both Micheaux's novels and his films are set in spaces and situations that were meaningful for audiences experiencing, either firsthand or through relatives, the dislocation of migration.

10. Jane Gaines, "Fire and Desire: Race, Melodrama, and Oscar Micheaux," *Black American Cinema*, ed. Manthia Diawara (New York: Routledge, 1993), 49. This chapter was written prior to the publication of Gaines' *Fire and Desire: Mixed-Race Movies in the Silent Era* (Chicago: University of Chicago Press, 2001), a comprehensive and compelling discussion of the links between exhibition, violence (real and imaginary), and censorship initiated by films like *Within Our Gates*.

11. Lawrence R. Rodgers, *Canaan Bound: The African-American Great Migration Novel* (Urbana: University of Illinois Press, 1997), 112.

12. Gaines, "Fire," 55.

13. Dr. Vivian is contrasted with two other suitors: Sylvia's first fiancé, Conrad Drebert (James D. Ruffin), a prospector who leaves her when he is fooled into believing that she is having an affair, and Larry Prichard (Jack Chenault), who is the archetype of the urban gangster and definitely not of her class; it is not surprising that Sylvia does not return his amorous feelings.

14. Thomas Cripps, " 'Race Movies' as Voices of the Black Bourgeoisie: *The Scar of Shame*," in *Representing Blackness: Issues in Film and Video*, ed. Valerie Smith (New Brunswick: Rutgers University Press, 1997), 57.

15. Gaines, "Fire." 74–75.

16. Ibid., 72.

17. Cripps, *Slow*, 196.

18. Ibid., 197.

19. Rodgers, *Canaan Bound*, 79.

20. Langston Hughes, "The Negro Artist and the Racial Mountain," in *Voices from the Harlem Renaissance*, ed. Nathan Irvin Huggins (New York: Oxford University Press, 1995), 309. This article was first published in *The Nation* in June 1926.

21. From "Another Negro Film: King Vidor Realizes Ambition by Making 'Hallelujah,' an Audible Picture," an unattributed article from the *New York Times*, June, 2, 1929. According to the author, Vidor could not get studio support for his idea until sound technology was introduced. Clippings file, Billy Rose Theater Collection, New York Public Library for the Performing Arts.

22. Streible, "The Harlem Theater," 222–25. See also Daniel J. Leab, *From Sambo to Superspade: The Black Experience in Motion Pictures* (Boston: Houghton Mifflin, 1976), 180.

23. Clyde Taylor, "Crossed Over and Can't Get Black: The Crisis of 1937–1939," *Black Film Review* 7.4 (1993): 24.

24. Ibid.

25. These early B-films were responsible for refining the practice of targeting a specific audience. Many independent producers churned out low-budget genre films, such as horror flicks and "teenpics," and marketed them specifically to the burgeoning postwar teen population. The same approach was also behind a number films produced during the height of blaxploitation. Significantly, some production companies, such as American International, were also responsible for a number of these films. For more on marketing to specific audiences, see John Hartmann, "The Trope of Blaxploitation in Critical Responses to *Sweetback*," *Film History* 6.3 (1994): 383–85, and Thomas Doherty, *Teenagers and Teenpics: The Juvenilization of American Movies in the 1950's* (Boston: Unwin Hyman, 1988), especially 3–16 and 42–70.

26. Leab, *From Sambo to Superspade*, 173.

27. Cripps, *Genre*, 41.

28. Charles Scruggs, *Sweet Home: Invisible Cities in the Afro-American Novel* (Baltimore: Johns Hopkins University Press, 1993), 63.

29. For more on Norman, see Gloria J. Gibson-Hudson, "The Norman Film Manufacturing Company," *Black Film Review* 7.4 (1993): 16–20, and Matthew Bernstein with Dana F. White, " 'Scratching Around' in a 'Fit of Insanity': The Norman Film Manufacturing Company and the Race Film Business in the 1920s," *Griffithiana* 62–63 (May 1998): 81–128.

30. Million Dollar Productions Inc. company information, the George P. Johnson Collection, Special Collections, UCLA.

31. Cited in Leab, *From Sambo to Superspade*, 175.

32. Mark A. Reid, *Redefining Black Film* (Berkeley: University of California Press, 1993), 17.

33. See, for example, both Manthia Diawara's *Black American Cinema* and Valerie Smith's *Representing Blackness*, wherein the collections of articles discussing pre-1970s films focus, with only one exception, on either *The Scar of Shame* or Oscar Micheaux exclusively. Additionally, two books focusing on Micheaux's life and works were published in 2000, J. Ronald Green's *Straight Lick: The Cinema of*

Oscar Micheaux (Bloomington: Indiana University Press, 2000) and Pearl Bowser and Louise Spence's *Writing Himself into History: Oscar Micheaux, His Silent Films, and His Audiences* (New Brunswick: Rutgers University Press, 2000), and another in 2001, Pearl Bowser, Jane Gaines, and Charles Musser's (eds.) *Oscar Micheaux and His Circle* (Bloomington: Indiana University Press, 2001). This flurry of publications indicates a replication in African American film studies of the concern with canon-building related to films with "serious" content or on auteur studies, the focus of the field as a whole. Only Clyde Taylor's article, "Crossed Over and Can't Get Black" focuses on genre films, whereas a more recent discussion of the African American gangsta' genre, Todd Boyd's *Am I Black Enough For You?: Popular Culture From the 'Hood and Beyond* (Bloomington: Indiana University Press, 1997), does not focus on African American gangster films, instead tracing the roots of the contemporary black gangsta' in film and music to *Scarface* and *The Godfather*. S. Craig Watkins, because he relies on Boyd's history, has a similar view in *Representing: Hip Hop Culture and the Production of Black Cinema* (Chicago: University of Chicago Press, 1998).

34. Rodgers, *Canaan Bound*, 95.

35. James De Jongh, *Vicious Modernism: Black Harlem and the Literary Imagination* (New York: Cambridge University Press, 1990), 15.

36. Rodgers, *Canaan Bound*, 75.

37. De Jongh, *Vicious Modernism*, 78.

38. Taylor, "Crossed Over," 24.

39. Sidney H. Bremer, in *Urban Intersections: Meetings of Life and Literature in United States Cities* (Urbana: University of Illinois Press, 1992), says of Harlem Renaissance literature: "practically every book includes a cabaret scene; its more formal counterpart, the charity ball; or its less formal counterpart, the rent party" (156). While not quite as common, many films include a cabaret scene inserted almost nondiegetically into the narrative. If, as Bremer asserts, "Harlem's social life was the result of its unique cultural status as the 'Negro Capital' or 'Mecca' or 'Promised Land'" in the 1920s (138), then it is likely that by the 1930s the social life is used as a sign of Harlem's cultural status.

40. Madison Thomas, "He Started It All!" 8. Citation unknown. Source from the Ralph Cooper clippings file, George P. Johnson Collection, Special Collections, UCLA.

41. See the discussion of Robinson in *Stormy Weather* in chapter 1.

42. *The Duke is Tops* was later re-released as *Bronze Venus* (1943), reflecting Lena Horne's increasing appeal following the release of *Cabin in the Sky* and *Stormy Weather* earlier in 1943. In this instance, film producers actually took advantage of the competition with Hollywood by piggy-backing onto the success of major releases.

43. Cripps, *Slow*, 328.

44. Donald Bogle, "'B' . . . For Black," *Film Comment* 21.5 (October 1985): 34.

45. Cripps, *Slow*, 328.

46. Cripps, *Genre*, 38.

47. Thomas, "He Started It All!" 8.

48. An additional factor is that more portable sound equipment was not available until after World War II. This directly affected how the city appeared in films from the mid-1940s on.

49. Taylor, "Crossed Over," 25.

50. Beverly Smith, "Harlem's Distress Intensified . . . ," *Herald Tribune* (February 10, 1930), cited in Jervis A. Anderson, *This Was Harlem: 1900–1950*, 7th ed. (New York: Noonday Press, 1993), 242.

51. Edward Buscombe, ed., *The BFI Companion to the Western* (London: BFI Publishing, 1988), 16.

52. Leab, "*Harlem Rides the Range*," 31. Citation unknown. Source from the *Harlem Rides the Range* clippings file, Billy Rose Theater Collection, New York Public Library for the Performing Arts.

53. See Virginia Wright Wexman, "The Family on the Land: Race and Nationhood in Silent Westerns," in *The Birth of Whiteness: Race and the Emergence of U.S. Cinema*, ed. Daniel Bernardi (New Brunswick: Rutgers University Press, 1996), 129–69, for a discussion of the contradictory ways in which silent Westerns negotiated the settlement of the West.

54. According to Gerald R. Butters Jr., in "Portrayals of Black Masculinity in Oscar Micheaux's *The Homesteader*," *Film/Literature Quarterly* 28.1 (2000), "the unrestricted nature of the American West would prove to be a feature of the cinematic landscape in which Micheaux could demonstrate African-American manhood" (55).

55. Peter Stanfield, "Country Music and the 1939 Western: From Hillbillies to Cowboys," in *The Movie Book of the Western*, ed. Ian Cameron and Douglas Pye (London: Studio Vista, 1996), 25.

56. Gary Saul Morson and Caryl Emerson, *Mikhail Bakhtin: Creation of a Prosaics* (Stanford: Stanford University Press, 1990), 375.

57. The most visible instance of Jeffries' claim appears in the documentary, *Midnight Ramble* (Pearl Bowser and Bestor Cram, 1994), in which Jeffries recounts a story that he says was inspirational: talking to a young boy and learning the child's belief that there were no black cowboys.

58. *Harlem on the Prairie Pressbook*, Billy Rose Theater Collection, New York Public Library for the Performing Arts.

59. Peter Stanfield, "Dixie Cowboys and Blue Yodels: The Strange History of the Singing Cowboy," in *Back in the Saddle Again: New Essays on the Western*, ed. Edward Buscombe and Roberta E. Pearson (London: BFI Publishing, 1998), 96.

60. Ibid., 115.

61. Stanfield, "Country," 25.

62. Leab, "Harlem," 30.

63. Cripps, *Slow*, 338.

64. Buscombe, *The BFI Companion*, 17.

65. Stanfield, "Country," 25.

Chapter 3

1. C.L.R. James, "Black People in the Urban Areas of the United States," in *The C.L.R. James Reader*, ed. Anna Grimshaw (Cambridge: Blackwell, 1992), 375.

2. August Meier and Elliott Rudwick, *From Plantation to Ghetto*, 3rd ed. (New York: Hill & Wang, 1976), 315.

3. Daniel J. Leab, *From Sambo to Superspade: The Black Experience in Motion Pictures* (Boston: Houghton Mifflin, 1976), 234; see also James P. Murray, "The Subject is Money," in *Black Films and Film-Makers*, ed. Lindsay Patterson (New York: Dodd, Mead, 1975), 249. The "Negro" box office is discussed as an important factor as early as 1962 in *Variety* (May 16, 1962). Also, a 1972 article appearing in *Newsweek* (August 28, 1972) refers to "the burgeoning black audience" (88). See also "The Black Movie Boom," in *Newsweek* (September 6, 1971): 66, and *Variety* (June 3, 1970).

4. For a more detailed history of blaxploitation, see Daniel Leab's *From Sambo to Superspade*; Donald Bogle's *Toms, Coons, Mulattoes, Mammies, & Bucks: An Interpretive History of Blacks in American Films*, 3rd ed. (New York: Continuum, 1995); Thomas Cripps' *Making Movies Black: The Hollywood Message Movie From World War II to the Civil Rights Era* (New York: Oxford University Press, 1993) and "*Sweet Sweetback's Baadasssss Song* and the Changing Politics of Genre Film," in *Close Viewings: An Anthology of New Film Criticism*, ed. Peter Lehman (Tallahassee: Florida State University Press, 1990); Ed Guerrero's *Framing Blackness: The African American Image in Film* (Philadelphia: Temple University Press, 1993); and Mark Reid's *Redefining Black Cinema* (Berkeley: University of California Press, 1993). For a discussion of the industrial conditions behind blaxploitation, see Jesse Algeron Rhines, *Black Film/White Money* (New Brunswick: Rutgers University Press, 1996). In my opinion, Guerrero gives the most comprehensive account of the multiple factors leading to blaxploitation.

5. Harold Cruse, *The Crisis of the Negro Intellectual* (New York: Morrow, 1967), 111.

6. Guerrero, *Framing Blackness*, 78.

7. Mel Watkins, *On The Real Side: Laughing, Lying, and Signifying—The Underground Tradition of African-American Humor that Transformed American Culture, From Slavery to Richard Pryor* (New York: Touchstone, 1994), 462. For more on this black urban folk figure, see also William H. Wiggins, "Jack Johnson as Bad Nigger: The Folklore of His Life," *Southern Folklore Quarterly* 30 (September 1966); Daryl Cumber Dance, *Shuckin' and Jivin': Folklore from Contemporary Black Americans* (Bloomington: Indiana University Press, 1987); and Langston Hughes and Arna Bontemps, eds., *The Book of Negro Folklore* (New York: Dodd, Mead, 1958). Lawrence Levine's *The Unpredictable Past* (New York: Oxford University Press, 1993) provides an in-depth genealogy of the slave tricksters, especially pp. 59–77.

8. Reid, *Redefining Black Cinema*, 79.

9. Cripps, *Making*, 289–90.

10. Reid, *Redefining Black Cinema*, 74.

11. Cripps, "*Sweetback*," 240.

12. Cited in James H. Cone, *Martin and Malcolm and America: A Dream or a Nightmare* (New York: Maryknoll, 1991), 1. From a speech given on April 3, 1964, to the congregation of the Cory Methodist Church.

13. Kenneth B. Clark, *Dark Ghetto: Dilemmas of Social Power* (New York: Harper & Row, 1965), 11.

14. Ibid.

15.   See Daniel P. Moynihan, *The Negro Family: The Case for National Action* (Washington, D.C.: U.S. Government Printing Office, 1965), and Oscar Lewis, "The Culture of Poverty." *Scientific American* 215.4 (October 1966).

16.   The cities have different histories of migration, settlement, and cultural significance, with Harlem's population dating from the early part of the twentieth century and consisting primarily of migrants from the southeastern part of the United States. Watts' black population was more recent, its bulk influenced by the war industry during World War II and pulling from the Southwest.

17.   Thanks to Manthia Diawara for first drawing my attention to the connections between the detective and the flâneur.

18.   As Mikhail Bakhtin argues, "it is precisely the chronotope that provides the ground essential for the showing-forth, the representability of events." See *The Dialogic Imagination*, ed. Michael Holquist, trans. Caryl Emerson and Michael Holquist (Austin: University of Texas Press, 1981), 250.

19.   There were also important technological developments between the late 1930s and the late 1960s that allowed for more mobile shooting situations. However, lighter and cheaper equipment does not guarantee that characters become a part of their urban environment, as can be seen in *Shaft* (2000), by John Singleton. For more on this film, see the epilogue.

20.   Bakhtin, *The Dialogic Imagination*, 247.

21.   Vincent Canby, "*Cotton Comes to Harlem,*" *New York Times*, June 7, 1970, 50; Clayton Riley, "*Cotton Comes to Harlem,*" *New York Times*, July 16, 1970, II:1.

22.   Guerrero, *Framing Blackness*, 81.

23.   Chester Himes wrote stories from prison for *Esquire* before finding critical and financial success (like many African American artists before him) in Paris, where he wrote the Grave Digger Johnson and Coffin Ed Jones detective stories as part of *La Série Noire*, the same series that included most of the film noir texts, authored by Dashiell Hammett, Raymond Chandler, and Cornell Woolrich, among others, and which, some say, provided film noir's name. Two other novels in the series have been adapted to film—Cotton's "sequel," *Come Back Charleston Blue* (1972), based on the novel *The Heat's On* (published in France in 1960), and *A Rage in Harlem*, Bill Duke's 1991 adaptation of *For Love of Immabelle* (Chatham, N.J.: The Chatham Bookseller, 1973), reissued as *A Rage in Harlem* (New York: Vintage Crime, 1991). In "*Noir* by *Noirs*: Towards a New Realism in Black Cinema," Manthia Diawara provides a compelling discussion of Harlem's relationship to film noir. Diawara reads Duke's adaptation of the Himes novel in the larger context of black film in the Reagan and Bush years and argues that there are continuities between noir themes and films from this time. See also Stephen F. Soitis, *The Blues Detective: A Study of African American Detective Fiction* (Amherst: University of Massachusetts Press, 1996).

24.   Cited in Dave McIntyre, "Harlem on My Mind," *The Evening News*, July 23, 1969, 62.

25.   Joel Doerfler, "A Minority of Multitudes," *Boston After Dark* (July 21, 1970). Clippings file, Billy Rose Theater Collection, New York Public Library for the Performing Arts.

26. Cited in Robert Lee, "Harlem on My Mind: Fictions of a Black Metropolis," in *The American City: Literary and Cultural Perspectives*, ed. Graham Clarke (New York: St. Martin's, 1988), 63.

27. Such references to the African diaspora reflect Davis' ideological and philosophical outlooks. *Kongi's Harvest* (1971) was Davis' ill-fated attempt to expand his filmmaking vision. Adapted from a Wole Soyinka play (with Soyinka in the lead role) and shot in Nigeria, the film failed to find a distributor, and was later disowned by Soyinka. For more on this, see Manthia Diawara's *African Cinema: Politics and Culture* (Bloomington: Indiana University Press, 1992) and Nwachukwu Frank Ukadike's *Black African Cinema* (Berkeley: University of California Press, 1994).

28. The original screenplay calls for Billie to be clad in rags and the chains of a slave. My suspicion is that this outfit might have been too controversial, especially in the links it makes between racial oppression and gender. The novel dispenses with the clothing altogether and has an almost nude Billie writhing on top of the cotton in a highly sexualized performance (in The Cotton Club rather than the Apollo). Of the three, this performance makes most explicit the sexual tensions underlying much of America's racial history.

29. Robin D. G. Kelley, *Yo' Mama's Disfunktional! Fighting the Culture Wars in Urban America* (Boston: Beacon Press, 1997), 23.

30. One of the changes made from the novel is the almost total deletion of Colonel Calhoun and his Back-to-the-South movement. In the novel, he is responsible for the robbery and the subsequent hiding of the money in the bale. Significantly, when Calhoun and his nephew open the Back-to-the-South offices in an attempt to recover the cotton, it sends the neighborhood into an uproar, complete with pickets and protests. Calhoun remains in the film, but he is stripped of any resemblance to his novelistic cousin; instead, he becomes nothing more than Deke's partner in the heist. The reasons why Davis would drop this from the film are unclear, especially considering that no reason for the cotton's presence is supplied by the film. It is my guess that, as with the original references to Billie's costume, this subject matter was considered too inflammatory, especially considering that Calhoun's company was offering northern blacks a form of indentured servitude (similar to what the northern industries had practiced during the Great Migration), and was using the argument that urban African Americans were better off on the plantation.

31. Lee, "Harlem," 64.

32. Burton Pike, "The City as Image," in *The City Reader*, ed. Richard T. LeGates and Frederic Stout (New York: Routledge, 1996), 246.

33. Gary Saul Morson and Caryl Emerson, *Mikhail Bakhtin: Creation of a Prosaics* (Stanford: Stanford University Press, 1990), 423.

34. Don L. Lee (Haki Madhubati), "The Bittersweet of Sweetback/Or, Shake Yo Money Maker," *Black World* 21.1 (November 1971): 43–44.

35. Cited in James P. Murray, "Running With *Sweetback*," *Black Creation* 3.1 (Fall 1971): 10.

36. See Newton's commentary on the film in *The Black Panther* 6 (June 19, 1971).

37. Lerone Bennett, Jr. "The Emancipation Orgasm: Sweetback in Wonderland," *Ebony* 26 (September 1971): 108. For a detailed overview of the critical responses to the film, see Jon Hartmann's "The Trope of Blaxploitation in Critical Responses to *Sweetback*," *Film History* 6.3 (1994): 382–404.

38. Van Peebles was familiar with the art film "scene," having made his American debut with *The Story of a Three Day Pass* at the San Francisco Film Festival in 1967. Furthermore, Van Peebles was making films in France in the mid- to late 1960s, so it is safe to assume that he was exposed to a number of different cinematic styles: European, Latin American, and American. It is a strong possibility that Van Peebles' desire for a revolutionary cinema was in keeping with the vision of a number of young filmmakers, like Jean Luc Godard, who were trying to break free from Hollywood conventions.

39. Reid, *Redefining Black Cinema*, 78.

40. Thulani Davis, "We've Got to Have It," *Village Voice*, June 20, 1989, 67.

41. Ibid., 68.

42. Cripps, "*Sweetback*," 252.

43. Ibid., 241.

44. David James, "Toward a Geo-Cinematic Hermeneutics: Representations of Los Angeles in Non-Industrial Cinema—*Killer of Sheep* and *Water and Power*," *Wide Angle* 20.3 (July 1998): 27.

45. Bennett, "The Emancipation Orgasm," 112; Lee, "Bittersweet," 47.

46. Guerrero, *Framing Blackness*, 91.

47. Cripps, "*Sweetback*," 238.

48. Ibid., 251.

49. Guerrero, *Framing Blackness*, 96.

50. Bogle, *Toms, Coons, Mulattoes, Mammies, and Bucks*, 239–40.

51. Guerrero, *Framing Blackness*, 96.

52. Ibid.

53. Thomas Doherty, "The Black Exploitation Picture: *Superfly* and *Black Caesar*," *Ball State University Forum* 24.2 (Spring 1983): 34.

54. Reid, *Redefining Black Cinema*, 78. Doherty makes a similar connection: "Throughout *Superfly* there is a strange tension between verisimilitude on the one hand (the accurate rendering of the ghetto milieu) and fantasy on the other (Priest's heroic triumph over authority). For the target audience, the verisimilitude lends credibility and validation to a medium that has seldom spoken to its culture" ("The Black Exploitation Picture," 35).

55. Toni Cade Bambara, "Reading the Signs, Empowering the Eye: *Daughters of the Dust* and the Black Independent Cinema Movement," in *Black American Cinema*, ed. Manthia Diawara (New York: Routledge, 1993), 120; Ntongela Masilela, "The Los Angeles School of Black Filmmakers," in *Black American Cinema*, ed. Manthia Diawara (New York: Routledge, 1993), 107.

56. Masilela, "The Los Angeles School," 108.

57. Cited in Steve Howard, "A Cinema of Transformation: The Films of Haile Gerima," *Cineaste* 14.1 (1985): 24.

58. Ibid.

59. Bambara, "Reading the Signs," 119–20. Julie Dash's *Daughters of the Dust* was the culmination of this focus on family, women, history, and folklore. Dash is associated with the LA Rebellion; however, she was not enrolled at UCLA with Gerima and Burnett.

60. Cited in Howard, "A Cinema of Transformation," 24

61. Masilela, "The Los Angeles School," 112.

62. Bambara, "Reading the Signs," 120.

63. Howard, "A Cinema of Transformation," 25.

64. Clyde Taylor, "The New Black Cinema Comes Home," *First World* (May/June 1977): 46.

65. Gerima utilized many Brechtian strategies, including alienation and distanciation, to produce a more active viewer. As Gerima has stated, in Tony Safford and William Triplett, "Haile Gerima: Radical Departures to a New Black Cinema." *Journal of the University Film and Video Association* 35.2 (Spring 1983), "Are the conventions helping or are they exhausted? Structure has to be questioned. Mainstream cinema is now novocaine, helpless and dependent. I want the viewer to participate. We should believe in debate and find our errors and solutions there. In making a film I try equally to combat an aesthetic that is enslaving human beings by, for example, violating the codes of cinema, and, at the same time, creating a structure in which the spectator can become an active participant. . . . At best, one has to see independent filmmaking as a different audience-building process" (61). See also Clyde Taylor: "Although Gerima has apparently absorbed the whole corpus of film technique, a Brechtian strategy stands out. Like Brecht, Gerima uses tedium, distraction, off-balance visual perspectives and discomforting sequences—whatever— to prevent his viewers from settling into a plushy escape-at-the-movies reverie and to force them to *think* out the political implications of the happenings before them" ("New Black," 47).

66. Taylor, "New Black," 46–47.

67. Janet Maslin, "A Thesis Project," *New York Times*, September 23, 1979, C8.

68. Cited in Safford and Triplett, "Haile Gerima," 62.

69. Davis, "We've Got to Have It," 238.

70. Bambara, "Reading the Signs," 120.

71. Davis, "We've Got to Have It," 253.

72. Ibid., 230.

Chapter 4

1. Although the South Side defines Dorothy/Mahogany (Diana Ross), it is not an impediment to her middle-class aspirations, which effectively allow her to leave it all behind. Her eventual choice to return to the neighborhood is undermined by the fact that her decision is made in order to complete the process of heterosexual coupling initiated at the beginning of the film. In short, Dorothy returns in order to "stand by her man," subsuming her identity to his political aspirations and foregoing a promising career as a fashion designer in Italy. For more on *Mahogany*'s gen-

der, race, and class relationships, see Robyn Weigman's "Black Bodies/American Commodities: Gender, Race, and the Bourgeois Ideal in Contemporary Film," in *Unspeakable Images: Ethnicity and the American Cinema*, ed. Lester D. Friedman (Urbana: University of Illinois Press, 1991), 308–28, and Jane Gaines' "White Privilege and Looking Relations—Race and Gender in Feminist Film Theory," *Screen* 29.4 (Autumn 1988): 12–27. For an updated rendering of black Chicago, see *love jones* (Theodore Witcher, 1997).

2.   Daniel J. Leab, *From Sambo to Superspade: The Black Experience in Motion Pictures.* (Boston: Houghton Mifflin, 1976), 262; Ed Guerrero, *Framing Blackness: The African American Image in Film* (Philadelphia: Temple University Press, 1993), 105.

3.   B. J. Mason, "The New Films: Culture or Con Game?" *Ebony* 28.2 (December 1972): 64.

4.   Cited in Guerrero, *Framing Blackness*, 102.

5.   Ibid., 99.

6.   Ibid., 105.

7.   The phrase "New Jack" comes from Barry Michael Cooper's "New Jack City." Cooper introduced the term in 1987 to refer to Detroit's violent inner-city culture. See Nelson George, *Buppies, B-Boys, Baps & Bohos* (New York: HarperCollins, 1992), 31.

8.   Spike Lee, *Spike Lee's Gotta Have It: Inside Guerrilla Filmmaking* (New York: Fireside, 1987), 62.

9.   S. Craig Watkins, *Representing: Hip Hop Culture and the Production of Black Cinema* (Chicago: University of Chicago Press, 1998), 98.

10.   Ibid., 182.

11.   This scene is quoted in French filmmaker Matthieu Kassovitz's, *La Haine* (1995), a homage to Lee and an adaptation of contemporary African American filmmaking styles and themes for a French context.

12.   Jesse Algeron Rhines, *Black Film/White Money* (New Brunswick: Rutgers University Press, 1996), 62.

13.   Watkins, *Representing*, 112.

14.   Ibid., 145.

15.   As Guerrero argues, "the start of the 1980's saw a disturbing resurfacing of images from Hollywood's pre-civil rights past, amounting to a cinematic style of appropriation and representation of African Americans that might best be described as 'neo-minstrelsy' " (*Framing Blackness*, 122).

16.   Lee, *Spike Lee's Gotta Have It*, 176.

17.   Rhines, *Black Film/White Money*, 123. We should be wary of Rhines' unproblematic adoption of such highly overdetermined and contested terminology. The term "underclass" implies a nihilistic attitude in its very terms because it suggests that "poverty . . . had become a permanent condition." See Nicholas Lemann, *The Promised Land: The Great Black Migration and How It Changed America* (New York: Vintage Books, 1991), 281. See also Robin D. G. Kelley, *Yo' Mama's Disfunktional!: Fighting the Culture Wars in Urban America* (Boston: Beacon Press, 1997), 15–42 and chapter 5 in this book.

18. Nelson George, "*Do The Right Thing*: Film and Fury," in *Five for Five: The Films of Spike Lee* (New York: Stewart, Tabori and Chang, 1991), 77.

19. This was noted as early as August 1986 by John Blake who, in the *Chicago Tribune*, suggested that Lee's filmmaking might help to "revitalize" independent cinema. John Blake, *Chicago Tribune*, August 13, 1986, 3.

20. Salim Muwakkil, "Spike Lee and the Image Police," *Cineaste* 26.4 (1990): 35.

21. For more on Lee's links to Brecht and to modernism as a whole, see Douglas Kellner, "Aesthetics, Ethics, and Politics in the Films of Spike Lee," in *Spike Lee's Do the Right Thing*, ed. Mark A. Reid (New York: Cambridge University Press, 1997), 73–106.

22. See Paula J. Massood, "*Summer of Sam* (rev.)" *Cineaste* 25.2 (2000): 62–64.

23. Spike Lee, "Five for Five," in *Five for Five: The Films of Spike Lee* (New York: Stewart Tabori and Chang, 1991), 12.

24. See Neil Smith, "New City, New Frontier: The Lower East Side as Wild, Wild West," in *Variations on a Theme Park: The New American City an the End of Public Space*, ed. Michael Sorkin (New York: Hill and Wang, 1992), 61–93; Mike Davis *City of Quartz: Excavating the Future in Los Angeles* (New York: Vintage, 1992); and Brian Willis, ed., *If You Lived Here: The City in Art, Theory, and Social Activism* (Seattle: Bay Press, 1991).

25. Polyphony is understood here in Bakhtinian terms as a "a multiplicity of distinct and even antithetical voices," cited in Robert Stam, "Bakhtin, Polyphony, and Ethnic/Racial Representation," in *Unspeakable Images: Ethnicity and the American Cinema*, ed. Lester D. Friedman (Urbana: University of Illinois Press, 1991), 255. See also Stam's *Subversive Pleasures: Bakhtin, Cultural Criticism, and Film* (Baltimore: Johns Hopkins University Press, 1989). The film's polyphony has been discussed by a number of other critics, including Victoria E. Johnson in "Polyphony and Cultural Expression: Interpreting Musical Traditions in *Do The Right Thing*," *Film Quarterly* 47.2 (Winter 1993–1994): 18–29. Guerrero makes mention of the film's polyphony in *Framing Blackness*.

26. Lisa Kennedy, "And Then There Was Nunn," *Village Voice*, June 20, 1989, 75.

27. Thomas Doherty, "*Do The Right Thing*," *Film Quarterly* 43.2 (Winter 1989–1990): 38.

28. Robin D. G. Kelley, *Race Rebels: Culture, Politics, and the Black Working Class* (New York: The Free Press, 1994), 206.

29. Johnson, "Polyphony and Cultural Expression," 24.

30. Muwakkil, "Spike Lee," 36. For example, Ice Cube makes his acting debut in *Boyz N the Hood*, Ice T appears in *New Jack City*, along with such old-school figures as Fabulous Freddy. For more on rap's influence on contemporary African American cinema, see Robin D. G. Kelley *Race Rebels*; Michael Eric Dyson, *Reflecting Black: African-American Cultural Criticism* (Minneapolis: University of Minnesota Press, 1993); Todd Boyd, *Am I Black Enough For You?: Popular Culture from the 'Hood and Beyond* (Bloomington: Indiana University Press, 1997); Tricia Rose, *Black Noise: Rap Music and Black Culture in Contemporary America* (Hanover, N.H.: Uni-

versity Press of New England, 1994); and Murray Foreman, *The 'Hood Comes First: Race, Space, and Place in Rap and Hip-Hop* (Middletown, Conn.: Wesleyan University Press, 2002).

31.   Manthia Diawara, *"Noir* by *Noirs*: Towards a New Realism in Black Cinema," *African American Review* 27.4 (1993): 528. For more on this subject, see William Grier's and Price Cobbs' *Black Rage* (New York: Basic Books, 1968).

32.   Johnson, "Polyphony and Cultural Expression," 25.

33.   The block includes a number of women residents but they are underdeveloped and one-dimensional, especially in contrast to the film's male characters. Lee's filmic representation of women has often been a matter of debate, dating back to Nola in *She's Gotta Have It* and continuing throughout his career. See especially, bell hooks' " 'whose pussy is this': a feminist comment," in *Talking Back: Thinking Feminist Thinking Black* (Boston: South End Press, 1989) and Michele Wallace's "Spike Lee and Black Women," in *Invisibility Blues: From Pop to Theory* (New York: Verso, 1990). The focus on female characters is subsumed under the larger (more vocal) discourse of the neighborhood, or shifted into a somewhat repressed reference to tensions generated by the intersections between race and gender, as seen in Mookie's forbidding his sister Jade to return to Sal's Famous in order to allay his (mostly imagined) fears that Sal is sexually interested in her. While the exchange between Mookie and Jade explores the long history of sexualized race relations, the effort fails because it is underdeveloped. Instead, the scene replicates exactly what Lee is attempting to deconstruct because the effect is to make Mookie appear reactionary, in part, because from a narrative standpoint, Sal's treatment of Jade is entirely in keeping with both of their characters. Furthermore, in her critiques of Mookie's laziness earlier in the film, Jade is already partially sympathetically aligned with Sal.

34.   Doherty, *"Do the Right Thing,"* 35.

35.   For many critics, there was no difference between Lee and the character he played on the screen. Thus, Mookie's actions were seen as directly related to Lee's ideological worldview. For the more hysterical reviewers, Lee became an advocate of violence (with condemnations similar to those heaped upon Malcolm X decades before). In fact, Mookie's actions were considered to be so reprehensible that most discussions of the film overlooked the more heinous crime—Radio Raheem's death at the hands of the NYPD.

36.   W.J.T. Mitchell, "The Violence of Public Art: *Do the Right Thing," Critical Inquiry* 16 (Summer 1990): 894.

37.   Ibid., 898.

38.   Jacquie Jones, "In Sal's Country," *Cineaste* 17.4 (1990): 34.

39.   Johnson, "Polyphony and Cultural Expression," 23.

40.   Lee, *Do*, 63–64.

41.   For example, see Catherine Pouzoulet, who argues that Lee's "refusal to depict realistically deviant behavioral patterns" was his "penultimate political mistake" in "The Cinema of Spike Lee: Images of a Mosaic City," in *Spike Lee's Do the Right Thing*, ed. Mark A. Reid (New York: Cambridge University Press, 1997), 41. Lee has maintained that it is racist to assume that drugs were a mandatory part of the cinematic urbanscape because no one ever asks white directors why drugs

are missing from their representations of white suburbia. Lee's response suggests an understanding of the politics of filmmaking and the constructed nature of the image in ways that seem to escape Pouzoulet.

42. Mitchell, "The Violence of Public Art," 895.

Chapter 5

1. Ed Guerrero, *Framing Blackness: The African American Image in Film* (Philadelphia: Temple University Press, 1993), 182; Jacquie Jones, "The New Ghetto Aesthetic," *Wide Angle* 13.3–4 (July–October 1991): 33; Manthia Diawara, "Black American Cinema: The New Realism," in *Black American Cinema*, ed. Manthia Diawara (New York: Routledge, 1993), 24.

2. In the late 1980s and 1990s most black-directed features cost between $1 million and $10 million, an amount still far below the industry average but greater than films in the 1970s. This change may be attributed to the industry's rising faith in African American directors and themes; however, it is more likely due to fluctuations in the overall structure of the industry. Also, directors like Rich, Lee, and Townsend worked independently from the industry (at least for their first films), with outside support coming in at the post-production and exhibition stage. This differs from Singleton, the Hughes brothers, and Mario Van Peebles, whose careers are much more enmeshed in the industry. See Jesse Algeron Rhines, *Black Film/White Money* (New Brunswick: Rutgers University Press, 1996), 152–60, for more on this.

3. Guerrero, *Framing Blackness*, 165.

4. Nina Easton cited in Jacquie Jones, "The New Ghetto Aesthetic," *Wide Angle* 13.3–4 (July–October 1991): 33.

5. Karen Grigsy Bates, " 'They've Gotta Have Us': Hollywood's Black Directors," *The New York Times Magazine*, July 14, 1991, VI:15.

6. Henry Louis Gates Jr., "Blood Brothers: Albert and Allen Hughes in the Belly of the Hollywood Beast," *Transition* 63 (1994): 171.

7. Paul Gilroy, *The Black Atlantic: Modernity and Double Consciousness.* (Cambridge, Mass.: Harvard University Press, 1993), 111.

8. Todd Boyd, *Am I Black Enough For You?: Popular Culture From the 'Hood and Beyond* (Bloomington: Indiana University Press, 1997), 92.

9. Robin D. G. Kelley, *Race Rebels: Culture, Politics, and the Black Working Class* (New York: The Free Press, 1994), 191.

10. Edward Soja, *Postmodern Geographies: The Reassertion of Space in Critical Social Theory* (New York: Verso, 1989), 223.

11. Lonnie Bunch, "A Past Not Necessarily Prologue: The Afro-American in Los Angeles," in *20th Century Los Angeles: Power, Promotion, and Social Conflict*, ed. Norman M. Klein and Martin J. Schiesl (Claremont, Calif.: Regina Books, 1990), 119.

12. Bunch, "A Past," 103. Walter Mosley's "Easy Rawlins'" novels and Chester Himes' *If He Hollers Let Him Go* effectively describe African American Los Angeles during the 1940s and 1950s. Easy Rawlins embodies the tensions of working in the

defense industry and the frustrations of attempting to hold on to self-respect in the face of mortgage payments. Easy is fired from his job, basically for being "too proud." It is this experience that leads him to accept his first case as a private detective. Himes' novel, possibly because it was a product of the time and the author's direct experiences in the defense industry, is much more dystopian. Himes' Bob Jones is also too proud for his own good. But rather than simply being fired for this, Jones is accused of rape after he refuses to conform to a white, female co-worker's preconceived notions of black men. Both novels incorporate the thriving migrant culture and vibrant atmosphere of the city's black neighborhoods. For Mosley, the city's African American sections add color and texture to the narrative as well as suggesting a cohesive community space that in Carl Franklin's cinematic adaptation of *Devil in a Blue Dress* takes on nostalgic overtones. For Himes, on the other hand, the continuing presence of the rural South in Los Angeles' culture signified the persistence of Jim Crow and racialized (and sexualized) repressions.

13. Mike Davis, *City of Quartz: Excavating the Future in Los Angeles* (New York: Vintage, 1992), 296.

14. William Julius Wilson, *The Truly Disadvantaged: The Inner City, the Underclass, and Public Policy* (Chicago: University of Chicago Press, 1987), 35.

15. Davis, *City of Quartz*, 304.

16. Wilson, *The Truly Disadvantaged*, 39.

17. Michael Eric Dyson, *Reflecting Black: African-American Cultural Criticism* (Minneapolis: University of Minnesota Press, 1993), 90.

18. Wilson, *The Truly Disadvantaged*, 36.

19. Davis, *City of Quartz*, 305.

20. *New Jack City* dates the introduction of crack cocaine to New York in 1984. Davis dates its appearance in Los Angeles to between 1985 and 1987 (*City of Quartz*, 312). The opening scenes of *Menace II Society* also acknowledge the introduction of drugs to Watts, specifically following the Watts Rebellion. Unlike *New Jack City*, however, *Menace* fails to place the introduction of crack on the scene in its history of the Watts' drug trade. Instead, there is a conceptual and temporal leap made from heroin in the 1970s to crack in the late 1980s and 1990s. While the crack economy plays a significant role in the film (for example, in the "lesson" we are given in how to prepare crack), this particular drug is not historicized in a manner similar to heroin.

21. Nelson George, *Buppies, B-Boys, Baps & Bohos* (New York: HarperCollins, 1992), 26–27.

22. Robin D. G. Kelley, *Race Rebels: Culture, Politics, and the Black Working Class* (New York: The Free Press, 1994), 192.

23. Ibid., 193.

24. Dyson, *Reflecting Black*, 97.

25. George Lipsitz, "We Know What Time It Is: Race, Class and Youth Culture in the Nineties," in *Microphone Fiends: Youth Music & Youth Culture*, ed. Andrew Ross and Tricia Rose (New York: Routledge, 1994), 19.

26. Kelley, *Race Rebels*, 208.

27. Guerrero, *Framing Blackness*, 166.

28. Jones, "Ghetto," 34. However, Jones makes a distinction between the two

media by arguing that "there is a profound dissimilarity between contemporary Black Hollywood cinema and rap music: as a phenomenon Black Hollywood is necessarily not of its own creation. And the reason . . . is economics" (33). I would contend that this distinction might have been more relevant in 1991 than it is in 2003.

29.   Thomas Doherty and Jacquie Jones, "Two Takes on *Boyz N the Hood*," *Cineaste* 18.4 (1991): 17.

30.   Peter Marcuse, "Not Chaos, But Walls: Postmodernism and the Partitioned City," in *Postmodern Cities and Spaces*, ed. Sophie Watson and Katherine Gibson (Cambridge, Mass.: Blackwell, 1995), 248.

31.   Charles Scruggs, *Sweet Home: Invisible Cities in the Afro-American Novel* (Baltimore: Johns Hopkins University Press, 1993), 17.

32.   According to Guerrero, "the feeling of confinement and limitation of opportunity that shapes all black life in Los Angeles' sprawling ghetto opens the film with a full-frame shot of a STOP sign as a fleet, silver airliner flies overhead and beyond the hood to distant lands and vastly broader social horizons." Guererro, *Framing Blackness*, 184.

33.   Scruggs, *Sweet Home*, 54.

34.   Marcuse, "Not Chaos," 249.

35.   Diawara, "Black," 22. In Los Angeles, television news is provided in an "helicopter-eye's-view" format, thus adding voyeurism to the surveillance and adding a familiarity to *Boyz*'s sights and sounds.

36.   Vertically built cities like New York and Chicago do not rely on helicopters for policing as much as Los Angeles. However, similar methods of surveillance and control are found in the architecture of high-rise housing projects—the literal "Watch Hills" of the ghetto. I will return to this point in chapter 6.

37.   Soja, *Postmodern Geographies*, 7.

38.   It is not simply ironic that the posters envisage Reagan in a cowboy hat and outfit. Reagan's presidency (and governorship of California) often appropriated the discourses of the Wild West and Manifest Destiny. It is, therefore, not too much of a jump to see the LAPD's "Operation Hammer," which was overwhelmingly endorsed by the Reagans (as part of Nancy's War on Drugs), as a continuation of the frontier mythology in which Native Americans were contained, controlled, and made safe for civilization. For more on this, see Michael Paul Rogin's *Ronald Reagan, The Movies and Other Episodes in Political Demonology* (Berkeley: University of California Press, 1988); Sidney Blumenthal and Thomas Byrne Edsall, eds., *The Reagan Legacy* (New York: Pantheon Books, 1988); Haynes Bonner Johnson's *Sleepwalking Through History: America in the Reagan Years* (New York: Doubleday, 1992); and Alexandra Keller's *Re-Imagining the Frontier: American Westerns Since the Reagan Administration* (unpublished Ph.D. diss., New York University, 1998).

39.   Andrew Ross cited in Grant Farred, "No Way Out of the Menaced Society: Loyalty Within the Boundedness of Race," *Camera Obscura* 35 (May 1995): 10–11.

40.   Reva also border crosses by earning her MA and moving up the economic ladder. While the film tries to offer an alternative version of black womanhood—with both Reva and Brandi—this is significantly undermined by its indictment of

Reva for leaving. Thus, Reva becomes another example of the black middle class that has left the ghetto. What is left in the hood are single mothers, on drugs, on welfare, and certainly not capable of raising their (male) children.

41. As Gilroy suggests, this optimism "is no longer plausible advice to the black listening public." See Paul Gilroy, "After the Love Has Gone: Bio-Politics and Etho-Poetics in the Black Public Sphere," *Public Culture* 7.1 (Fall 1994): 53.

42. Dyson, *Reflecting Black*, 93.

43. Diawara, "Black," 24.

44. Kelley, *Race Rebels*, 202.

45. Ibid., 195.

46. S. Craig Watkins, *Representing: Hip Hop Culture and the Production of Black Cinema* (Chicago: University of Chicago Press, 1998), 209. Watkins offers his own readings of the two films (196–231). While our two discussions are similar in some respects, Watkins fails to fully take into account the specifics of the film's visual and aural strategies.

47. Ella Shohat and Robert Stam, *Unthinking Eurocentrism: Multiculturalism and the Media* (New York: Routledge, 1994), 180.

48. Doherty, "Two," 19.

49. Atlanta has its own history as an urban utopia, appearing as such in the writings of W.E.B. DuBois and in the films of Micheaux, Lee, Singleton, and the Hughes brothers. Often the city is associated with the "Talented Tenth," and it has begun to symbolize in a similar utopia as Harlem during the 1920s.

50. O-Dog's crime and its televisual representation references an actual event in Los Angeles in which a Korean shop owner (Soon Ja Du) shot an African American woman (Latasha Harlins) because she suspected Harlins of a crime. This event was recorded on surveillance tape and was repeatedly aired by Los Angeles television stations during the 1992 riots, as if to suggest that the looting and other activities were responses to this act rather than to the acquittal of the LAPD officers who assaulted Rodney King. Elaine H. Kim, "Home is Where the *Han* Is: A Korean-American Perspective on the Los Angeles Upheavals," in *Reading Rodney King, Reading Urban Uprising*, ed. Robert Gooding-Williams (New York: Routledge, 1993), 234.

51. Amy Taubin, "Girl N the Hood," *Sight & Sound* 3.8 (August 1993): 17.

52. Cited in Gates, "Blood Brothers," 174.

53. Cited in ibid., 175.

54. Rodia's Watts Towers appear in other films set in the hood, most notably *Colors*, where it is the backdrop in a scene in which Sean Penn's character wrecks a cruiser after a high-speed chase with a group of suspected gang members. Just as the Hollywood sign is the central metaphor for one visual construction of LA, the Watts Towers similarly connotes another construction. Even if you've never seen it in LA, the Towers' location has already been announced in a history of cinematic representations.

55. By this time, the bird's-eye-view strategy of articulating black city space was familiar, having appeared in *New Jack City, Straight Out of Brooklyn*, and *Candyman* as a means of introducing Chicago's Cabrini-Green housing projects and the sur-

rounding neighborhoods. In *Menace*, such a strategy may also be an inversion of the LAPD's use of helicopters to patrol the neighborhood. Rather than just observing, the film will enter the space.

56. This b-boy/gangsta' figure had other incarnations in hood films from this time period, most notably in *New Jack City*'s Nino, *Juice*'s Bishop, and *Above the Rim*'s Birdie. These characters, however, fulfill different functions. First, Nino's actions are constrained by genre conventions. He is much more of a traditional gangster in the *Scarface* mold than a gangsta'. In the latter two examples the characters' behaviors are explained away as psychological imbalances rather than as nihilism or gangsta'ism, therefore supporting the sociological argument that inner-city behaviors are pathological. With Mars, Raheem, Doughboy and his friends, Caine, or O-Dog there is no indication that a psychological problem is the root of their behavior. If any reason is presented, it is more related to economic, social, political, and cultural pressures. For more on the links (and differences) between gangsters and gangstaz, see Boyd, *Am I Black Enough*, 82–104.

57. Farred, "No Way Out," 11.

58. Ibid., 12.

59. Ibid.

60. Davis, *City of Quartz*, 290.

61. This individualist ideology can be traced back to the earliest African American films made by the Douglass and Lincoln Companies. The ideal figure of the individual maintains the status quo in films like *Boyz*, because while the individual, through hard work and perseverance, overcomes the social inequities contained within a particular social hierarchy (like the majority of Sidney Poitier's roles), this is accomplished, in part, to secure a place within that hierarchy. If viewed in this manner, *Boyz* remains firmly entrenched within the ideology of the American Dream. Through hard work and determination, Tre survives his youth and goes on to college.

62. Cornel West, "Nihilism in Black America: A Danger that Corrodes from Within," *Dissent* (Spring 1991): 222–23.

63. Boyd, *Am I Black Enough*, 101.

64. Gilroy, "After," 70.

65. Kelley, *Race Rebels*, 198.

66. Ibid., 194.

67. I'm indebted to Robert Stam for this suggestion.

68. See Boyd, *Am I Black Enough*, pages 13–39 and Watkins, *Representing*, 63–76, for an in-depth discussion of these generational differences.

69. Cited in Houston A. Baker, "Scene . . . Not Heard," in *Reading Rodney King: Reading Urban Uprising*, ed. Robert Gooding-Williams (New York: Routledge, 1993), 47.

70. Mike Davis traces the transformation of the civil rights movement to the Black Panthers. With the dismantling of the Panthers in South Central, area gangs grew in influence, some as outcroppings of Panther activities. As Davis argues, by the 1970s and 1980s, the gangs had lost much of the original political ideology at the core of the Panther movement. What they retained, however, were specific atti-

tudes about black masculine agency. See Davis (*City of Quartz*, 296). Nelson George identifies a similar generation gap between the hip-hop generation and the "black thirtysomethings." He claims, this tension has "long been a subtext in the black music biz [and] is now manifesting itself in black film." Nelson George, "Menaces to Society: Brothers Grim—the Hugheses' Film is Hip-Hop Dark," *Village Voice*, May 25, 1993, 23.

71.   Boyd, *Am I Black Enough*, 103.

72.   Gilroy, "After," 53.

73.   It is impossible to claim, like Boyd, that the film is apolitical. Instead, the Hugheses demonstrate a tendency of gangsta' culture, which George identifies as a fundamental contradiction in the twins' words. As he observes, "When asked about negative images of black life in *Menace* the more gregarious Allen replies with an answer typical of the culture, 'My answer is that I'm not out here to be a teacher.' Continuing on, he then, like a rapper-philosopher, contradicts himself by embracing the teaching metaphor: 'You don't learn from a positive film or from *The Cosby Show*. You can learn from the negative about what needs to be changed. What can you learn from a middle-class lifestyle?' " ("Menaces," 21). Likewise, Gilroy teases out a similar sort of discrepancy in rapper Snoop Dogg's words: "Understandably Snoop asserts that his work has no political significance whatsoever. When pressed to operate in that restricted mode his rather conventional opinions seem to be a long way from anything that could reasonably be called nihilist. 'As far as me being political, the only thing I can say is the mutha-fuckin' U.S. can start giving money to the hood, giving opportunity and starting business, something to make niggas not want to kill each other. Give them some kind of job and finances cos' the killin ain't over love nor money. They are killin and jackin one another 'cos their ain't no opportunity' " ("After," 72).

74.   Diawara, "Black," 25.

75.   Ibid., 11.

76.   Soja, *Postmodern Geographies*, 215.

77.   The films are primarily, if not solely, concerned with representing the struggle for survival of young African American *men* in the inner city. This project's masculinist agenda displaces and renders invisible the experiences of black women, unless it is in the roles of bitches or "ho's." Only Leslie Harris' *Just Another Girl on the IRT* (1992) moves away from these parameters. However, the fact that her film, in comparison to other hood films, did not fare well in the box office is an indication of the greater commercial appeal of the male-centered stories.

Chapter 6

1.   Reece Auguiste, "The Migrants Tale: A Symphony for Our Time," *Black Audio Film Collective Artist Statement*. <http://gertrude.art.uiuc.edu/@art/LOT project/bafetext.html>.

2.   See Teshome Gabriel, "Thoughts on Nomadic Aesthetics and the Black Independent Cinema: Traces of a Journey," in *Blackframes: Critical Perspectives on Black Independent Cinema*, ed. Mbye B. Cham and Claire Andrade-Watkins (Cambridge,

Mass.: The MIT Press, 1988), 62–79; James Clifford, *Routes: Travel and Translation in the Late Twentieth Century* (Cambridge, Mass.: Harvard University Press, 1997); Stuart Hall, "Subjects in History: Making Diasporic Identities," in *The House that Race Built*, ed. Wahneema Lubiana (New York: Random House, 1997), 289–99; and Paul Gilroy, *The Black Atlantic: Modernity and Double Consciousness* (Cambridge, Mass.: Harvard University Press, 1993).

    3. Ed Guerrero, *Framing Blackness: The African American Image in Film* (Philadelphia: Temple University Press, 1993), 182.

    4. See Paula J. Massood, "Ghetto Supastar: Warren Beatty's *Bulworth* and the Politics of Race and Space," *Literature/Film Quarterly* 30.4 (2003).

    5. Jesse Algeron Rhines, *Black Film/White Money* (New Brunswick: Rutgers University Press, 1996), 157. As the following figures (domestic box office) indicate, hood films earned an extremely high rate of return:

    Boyz N the Hood—cost $6 million, made $60 million (Rhines, *Black Film/White Money*, 75)

    Straight Out of Brooklyn—cost $300,000, made $2.7 million (<www.imdb.com>)

    New Jack City—cost $8.7 million, made $47 million (Guerrero, *Framing Blackness*, 186)

    Menace II Society—cost $3.5 million, made $30 million (<www.imdb.com>)

    See also S. Craig Watkins, *Representing: Hip Hop Culture and the Production of Black Cinema* (Chicago: University of Chicago Press, 1998), 183–95.

    6. This is related to the intellectual environment of the 1980s and 1990s, which experienced an expanded interrogation into the structures of representation and identity, particularly concerning race, ethnicity, gender, and sexuality.

    7. Watkins addresses a similar question in *Representing*. Unlike my discussion, he disputes the links between the two time periods on the basis of the fact that hood films do not fit the criteria of exploitation films. See pp. 171–76.

    8. Cited in Alex McGregor (1993), "Cowboyz 'n' the Hood," *Time Out* (London), November 17, 1993, 19. Thanks to Alexandra Keller for this reference.

    9. All the African American directors who debuted with features and then received backing for a second film were male. Julie Dash, Darnell Martin, and Leslie Harris were less fortunate than their male counterparts, even though Dash's *Daughters of the Dust* received critical accolades. A glance at the box office histories of their films might provide part of the reason why they have not made second features: Harris's *Just Another Girl on the IRT* made only $500,000 in its first year, Dash's *Daughters of the Dust* made $1.6 million domestically, and Martin's *I Like It Like That* lost money, earning $2 million domestically on a $5.5 million investment. (Martin, however, does have a multipicture deal with a studio.) Possibly indicating a move away from this trend, *Eve's Bayou* (1997) was made for between $3 million and $5 million dollars and earned $14 million by January 1998 (David Lugowski, in conversation).

    10. Within a few months of *The Inkwell*, Spike Lee released *Crooklyn*, which focuses on the similar themes of youth and childhood. Semiautobiographical, Lee's film is set in Brooklyn during the 1970s; however, it also shifts to the South at a certain stage. This move represents not only a thematic shift, but also a stylistic one

because the new setting is cinematically demarcated through the use of a different film stock and a decompressed, anamorphic lens.

11.　None of the subsequent films, except possibly *Higher Learning*, enjoyed nearly the same domestic box office returns as the debuts. For example:

Van Peebles—*Posse* grossed $18 million, while *Panther* brought in $7 million

Singleton—*Poetic Justice* brought in $28 million, while *Higher Learning* made $38 million

Rich—*The Inkwell* made $9 million

Hugheses—*Dead Presidents* grossed $24 million

While the above figures are significant, they indicate only a small investment-to-profit ratio, since the films were made with higher production costs. As a frame of reference, the big money-makers by African American directors were *Sister Act 2* ($57 million), *A Low Down Dirty Shame* ($29 million), *Waiting to Exhale* ($66 million), *Don't Be a Menace to Society While Drinking Your Juice in the Hood* ($40 million), *A Thin Line Between Love and Hate* ($35 million), *Set It Off* ($36 million [in first 4 months]), and *Soul Food* ($43.5 million [by January 1998]). With the exception of the *Set It Off*, all of these examples are of other genres, most notably comedy, and are anchored by African American superstars with crossover appeal—Whoopee Goldberg, Whitney Houston, Martin Lawrence, and, to a lesser extent, the Wayans brothers and Queen Latifah (the latter two examples being buoyed by their Fox network television sitcoms). Comedy has been the "most prolific genre in terms of black themes, casts, and images, and the only genre that has continuously engaged black talent since the collapse of the initial blaxploitation boom." The reason for this continuity and success, according to Ed Guerrero, is that "black comedy provides a deflected, mostly non-threatening space within which America can tentatively engage its ubiquitous race problem" (*Framing Blackness*, 190).

12.　M. M. Bakhtin, *The Dialogic Imagination*, ed. Michael Holquist, trans. Caryl Emerson and Michael Holquist (Austin: University of Texas Press, 1981), 252.

13.　Gary Saul Morson and Caryl Emerson, *Mikhail Bakhtin: Creation of a Prosaics* (Stanford: Stanford University Press, 1990), 426.

14.　The conversation might also be Cundieff's satirical critique of cultural critics such as Trey Ellis, whose "New Black Aesthetic" identifies "little round glasses" as one of the primary characteristics of its practitioners. In his article, Ellis mentions the glasses twice, and suggests that this is one of the ways that "NBA" style is differentiated from hip-hop style. See Trey Ellis, "The New Black Aesthetic," *Callaloo* 12.1 (Winter 1989): 233–43.

15.　Rhines, *Black Film/White Money*, 161–62.

16.　The play on the idea of "crossing over" is meant to draw attention to the ways in which some of the films with chronotopic motifs from the hood also found new markets. For example, a multigenerational, ethnic, class, and gender audience was drawn to *Devil in a Blue Dress*'s noir/detective narrative, its setting in 1950s Los Angeles, its casting of Denzel Washington as the lead, and by the fact that it is an adaptation of a best-selling novel.

17.　See Alexandra Keller, *Re-Imagining the Frontier: American Westerns Since the Reagan Administration* (unpublished Ph.D. diss., New York University, 1998).

As Keller posits, the film's allusions work to "legitimize" Van Peebles' project. In order for *Posse*'s revisionist strategies to be effective, Van Peebles first had to prove his familiarity and dexterity with the genre; he had to show his inside knowledge before offering an outsider perspective. Only then could he begin to deconstruct the mythology of the Western.

18.   Ice Cube, Ice-T, and Tupac Shakur diversified their roles in a similar manner as Singleton's and the Hugheses' later narratives moved away from the hood. For instance, Ice-T appeared in *Trespass* (1992), *Surviving the Game* (1994), *Johnny Mnemonic* (1995), and the television police-drama *Players*. Shakur's matinee-idol looks and crossover appeal were utilized most effectively in *Gridlock'd* (1997) and *Gang Related* (1997), both of which were buddy films, teaming him up with Timothy Roth and Jim Belushi, respectively. Even Ice Cube diversified, with *Trespass*, *Anaconda* (1997), and *Dangerous Ground* (1997). The increasing marketability of rappers-turned-movie-stars can be traced in the careers of LL Cool J and Will Smith, both of whom developed thriving screen careers in the second half of the 1990s, but who have done so outside of the hood film. Smith, in particular, has capitalized on his cross-over appeal by breaking into the action genre with *Independence Day* (1996) and *Men in Black* (1997), and his own attempt at a Western, *Wild Wild West* (1999), all of which capitalized on his musical talent for their soundtracks. LL Cool J also has starred on screen and on the sound track of films like *Deep Blue Sea* (1999) and *Any Given Sunday* (1999).

19.   The Promised Land saloon is itself an interesting link back to chapter 1 and Zeke's (from *Hallelujah*) sermon about taking a train to heaven, the Promised Land. By the time we get to *Posse*, The Promised Land is a saloon, a place in black-cast musicals that was more closely aligned with sin and temptation. Here it is not such a place.

20.   The film is following a strategy similar to many hood and blaxploitation films—the inversion of good and bad, with lines drawn along racialized boundaries. Thus cops, almost always white, are the outlaws, and "outlaws" (whether real or mythic) are good. Furthermore, the genealogy of such a tendency can be traced back to such outlaw figures as the trickster. Thus Jessie Lee shares the same lineage with Sweetback (and many of the shots of Jessie Lee echo earlier shots of Sweetback). The difference is that Van Peebles Jr. constructs a much more "moral" film than his father. This could be because Mario was also working within the moral framework of the Western, because *Posse* was more closely aligned with industrial ideology than Melvin's film (which was made independently of the industry), or because Mario is a different generation than his father.

21.   Morson and Emerson, *Mikhail Bakhtin*, 374.

22.   Lynne Kirby, *Parallel Tracks: The Railroad and Silent Cinema* (Durham: Duke University Press, 1997), 156.

23.   Da Mayor and Mother Sister actually are chronotopes themselves. Da Mayor and Mother Sister are the community's elders, and they also represent a particular African American geography—the presence and continuation of southern tradition in northern industrial areas.

24.   Kevin Lynch, *The Image of the City* (Cambridge, Mass.: MIT Press, 1960), 1.

25. Cited in Stephen Schaefer, "Spike Makes 'Clockers' Timely," *New York Post*, August 25, 1995, 47.

26. Cited in Jonathan Bernstein, "Spike Lee," *The Face* (December 1997): 202.

27. *Boyz* offers perhaps the 1990s most sympathetic rendering of an inner-city African American youth. But, as my discussion in the previous chapter suggests, Tre does not strictly apply here because he neither deals nor uses drugs, nor is he involved with gangs. In fact, as a college-bound overachiever, Tre is the epitome of the American Dream.

28. As Lee states: "I really wasn't interested in telling a cop's story. I was much more passionate about telling the story of this young African-American kid who comes from a strong family, who's gone off the straight and narrow and has turned to a life of drugs" (cited in ibid., 202).

29. This is also a successful transformation to an alternative morality than that conventionally seen in American filmmaking. Strike might be a drug dealer, he might even teach young Tyrone how to clock, but he's not a murderer.

30. On this phenomenon, see Todd Boyd, *Am I Black Enough For You? Popular Culture From the 'Hood and Beyond.* (Bloomington: Indiana University Press, 1997); Michael Eric Dyson, *Reflecting Black: African-American Cultural Criticism* (Minneapolis: University of Minnesota Press, 1993); and Lisa Kennedy's discussion of Quentin Tarantino, in which Tarantino observes, "Someone said to me at Sundance when *Reservoir Dogs* was there, 'You know what you've done, you've given white boys the kind of movies black kids get. You know like *Juice*, and . . . *Menace II Society*, looking cool, being bad, with a fuck you attitude,'" from "Natural Born Filmmaker: Quentin Tarantino Versus the Film Geeks," *Village Voice*, October 25, 1994, 32.

31. Cited in David Bradley, "Spike Lee's Inferno, The Drug Underworld," *New York Times*, September 20, 1995, 32.

32. Lee, like his younger counterparts, also moved out of the city with his second feature, *School Daze*, which was set on a college campus.

33. Ernest Quimby, "Bedford-Stuyvesant," in *Brooklyn USA: The Fourth Largest City in America*, ed. Rita Seiden Miller (New York: Brooklyn College Press, 1979), 229.

34. Ibid., 232.

35. David McCullough, *Brooklyn—And How It Got That Way* (New York: Dial Press, 1983), 212.

36. Bradley observes "Crooklyn . . . owes its brownstone ethos to no one but Spike Lee" ("Spike Lee's Inferno," 32).

37. Historian Ernest Quimby observes that "Anti-blockbusting campaigns, urban renewal, and the construction of exclusively low-income housing projects . . . erode[d] the sense of community, prevent[ed] social mobility, thwart[ed] economic and political mobilization, and allow[ed] the containment and administrative manipulation of Blacks" ("Bedford-Stuyvesant," 236).

38. Cited in Laurie Werner, *USA Weekend*, September 15–17, 1995, 10.

39. Almost the entire film is set in Brooklyn. The story shifts only once to another location: when Rocco visits the Manhattan boutique that had previously employed Victor as a security guard.

40. Georgia Brown and Amy Taubin, "Clocking In: Two Critics Rate Spike Lee's Ultimate Hood Movie," *Village Voice*, September 19, 1995, 71.

41. Richard Price, *Clockers* (Boston: Houghton Mifflin, 1992), 4.

42. It is ironic that while the film details many of the clockers' transactions, selling crack to an assortment of neighborhood residents (including pregnant women), it is not these activities that will cause Rodney's downfall. Instead, it is a group of kids from the suburbs who incriminate Rodney when they are caught with drugs purchased from Rodney's store. In this instance, the interlopers do the most damage.

43. According to Michel Foucault, a heterotopia is a "countersite" in which "all the other real sites that can be found within the culture are simultaneously represented, contested, and inverted." Foucault's heterotopias are both lived spaces and "other" spaces that are "absolutely different from all the sites that they reflect and speak about." See Foucault's "Of Other Spaces," trans. Jay Miskowiec, *diacritics* 16.1 (Spring 1986): 24.

44. The film's concern with the intersections between the manufactured and the real are introduced in its opening credits, which appear over photographic recreations of the victims of actual drug-related homicides. This, more than Singleton's statistics, graphically points to the dangers of inner-city living.

45. Kirby, *Parallel Tracks*, 10.

46. Gilroy, *The Black Atlantic*, 133.

47. Price, *Clockers*, 622.

48. Kirby, *Parallel Tracks*, 78–80.

49. Brown and Taubin, "Clocking In," 71. See also Stephen Schaefer "Spike Makes 'Clockers' Timely," *New York Post*, August 25, 1995, 47; Stanley Kauffman, "Controlled Substances," *The New Republic* (October 2, 1995): 38–39; Kenneth Turan, "World of Spike Lee's 'Clockers' Unsettling," *Daily Press*, September 16, 1995, D3; Jack Matthews "Spiked Urban Brew: A Potent 'Clockers,' Fermented in Lee's Bitter Juices," *Newsday*, September 13, 1995, B1, B3; David Bradley "Spike Lee's Inferno, The Drug Underworld," Anthony Lane, "Cracking Up," *The New Yorker* (September 18, 1995): 107–8; David Sterrit, "Spike Lee's Urban Playground Feels a Lot Grittier in 'Clockers'," *Christian Science Monitor* (September 13, 1995): 13.

50. Gilroy, *The Black Atlantic*, 18.

51. Ibid., 111.

52. Ibid., 133.

53. Charles Scruggs, *Sweet Home: Invisible Cities in the Afro-American Novel* (Baltimore: Johns Hopkins University Press, 1993), 4.

54. Manthia Diawara, "*Noir* by *Noirs*: Towards a New Realism in Black Cinema," *African American Review* 27.4 (1993): 530. See also Shohat and Stam's discussion of the train in Lee's *Malcolm X*, in which the train "evokes for blacks both subordinate service roles and the opportunity for travel." Ella Shohat and Robert Stam, *Unthinking Eurocentrism: Multiculturalism and the Media* (New York: Routledge, 1994), 352.

55. Diawara, "*Noir* by *Noirs*," 535.

56. Gilroy, *The Black Atlantic*, 133.

Epilogue

1. This has been noted by the popular press. For example, in *Time*, George Tillman Jr., writer and director of *Soul Food*, states: "There are sex comedies, hood films. We're trying to get away from that." The author of the articles cites *Soul Food*, *Eve's Bayou*, *Amistad*, and *Beloved* as a step in that direction. Christopher John Farley, "Cooking Up a Hit," *Time* (October 31, 1997): 87.

2. Rock's career has been very diverse thus far. Like many of the directors discussed in the latter half of this study, he debuted as a performer in a hood film, *New Jack City*. Since then he has appeared in a wide array of films, often opting for low-budget, art house films like *Dogma* and *Nurse Betty*, although he has also appeared in blockbuster action films like *Lethal Weapon 4* (Richard Donner, 2000).

3. *Leprechaun 5* is an undisguised attempt at capitalizing on the appeal of hood films. It can only do so, however, by combining hood conventions with those from other genres, such as the horror film and the comedy. Nonetheless, it retains certain characteristics of the earlier films, such as setting and the casting of rappers Coolio and Ice-T, one of the early rappers to perform in such films (his first appearance was in Mario Van Peebles' *New Jack City* in 1991).

4. A December 2000 Director's Guild of America press release entitled, "DGA Annual Report on Women and Minority Hiring Reveals Bleak Industry Record in 1999," indicates a slight decrease in hiring (especially for minority and women directors working in tape) in 1999. Yet the DGA data also indicate that the percentage of the total (DGA) days worked by African American directors increased from 2.1 percent in 1991 to 4.6 percent in 1999 (the same percentage as in 1998, and therefore not a decrease for African American directors). These figures are for African American directors working in film and tape combined (with film including theatrical and nontheatrical releases). The percentage of the total days worked for African American directors in film in 1999 was 5.4 percent and only 2.4 percent for tape (television), indicating the television networks' continued resistance to African American personnel (a main theme of *Bamboozled*). Additionally, according to Janine Alexander in the DGA's publicity office, African American membership has increased slightly, from 3 percent in 1991–1997 to 4 percent in 1998–1999 (in interview with author). DGA press release available at www.dga.org.

5. A recent example of this trend is Gina Prince-Bythewood's *Disappearing Acts* (2000), a love story based on a Terry McMillan novel and made for HBO. Cable has also provided more experienced directors with work; for example, Charles Burnett made *Nightjohn* for HBO and Julie Dash directed a segment for HBO's *Subway Stories* (1997). Dash directed *Funny Valentines* (1999) and *Incognito* (1999) for BET and *Love Song* (2000) for MTV.

6. The film was actually shot in Toronto, so Chicago's spaces were limited to the establishing shots of the city and the projects. The streets surrounding the projects were a set. Moreover, Toronto was used as the location for the Mississippi scenes, an even more interesting choice since one of the themes of the film is the attempt to keep industry in the Delta region.

7. A definite class and gender bias exists in the film's suggestion that Loretta's problems are related to part of the urban underclass: a single mother who is unem-

ployed and addicted to alcohol and drugs. She is therefore powerless when faced with the temptations of the city and can only change through the initial agency of others (her mother and uncle). Will, on the other hand, is a successful corporate lawyer, a member of the upper-middle class, whose distance from the family is based more on his own choices than any lack of agency. In other words, Will's situation came through free choice. Loretta's did not.

8.   Jacquie Jones, "The Black South in Contemporary Film," *African American Review* 27.1 (1993): 20.

9.   Ibid., 23.

10.   As S. Craig Watkins argues, "a combination of public scorn, new methods of containment, and censorship, youthful exuberance, and high-profile celebrity deaths [and arrests] gradually undermined the appeal of the gangsta motif." S. Craig Watkins, *Representing: Hip Hop Culture and the Production of Black Cinema* (Chicago: University of Chicago Press, 1998), 237.

11.   Cited in Rod Dreher, " 'Down,' Not Out," *New York Post*, December 26, 1998 34.

12.   Vern E. Smith and Daniel Pedersen, "South Toward Home," *Newsweek* (July 14, 1997), 39. Smith and Pederson gathered some of their information from interviews with actual migrants, but the bulk of their empirical information came from Frey's study. For more on this see, William H. Frey, "Black Movement to the South and Regional Concentrations of the Races," *Population Today* 26.2 (February 1998). See also Randolph E. Schmid, "Blacks Coming Back to South," from *The Tallahassee Democrat*, January 29, 1998, 1A and 4A. The Schmid article was picked up by *The Tallahassee Democrat* from The Associated Press and was based on the Frey findings.

13.   Smith and Pedersen, "South Toward Home," 36.

14.   Dreher, " 'Down,' Not Out," 34.

15.   Ed Guerrero, *Framing Blackness: The African American Image in Film*. (Philadelphia: Temple University Press, 1993), 10.

16.   Some critics in the 1970s feared that blaxploitation was really a return to minstrelsy, See Gordon R. Watkins, "Another Step Backwards: New Black Movies, Another Age of Minstrelsy," *Millimeter* (November 1973): 10–11, 18–20.

17.   An interesting variation on the South appears in David Gordon Green's *George Washington* (2000), a quirky film set in the South and which, according to its director, was an attempt at creating an integrated southern utopia.

18.   For more on Singleton's *Baby Boy*, see Paula J. Massood, "From Homeboy to *Baby Boy*: Masculinity and Violence in the Films of John Singleton," in *New Hollywood Violence*, ed. Steven Schneider (Manchester: Manchester University Press, forthcoming 2003).

19.   *Shaft* (2000) dispenses with sexual content in lieu of violence. In fact, Shaft Jr. only engages in sexual activity under the film's opening titles. Otherwise, his activities are only alluded to dialogue.

20.   This is an inversion of *Dark Manhattan*'s mobility narrative. In the former film, Curly longs to be accepted by the people uptown. Both men, it seems, do not know their place.

Index

Above the Rim, 143, 181
action film. *See* genre
African cinema, 95
Ahearn, Charlie, 122
Aiello, Danny, 135
Alice, Mary, 212
American International Pictures, 232n. 25
American Pimp, 165, 219
"America's Most Wanted," 162, 172
Amistad, 179, 216
Amos 'N' Andy, 208
Anderson, Eddie, 31, 32
Anderson, Jervis, 68
Anderson, Steve, 181
Angelou, Maya, 3, 211–12, 215, 216
Angola, 113
antebellum idyll. *See* chronotope
Apollo Theater (Harlem), 61, 67, 85, 90,
  129, 220
Armstrong, Louis, 37
Associated Features, 71
Atlanta (Georgia), 142, 168, 213. *See also*
  migration
Auguiste, Reece, 175
Autry, Gene, 70, 72–73

Baby Boy, 176, 210, 220, 255n. 18
"bad niggers," 83, 99, 160, 164–65, 219,
  235n. 7
Bailey, Donna, 125
Baker, Josephine, 119
Bakhtin, Mikhail, 4–7, 14, 17, 25, 160, 179,
  228n. 9, 236n. 18. *See also* chronotope;
  dialogism; heteroglossia; polyphony

Bale, Christian, 222
Bambara, Toni Cade, 114
Bamboozled, 6, 142, 188, 207–9, 210, 218,
  225
BANG (Blacks Against Narcotics and
  Genocide), 119
Baraka, Amiri, 88
Barclay, Paris, 181
Bargain With Bullets, 62
Barry, Marion, 119
Bassett, Angela, 157
Baudelaire, Charles, 85
b-boy, 128, 135, 136–37, 160, 247n. 56
Beastie Boys, The, 124
Beat Street, 122, 125, 136
Beatty, Warren, 176, 181
Bed-Stuy. *See* Brooklyn
Belafonte, Harry, 80–81
Beloved, 179, 216, 217
Berlin, Irving, 18
Best Man, The, 210
BET (Black Entertainment Television),
  159, 211, 254n. 5
Betrayal, The, 149
B-film, 232n. 25
Bible, 25
Bicycle Thieves, 131
Big Sea, The, 13
"Bird in the Hand, A," 160
Bird, Larry 134
Birmingham (Alabama), 142
Birth of a Nation, 32, 45, 50, 118
Birth of a Race, 46
black aesthetic, 116

Black Audio Film Collective, 175
black arts movement, 90, 97, 108
black-cast musicals. *See* genre; *see also*
    musicals
Black Film/White Money, 181
black ghetto chronotope. *See* chronotope
black nationalism, 81, 83, 88, 115, 117, 152
Black Panthers, 94, 115, 247–48n. 70
black power, 88, 98, 141
blaxploitation. *See* genre
Blazing Saddles, 182
blockbusters. *See* genre
Blow, Kurtis, 123
blues, 20, 28, 55
Body and Soul, 49
Bogle, Donald, 103
Bond, James, 120
Boston (Massachusetts): *Within Our Gates*,
    50
Box, The, 159
Boyd, Todd, 171
Boyz N the Hood, 2, 97, 143, 145, 148, 151,
    152, 153–62, 163, 164, 165, 166–67, 168,
    169, 170, 171, 173, 174, 177, 178, 179,
    181, 188–89, 190, 210, 220, 222, 252n.
    27. *See also* gender; hood chronotope;
    hood films
Bradford, Roark, 229n. 22
break-dancing, 122
Breathless, 95
Brecht, Bertold, 131, 239n. 65
Broadway, 23, 30
Bronx, The (New York), 122, 223
Bronze Buckaroo, The, 71, 185
Bronze Venus, 233n. 42. *See also The Duke is
    Tops*
Brooklyn (New York), 122–23, 125, 130,
    136, 188; Bed-Stuy, 125, 130–31, 143,
    192–93, 197; *Clockers*, 189, 191–92,
    193–94, 252n. 39; *Do The Right Thing*,
    125, 130–31, 143; Fort Greene, 133; Fort
    Greene Park, 129–30; Fulton Mall, 129;
    hood films, 220–21; *She's Gotta Have It*,
    125–26, 127–30. *See also* migration
Brooklyn chronotope. *See* chronotope
Brooks, Mel, 182
Brotherhood of Sleeping Car Porters, 31
Brown v. Board of Ed, 15
Brown, Ada, 39
Brown, Jim, 82

Buell, Jed, 59, 71, 72
The Bull-Dogger, 70
Bulworth, 176, 181–82, 249n. 4
Bumpers, Eleanor, 140
Burnett, Charles, 107, 108, 109, 216
Buscombe, Edward, 69, 76
Bush, George Sr., 2, 147, 151, 157, 163
Bush Mama, 86, 90, 93, 107–116, 117, 140,
    163, 224. *See also* black ghetto
    chronotope; gender
Busta Rhymes, 220
B-Western. *See* genre

CAB (Coalition Against Blaxploitation), 119
cabarets, 61, 62, 75, 233n. 39
Cabin in the Sky, 4, 12, 14, 16, 17, 25, 30–38,
    40, 41, 112, 207. *See also* antebellum idyll;
    black-cast musicals; gender
Cabral, Amilcar, 108
Cain and Abel, 21
Call of His People, The, 48
Calloway, Cab, 39, 41, 42
*Call to Home: African Americans Reclaim the
    Rural South*, 215
Cambridge, Godfrey, 87
Candyman, 181–82
Cannon, J. D., 92
Carmen Jones, 15, 43, 229n. 13
Carwash, 118
Casino, 190
Caught Up, 176
CB-4, 180, 181
Chenault, Lawrence, 55
Chestnutt, Morris, 155
Chicago (Illinois), 192, 193, 239–40n. 1;
    black ghetto chronotope, 85; *Down in the
    Delta*, 213–13, 214; hood films, 182; race
    films, 48; *Stormy Weather*, 39, 40; *Two
    Gun Man From Harlem*, 73, 75; *Within
    Our Gates* controversy, 51–52. *See also*
    migration
chronotope, 4–7, 14, 199, 209, 227n. 5,
    236n. 18, 251n. 23; antebellum idyll, 7,
    14–19, 22, 25–26, 30, 33, 35, 37, 38–39,
    40, 41, 79, 80, 84, 85–86, 90, 99, 100,
    120, 180, 208–209, 217, 218; black
    ghetto, 7, 79, 81, 84–86, 93, 100, 117,
    179–80, 182; Brooklyn, 130; gangsta',
    215; Harlem, 7, 46, 60–61, 71, 84; hood,
    7, 145–49, 162, 173, 176, 182, 186–87,

196; idyllic, 14, 17, 25. *See also* Mikhail Bakhtin; chronotopic motif

chronotopic motif, 71, 100, 179–80, 186, 250n. 16; antebellum idyll, 91–92, 99–100; Harlem, 60, 69, 71–72, 76, 77; hood, 179–180; Africa, 100–101

Chuchster, Simon, 95

Cinema Nôvo, 95

cinema verité, 129, 146, 164

"City of Harlem, The," 88

"City of Refuge," 13–14, 21

civil rights movement, 81, 141, 150, 186, 215

Civil War, 214, 216, 217

Clark, Kenneth, 84

Clark, Larry, 107

Cleopatra Jones, 90, 101, 119, 120

Cleopatra Jones and the Casino of Gold, 120

Cleveland (Ohio). *See* migration

Clockers: film, 3, 4–5, 133, 175–176, 188–205, 209, 212, 215, 220, 224; novel; 189–90. *See also* gender; hood chronotope

Cohen, Larry, 220

Collette, Toni, 221

Colored Players, The, 47, 48, 49, 52, 58. *See also The Scar of Shame*

Colors, 140, 155, 160, 246n. 54

Columbia Pictures, 177

comedy. *See* genre

Communist Party, 64

Compton (California): *Boyz N The Hood*, 155, 167; hood films, 148–49

Connelly, Marc, 12, 23, 31

Cooley High, 118

Cooper, Ralph, 57, 58–59, 61–62, 64, 65, 68, 70, 124. *See also Dark Manhattan*

CORE (Congress of Racial Equality), 119

Cotton Club, The (Harlem), 28, 85

Cotton Comes to Harlem: film, 85, 86–93, 96, 97, 98, 100, 101, 103, 104, 107, 109, 110, 115, 134, 138, 237n. 28, 30; novel, 87, 237n. 30. *See also* black ghetto chronotope; blaxploitation; gender

crack cocaine, 151, 244n. 20

Crimson Skull, 70

Cripps, Thomas, 52

Crisis, The, 3

Crooklyn, 192, 249 50n. 10

Cuba, 183, 185

Cuban cinema, 95

"Culture of Poverty, The," 28, 84

Cundieff, Rusty, 178, 180, 181, 250n. 14

Dark Ghetto, 84

Dark Manhattan, 57, 58–59, 60–61, 71, 73, 76, 85, 86, 124, 255n. 20. *See also* Harlem chronotope; race films

Dash, Julie, 152, 212

Dassin, Jules, 80

David, Keith, 195

Davidson, Tommy, 207

Davis, Mike, 149, 150

Davis, Ossie, 85, 86, 134, 237n. 27. *See also Cotton Comes to Harlem; Do The Right Thing*

Davis, Tamra, 180, 181

Davis, Zeinabu irene, 212

Day, Cora Lee, 114

Dead Presidents, 178, 179, 181, 210

Dee, Ruby, 134

defense industry, 31–32, 149

Demme, Jonathan, 216

DeNiro, Robert, 190

De Palma, Brian, 147

Depression, 29, 46, 47, 56, 61, 68, 72

DeSica, Vittorio, 131

Detroit (Michigan), 192, 193. *See also* migration

Devil in a Blue Dress, 179, 243–44n. 12

DGA (Director's Guild of America), 254n. 4

Diallo, Amadou, 223

dialogism, 5, 180, 182–83. *See also* Mikhail Bakhtin

diaspora, 4, 101, 113, 119, 134–35, 173, 175, 200, 202, 237n. 27, 248–49n. 2

Diawara, Manthia, 173, 203

Dickerson, Ernest, 124, 145, 172

direct cinema, 129

Dirty Harry, 96

Dogma, 210

Dolemite, 101

Don't Be a Menace to South Central While Drinking Your Juice in the Hood, 181

"Dopeman," 160

Do The Right Thing, 124, 130–43, 155–56, 171, 188, 192, 197, 223, 224, 242–43n. 41. *See also* gender

Douglas, Gordon, 86

Down in the Delta, 37, 211–218, 223–24

Down to Earth, 210
Drazan, Anthony, 181
DuBois, W.E.B., 55, 186, 200, 246n. 49
Dudley, Sherman, 58, 59
Duke, Bill, 178, 236n. 23
Duke is Tops, The, 233n. 42. *See also Bronze Venus*
Dunham, Katherine, 39, 42
Dutton, Charles, 168
dystopia, 13, 103, 161, 201, 215, 216, 219

Earth, Wind, & Fire, 100
Eastwood, Clint, 96
Edison, Thomas, 45, 56
Edson, Richard, 137
Eisenstein, Sergei, 132
Ellington, Duke, 37, 72
Ellison, Ralph, 64, 87
Esposito, Giancarlo, 134
Eve's Bayou, 179, 210
Executive Order 8802, 31, 38, 43, 79, 149

"Fade to Black," 123
Fair Employment Practices Committee, 31, 79
Fanon, Franz, 108
Farrakhan, Louis, 160
Farred, Grant, 167
Fat Boys, The, 123
Fear of a Black Hat, 180–81, 191
Felder, Robert, 42
femme fatale, 33
"Fight the Power," 135, 141
Fishburne, Laurence, 155
Fisher, Rudolph, 11, 13
Five Stairsteps, 159
flânuer, 85, 236n. 17
Fleming, Victor, 14, 129
Flying Ace, The, 58
Fort Greene. *See* Brooklyn
Fort Greene Park. *See* Brooklyn
Ford, John, 70, 183
40 Acres and a Mule Filmworks, Inc., 124
Foster Photoplay Company, 45, 47
Foster, William, 47, 48
Foucault, Michel, 156, 194–95, 224, 253n. 43
Fountaine, William, 21
Four Blackbirds, 70, 75
4 Little Girls, 142

Four Tones, 70, 75
Foxy Brown, 90, 101
Foxx, Redd, 90
Framing Blackness, 87
Franklin, Carl, 178, 243–44n. 12
Frazier, Sheila, 102
Freed, Arthur, 32
Freeman, Al Jr., 212
French New Wave, 108, 131–32
Fresh, 181
Frey, William H., 215
From Hell, 179
From Plantation to Ghetto, 215
Fuller, James, 26
Fulton Mall. *See* Brooklyn

Gaines, Jane, 48, 51, 52–53, 231n. 10
Gang in Blue, 179
gangs, 149, 160, 171
gangsta' chronotope. *See* chronotope
gangsta' rap, 148, 152, 169, 170, 177, 180, 191, 209, 215, 218; aesthetic, 147, 182. *See also* chronotopic motif
gangster film. *See* genre
Gang War, 62, 64, 65, 68
Garrison, Harold, 16
Garvey, Marcus, 89, 186
Gator and the Pickaninny, The, 45
Gaye, Marvin, 164
gender, 248n. 77, 249n. 9, 254n. 4, 254–55n. 7; *Boyz N the Hood*, 161, 245–46n. 40; *Bush Mama*, 112–13; *Cabin in the Sky*, 33–35; *Clockers*, 191; *Cotton Comes to Harlem*, 89–90; *Do The Right Thing*, 242n. 33; *The Green Pastures*, 26–27; *Hallelujah*, 21–22
generation gap, 140–42, 170–71
genre: action film, 219, 222–23; black-cast musical (*see* musicals); blaxploitation, 1, 2, 3, 5, 6, 79, 82–84, 87, 89, 101, 102, 117–21, 126, 127, 145–47, 160, 177, 181, 182, 184, 210, 218, 219–221, 235n. 4 (*see also Cotton Comes to Harlem; Shaft* [2000]; *Superfly; Sweet Sweetback's Baadasssss Song*); blockbusters, 120–124, 131; B-Western, 72; comedy, 57, 69; folk musical (*see* musicals); gangster film, 15, 46, 57, 61, 62, 64–65, 66, 68, 69, 70, 71, 75, 124, 125, 162, 232–33n. 33 (*see also Dark Manhattan*); hip-hop film, 122–24

historical drama, 153; hood film, 1, 2, 3, 5, 8, 145–49, 153, 173, 175–82, 184, 185, 187–88, 190–91, 196, 205, 209, 210, 215, 219, 220–221, 222–23 (*see also Boyz N The Hood; Clockers; Menace II Society*); horror, 102; martial arts films, 120; melodrama, 15, 57, 152; plantation genre, 216–17; rap film, 158; show musical (*see* musicals); social drama, 57; sports film, 57; teen comedy, 152; uplift melodrama, 57 (*see also The Scar of Shame*); Westerns, 5–6, 15, 46, 57, 59, 64, 69–71, 75, 96, 102, 176, 182, 183, 185, 186–87 (*see also Posse; Two Gun Man From Harlem*)

George, Nelson, 130

George Washington, 255n. 17

Gerima, Haile, 86, 107–09, 114, 115, 117, 132, 136, 140, 163, 216, 224, 239n. 65. *See also Bush Mama*

ghetto, 84

Ghostface Killer, 181

Giant of His Race, A, 48

Gilroy, Paul, 169–70, 199–200, 202, 204

Glover, Savion, 207

Godard, Jean-Luc, 95

Goines, Donald, 105

Gomez, Nick, 181

Gone With The Wind, 14, 32

Gooding, Cuba Jr., 154

Gordy, Berry, 118

gospel, 28

graffiti, 122

Gray, F. Gary, 176, 178

Great Migration, The, 12–14, 20, 52, 81, 192, 209

Green Pastures, The, 12, 14, 16, 17, 22–30, 32, 33, 37, 62, 216, 230n. 30. *See also* antebellum idyll; black-cast musical; gender

Grier, Pam, 218–19

Griffith, D. W., 32, 45, 50, 64, 118

griot, 124, 214

Guerrero, Ed, 87, 99, 216–17

Guiliani, Rudolph, 223

Guillermin, John, 119

Hallelujah, 12, 14, 15, 16–22, 23, 25, 26, 27, 28, 32, 33, 36, 37, 42, 56, 229n. 15. *See also* antebellum idyll; black-cast musical; gender

Hall Johnson Choir, 28

Harlem (New York), 97, 129, 192, 194; as motif (*see* chronotopic motif); as promised land, 12–13, 60; black ghetto chronotope, 84–85; *Cotton Comes to Harlem*, 86–89 *passim*; *Dark Manhattan*, 62, 65–69 *passim*; hood films, 220–21; race films, 46, 48, 60; role in literature, 12–14, 60–61, 66–67; *Stormy Weather*, 39, 40; *Superfly*, 102–3, 106; *Two Gun Man From Harlem*, 73–76; Westerns, 69, 71–72. *See also* migration

Harlem chronotope. *See* chronotope

Harlem Nights, 179

Harlem on the Prairie, 71, 72, 185

Harlem Renaissance, 3, 12–13, 28, 55, 60, 67, 233n. 39

Harlem riot (1935), 68, 83. *See also* urban uprising

Harlem Rides the Range, 59, 71, 72, 73, 185

Harlem Studio Museum, 104

Harris, Edna Mae, 26

Harris, Leslie, 248n. 77

Harrison, John Kent, 216

Harry, Debbie, 122–23

Hassen, Kulani, 214

Hawks, Howard, 64

Hayes, Isaac, 184, 220

Haynes, Daniel L., 17

HBO (Home Box Office), 211, 254n. 5

Hearts in Dixie, 42, 229n. 15. *See also* black-cast musical

Henderson, Harry, 52

Herald Tribune, 68

Hernden, Cleo, 64

Heron, Gil-Scott, 111

heteroglossia, 52, 130–31, 135, 160. *See also* Mikhail Bakhtin

heterotopia, 194, 253n. 43

Heyward, DuBose and Dorothy, 229n. 22

Hicks, Tommy, 124, 125

Higher Learning, 179, 181, 210, 220

Hill, Walter, 180

Himes, Chester, 87, 119, 203, 236n. 23, 243–44n. 12

Hines, Earl, 72

hip-hop, 159, 177, 185, 215

hip-hop films. *See* genre

historical drama. *See* genre

Hollywood Pictures, 71
Hollywood Shuffle, 131, 133
Home of the Brave, 80
Homesteader, The (film), 49, 70, 234n. 54
Homesteader, The (novel), 49
Hoodlum, 179
Hong Kong, 120
hood chronotope. *See* chronotope
hood film. *See* genre
Hopper, Dennis, 140
Horne, Lena, 33, 39, 62, 233n. 42
horror film. *See* genre
House Divided, A, 216
House Party, 133, 146
Hudlin Brothers, 146, 152
Hughes, Albert and Allen, 2, 6, 145, 147,
    153, 162, 163, 170, 171, 172, 173, 176,
    177, 178–79, 190, 210, 219. *See also*
    Menace II Society
Hughes, Allen, 163
Hughes, Langston, 13, 55, 119

Ice Cube, 148, 158, 159, 160, 182, 241–42n.
    30, 251n. 18
Ice-T, 241–42n. 30, 251n. 18
I'm Gonna Git You Sucka, 218, 220
independent film, 122, 126
idyllic chronotope. *See* chronotope
Ingram, Rex, 24, 31, 33
Inkwell, The, 178, 210
integration, 32, 141, 185
Invisible Man, 64
Italian Neorealism, 108, 131
Ivory, James, 216

Jack the Ripper, 179
Jackie Brown, 218
Jackson, Jesse, 119
Jackson, Samuel L., 134, 164, 219
James, C.L.R., 79, 82
jazz, 5, 20, 26, 28–29, 55, 73, 158
Jazz Age, 20, 22
Jazz Singer, The, 56
Jefferson in Paris, 216
Jeffries, Herb, 59, 70, 71–73, 75, 76, 234n.
    57. *See also Two Gun Man From Harlem*
Jezebel, 32
Jim Crow car. *See* trains
Joe's Bed-Stuy Barbershop: We Cut Heads,
    124–25, 142, 192

Johns, Tracy Camilla, 126
Johnson, Charles S., 12, 48, 55
Johnson, George and Noble, 47, 48, 49,
    231n. 9
Jones, Barbara O., 108
Jones, Jacquie, 139
Jones, LeRoi. *See* Amiri Baraka
Johnstone, Norma, 52
Juice, 143, 145, 181, 191, 192, 196
Just Another Girl on the IRT, 196, 248n. 77

Kahn, Richard C., 59, 71, 75
Kane, Big Daddy, 183, 184
Kansas, 168
Kansas City (Missouri): *Dark Manhattan*, 66
Kassovitz, Matthieu, 240n. 11
Keighley, William, 12, 23
Keitel, Harvey, 190
Kelley, Robin D. G., 90, 148, 151
Kerner Commission on Civil Disorders, 6
King, Martin Luther Jr., 83, 98
King, Rodney, 2, 148, 172, 185, 186, 246n.
    49
Kirby, Lynne, 199, 202
Koalo, Mpho, 212
Kongi's Harvest, 237n. 27
Kraft, Renna, 110
Krush Groove, 121, 122–23, 124, 128, 136,
    158–59
Ku Klux Klan, 49, 70, 185

LaBute, Neil, 210
La Haine, 240n. 11
Lane, Charles, 185
LAPD, 140, 224, 246–47n. 55; *Boyz N The
    Hood*, 150–56, 157; *Bush Mama*, 109,
    110–11; *Menace II Society*, 166–67;
    "Operation Hammer," 245n. 38; *Sweet
    Sweetback's Baadasss Song*, 94, 95, 98;
    Watts, 98
L.A. Rebellion. *See* L.A. School of Black
    Filmmakers
L.A. School of Black Filmmakers, 107–8,
    113, 132
Larkin, Alile Sharon, 107
Lathan, Stan, 122, 123, 124
Leab, Daniel, 57, 73
Legree, Simon, 230n. 28
Lee, Malcolm D., 210, 211
Lee, Spike, 3, 4, 6, 7, 101, 121–43, 145, 146,

152, 159, 166, 175–76, 180, 181, 184,
    188–193, 196–97, 198, 199–200, 201,
    204–05, 207–09, 211, 215, 223, 224. *See
    also Clockers; Do The Right Thing; Joe's
    Bed-Stuy Barbershop: We Cut Heads; She's
    Gotta Have It*
Lemmons, Kasi, 210, 211, 212
Lenox Lounge (Harlem), 221
Leprechaun 5: In the Hood, 210, 254n. 3
"Let My People Go," 29
Lewis, Oscar, 84
Lil' Kim, 181
Lincoln Motion Picture Company, 47,
    231n. 9
LL Cool J, 124
Locke, Alain, 12, 24, 45, 55, 67
Lockhart, Calvin, 88
Long, Nia, 156
Los Angeles (California), 136, 149–56, 173,
    192, 193, 209; blaxploitation, 220; *Dark
    Manhattan*, 66; hood films, 145, 148–49,
    152, 153, 186–87, 192; race films, 48;
    Stormy Weather, 39, 40, 41; *Sweet
    Sweetback's Baadasss Song*, 95–97 *passim*,
    106. *See also* migration
Lost Boundaries, 80
Lost Boyz, The, 181
Love and Basketball, 210, 211
love jones, 211
Love, Peewee, 198
Lucas, Charles D., 50
lynching, 14, 49, 50–51
Lynch, Kevin, 188

Mahogany, 118, 239–40n. 1
Malcolm X, 84, 89, 114, 160, 188
Malcolm X, 192
A Man Called Adam, 80
Manhattan, 128, 193
Mankiewicz, Joseph L., 80
Mann, Anthony, 183
martial arts films. *See* genre
Martin, Darnell, 212
Masilela, Ntongela, 107
Maslin, Janet, 114
Mayfield, Curtis, 103
M.C. Eiht, 148
McGarrity, Everett, 21
McHenry, Doug, 178
McKinney, Nina Mae, 17

Meier, August, 215
melodrama. *See* genre
Memphis (Tennessee), 191; *Stormy
    Weather*, 39, 40
Menace II Society, 2, 128, 143, 146, 147, 148,
    151, 152, 153, 154, 160, 162–74, 176,
    177, 178, 188–89, 190, 191, 192, 199,
    210, 212, 222. *See also* hood chronotope;
    hood films
Men of Honor, 211
message movies. *See* problem pictures
Mexico, 94, 95
MGM, 31, 32
Micheaux Book and Motion Picture
    Company, 47
Micheaux, Oscar, 47, 48, 49–51, 57, 65, 70,
    97, 108, 133, 143, 231n. 9, 232–33n. 33,
    234n. 54. *See also Within Our Gates*
Middle Passage, 11
Midnight Ramble, 234n. 57
migration, 3, 11–14, 30, 31–32, 38, 39, 47,
    81–82, 115, 134, 175, 176, 186–88, 198,
    200–01, 209, 213, 214–15, 217;
    narratives, 51, 66; reverse (to the South),
    125, 215–16, 255n. 12; to Atlanta, 216; to
    Brooklyn, 192–94; to Chicago, 3, 12, 51,
    213; to Cleveland, 12; to Detroit, 12; to
    Harlem, 3, 11–12, 236n. 16; to Los
    Angeles, 31–32, 149; to Oakland, 31–32;
    to Pittsburgh, 12; to San Diego, 31–32; to
    San Francisco, 31–32; to Watts, 236n. 16
Miller, Fournoy E., 39, 59, 70, 72
Million Dollar Productions, 58–59, 62, 65
Minnelli, Vincente, 4, 12, 32, 36, 38, 129,
    207
minstrelsy, 30, 45, 126, 207
Mississippi, 213
Mississippi Delta, 23, 212–13, 214
Mobb Deep, 181
Mo' Better Blues, 179
mobility, 115–16, 137–38, 157, 202–3, 195
mockumentary, 180–81
Moon Over Harlem, 64, 67, 68–69
Moses, Lucia Lynn, 52
Moreland, Mantan, 70, 72, 208
Mosley, Walter, 243–44n. 12
Moynihan, Daniel P., 84, 161; Moynihan
    Report, 6, 116, 127, 154, 168
MPLA (Movimento Popular de Libertacao
    de Angola), 113, 114

MTV, 122–23, 159, 254n. 5
Murnau, F. W., 17
Murphy, Eddie, 121, 126, 128, 210
Murray's Dude Ranch, 75
Muse, Clarence, 62
musicals: black-cast musicals, 3, 5, 7, 12,
    15–16, 17, 30, 32, 39, 41, 42, 46, 60, 69,
    81, 100, 115, 207, 208–9, 217 (see also
    Cabin in the Sky; The Green Pastures;
    Hallelujah; Stormy Weather); Broadway,
    30; folk, 39; show, 40; Western, 70, 71
The Musketeers of Pig Alley, 64
Muwakkil, Salim, 131

NAACP, 32, 38, 43, 56, 83, 119
Naremore, James, 36, 38
"Negro Artist and the Racial Mountain,
    The," 55
Negro-cycle films. See problem pictures.
Negro Family, The, 84
New Black Realism, 145
New Deal, 68
New Jack Cinema, 177; aesthetic, 121, 143,
    145, 177
New Jack City, 2, 145, 177, 179, 183, 185,
    196, 210, 244n. 20
New Jersey, 191; hood films, 145, 192
New Jersey Drive, 181, 192
New Negro (ideology), 13, 24, 55, 67–68,
    71
New Negro, The, 12, 67
New Orleans (Louisiana), 183
New South, 218
Newsweek, 171, 215
New Testament, 24
Newton, Huey, 94
New York City (New York), 179, 188, 209,
    223; blaxploitation, 220; hood films, 145,
    192; race films, 48; Shaft (1970), 221;
    Shaft (2000), 220, 221–22; Stormy
    Weather, 39, 40, 42; Two Gun Man From
    Harlem, 73, 75
New York Age, 48
New York University, 124
Nicholas Brothers, The, 39, 42
Nightjohn, 216
nihilism, 141, 143, 169–72, 205, 248n. 73;
    as style, 172. See also vernacular nihilism
Niles, Polly, 103

Noah, 26, 28
Norman Film Manufacturing Company, 58,
    70, 232n. 29
Norman, Richard, 58
No Way Out, 80
Nunn, Bill, 134
Nurse Betty, 210
The Nutty Professor, 210
NYPD: Do The Right Thing, 138–40; Shaft
    (2000), 223–24; Street Crimes Unit, 223;
    Superfly, 102

Oakland (California): black ghetto
    chronotope, 85; hood films, 145. See also
    migration
Old Testament, 24
Ol' Man Adam an' His Chillun, 229n. 22
O'Neal, Ron, 102, 164
125th Street (Harlem), 67, 85, 89, 129, 221
OPEC, 150
Operation PUSH (People United to Save
    Humanity), 119
Original Gangstas, 220
OWI (Office of War Information), 77

Pace, Judy, 88
panopticon, 156, 194–95. See also Michel
    Foucault
Panther, 179
Paris, 41, 84, 119
Park, Robert, 84
Parks, Gordon Jr., 86, 101
Parks, Gordon Sr., 85, 220
Peckinpah, Samuel, 183
Pederson, Daniel, 215, 216
Penn, Leo, 80
Pettus, William E., 52
Phifer, Mekhi, 190, 220
Philadelphia (Pennsylvania): race films, 48;
    The Scar of Shame, 53, 54
Pickett, Bill, 70, 72
Pinket, Jada. See Jada Pinkett Smith
Pinkett Smith, Jada, 168, 208
plantation genre. See genre
Pittsburgh (Pennsylvania). See migration
Plessy v. Ferguson, 15
Poetic Justice, 178, 181, 210, 220
Poitier, Sidney, 80–81, 82, 86, 127
Pollack, Jeff, 181

Polk, Oscar, 31
polyphony, 186, 241n. 25. *See also* Mikhail
    Bakhtin
Pooh Man, 148, 168
Popkin, Harry and Leo, 58, 62
Porgy, 229n. 22
Posse, 6, 176, 178, 179, 182–87, 189, 200,
    210, 251n. 20. *See also* Westerns
Preer, Evelyn, 50
Price, Richard, 4, 189–90, 193, 220
Prince-Bythewood, Gina, 210, 211, 212
problem pictures, 77, 80–81
Production Code, 35
Pryor, Richard, 121, 126, 128
Public Enemy, 124, 135
public housing, 125, 194–96, 197, 245n. 36
Pullman porter, 199, 201–3, 231n. 9
Pulp Fiction, 218
"Pusherman," 103, 160

Queens (New York), 193

race films, 3, 15, 43, 46–49, 55–60, 65, 69,
    77, 79, 86, 103, 107–8, 208–9, 215
A Rage in Harlem (film), 179, 236n. 23
A Rage in Harlem (novel), 203, 236n. 23
Randol, George, 58, 59, 61, 65
Randolph, A. Philip, 31
rap, 122, 124, 177, 180, 184–85, 197,
    241–42n. 30, 244–45n. 28; aesthetic, 153;
    films (*see* genre)
Rappaport, Michael, 208
"Rapture," 123
Rashomon, 126
Reagan, Ronald, 2, 147, 151, 157, 158, 163,
    172, 245n. 38
realism, 146, 159, 253n. 44
"reality effect," 227n. 8
Realization of a Negro's Ambition, The, 48
Reconstruction, 217
Red Summer of 1919 (Chicago), 51
Reid, Mark, 106
religion, 19, 20, 25–26
Reol Productions, 48
Retour en Afrique, 87
The Return of Superfly 219, 220
Rich, Matty, 2, 145, 146, 153, 172, 176,
    177, 178, 180, 194, 210
Ritter, Tex, 70

Rhines, Jesse Algeron, 181
rhythm and blues, 100, 184
Robinson, Bill "Bojangles," 39, 61
Robinson, Jackie, 134, 137
Robinson, Mabel, 88
Robson, Mark, 80
Rock, Chris, 210, 254n. 2
Rodgers, Lawrence, 51, 55
Rodia, Simon, 165, 246n. 54
Rolle, Esther, 212
Roosevelt, Franklin D., 31
Roots, 217
Rose, Bernard, 181
Rosewood, 179
Rosie the Riveter, 149
Ross, Diana, 121
Ross, Monty, 125
Roundtree, Richard, 220
Rudwick, Elliot, 215
Run-DMC, 122–23, 158
Russell, Nipsy, 184, 195

Sack Amusement Enterprises, 71, 74
Sambo, 45
San Diego (California). *See* migration
San Francisco (California), 96. *See also*
    migration
Sankofa, 216, 217
Savage, John, 134
Scales, Hubert, 95
Scarface, 64
Scar of Shame, The, 49, 52–55, 58, 65, 67,
    232–33n. 33. *See also* race films
School Daze, 142, 188, 192
Schultz, Michael, 118, 122
Scorsese, Martin, 133, 147, 190
Scott, Darin, 176
Scruggs, Charles, 155
Segal, Steven, 162
segregation, 15, 31, 186
Sembene, Ousmane, 108
Set It Off 176
Shadyac, Tom, 210
Shaft (1971), 87, 89, 101, 102, 104, 105,
    107, 111, 118, 119, 133, 146, 220. *See also*
    black ghetto chronotope; blaxploitation
Shaft (2000), 3, 219–24. *See also* action film;
    blaxploitation
Shaft in Africa, 119

Shaft Returns, 220

Shakur, Tupac, 257n. 18

Sheila E., 124

She's Gotta Have It, 121, 125–30, 133, 134, 135, 136, 159, 160

Shine, 83

Shohat, Ella, 160

Shore, Sig, 119, 219

ShowTime, 211

Siegel, Don, 96

signs, 66–67, 97, 104, 154–55, 167–68, 221

singing cowboy, 70, 72–73

Singleton, John, 2, 3, 97, 145, 146, 153, 162, 163, 165, 166, 167, 168, 172, 173, 176, 177, 178–79, 180, 181, 210, 219, 220, 224. *See also Boyz N The Hood; Shaft* (2000)

Small's Paradise (Harlem), 85, 104

Smith, Bessie, 56

Smith, Cauleen, 212

Smith, Kevin, 210

Smith, Vern E., 215, 216

Snipes, Wesley, 212

social drama. *See* genre.

sound: *Bush Mama*, 111–12, 164; *Menace II Society*, 163–64; transition to, 56

Sounder, 120

soundies, 56

South Central, 181

South Central (California), 136, 149–50, 179, 220; *Boyz N The Hood*, 155; hood films, 148–49, 153, 174, 182, 220–21; *Menace II Society*, 162–63

Soviet film, 131

Soviet montage, 132

speech idioms: *Boyz N The Hood*, 159–60; *Cotton Comes to Harlem*, 93; *Do The Right Thing*, 134–35; *The Green Pastures*, 26; *Joe's Bed-Stuy Barbershop: We Cut Heads*, 125; *Posse*, 185; *She's Gotta Have It*, 128; *Stormy Weather*, 41; *Two Gun Man From Harlem*, 73

Spera, Rob, 210

Spielberg, Steven, 216

sprituals, 5, 18, 20, 28

Spinal Tap, 180

Spivey, Victoria, 17

sports film. *See* genre.

Stack, Carol, 215

Stagecoach, 70

Staggerlee, 83, 89

Stam, Robert, 160

Stanfield, Peter, 72, 76

Step 'N' Fetchit, 208

Stewart, Michael, 140

Sticky Fingaz, 204

St. Jacques, Raymond, 87

St. Louis Blues, The, 56

Stock Market Crash (1929), 56

Stone, Andrew, 12

Stormy Weather, 12, 14, 30, 38–42, 60, 79, 124, 230n. 34. *See also* antebellum idyll; black-cast musicals

Story of a Three Day Pass, The, 238n. 38

Straight Out of Brooklyn, 2, 143, 145, 146, 177, 192, 194, 196, 210, 212. *See also* hood chronotope; hood films

"Sucker MCs," 158

suburban space, 54

subways, 135, 192–93, 195, 222

Summer of Sam, 133, 188

Sunrise 17

Superfly, 86, 89, 93, 101–07, 109, 110, 111, 115–19 *passim*, 129, 133, 160, 164, 238n. 54. *See also* black ghetto chronotope; blaxploitation

Superfly TNT, 119

Sweet Sweetback's Baadassss Song, 86, 87, 93, 94–101, 102, 103, 105–10 *passim*, 115, 117, 118, 133, 146, 160, 163, 179–80, 184, 219. *See also* black ghetto chronotope; blaxploitation

Sweet, Vonte, 166

Symbol of the Unconquered, The, 48, 49, 70

Tarantino, Quentin, 218

Tate, Larenz, 162

Taylor, Clyde, 57, 114

Taubin, Amy, 194

TBS, 211

teen comedy. *See* genre

teenpic, 232n. 25

Temple, Shirley, 61

Tennant, William, 120

Ten Nights in a Barroom, 58

Ten Pickaninnies, 45

Terrell, John Canada, 126

Tillman, George, 211

They Call Me Mr. Tibbs, 86
Third Cinema, 95, 108
Tone Loc, 183, 184, 185
Topsy, 46, 90
Townsend, Robert, 131, 146
trains, 4, 7, 20, 187, 195, 196, 198, 199–203,
    204, 253n. 54; Jim Crow car, 202
Trespass, 181–82
trickster, 89, 92, 164, 170, 219, 251n. 20
Turner, Tyrin, 162
Turturro, John, 137, 197
Two Gun Man From Harlem, 5, 71, 73–74,
    183, 185. *See also* Harlem chronotope;
    race films; Westerns
Tyson, Mike, 134

Ulmer, Edgar, 64, 69
Uncle Tom, 45, 46, 90
Uncle Tom's Cabin, 45, 90, 230n. 28
Underworld, 65
University of California, Los Angeles, 107
University of Chicago, 84
uplift, 47
uplift melodrama. *See* genre
Up Tight, 80
urbanism, 30
urban underclass, 128, 240n. 17
urban uprising, 83–84; Chicago (1919), 83;
    Harlem (1935), 68, 83; Los Angeles
    (1992), 163, 171, 185–86, 246n. 50; Watts
    (1965), 2, 97, 98, 109, 149, 150, 156, 163,
    165, 168, 171–72
USA Network, 211

Van Peebles, Mario, 2, 6, 145, 172, 176,
    177, 178–79, 182, 183–84, 186, 210. *See
    also New Jack City; Posse*
Van Peebles, Melvin, 6, 86, 94–95, 97–98,
    108, 132, 133, 136, 184, 238n. 38. *See also
    Sweet Sweetback's Baadasssss Song*
Variety, 73
vaudeville, 45
vernacular nihilism, 169–70. *See also*
    nihilism
Vertov, Dziga, 108, 187
VH1, 159
Vidler, Anthony, 1
Vidor, King, 12, 16–17, 19, 42

Vietnam War, 179

Wallace, Emmett, 40
Waller, Fats, 39
Walton, Lester, 48, 55
Warner Brothers, 230n. 30
Washington, Isaiah, 193
Watermelon Contest, 45
Waters, Ethel, 33, 62
Watts (California), 136, 149–50; black
    ghetto chronotope, 84–85; *Bush Mama*,
    110, 113, 114, 115; hood films, 148–49,
    153; idiom, 97–98; *Menace II Society*, 163;
    Sweet Sweetback, 94–95, 96–97. *See also*
    migration
Watts Rebellion, 2, 97, 98, 109, 149, 150,
    156, 163, 165, 168, 171
Watts Towers, 165, 246n. 54
Wayans, Keenan Ivory, 181, 218
Wayne, John, 96
Weathers, Johnny, 108
Weitz, Chris and Paul, 210
Werker, Alfred L., 80
West, Cornel, 169
Westerns. *See* genre
Western musicals. *See* musicals
West Indies, 217
White Men Can't Jump, 181
White, Steve, 197
White, Walter, 32, 79, 119
Whitten, Margaret, 76
Who's The Man?, 181
Wild Style 122, 123
Williams, Spencer, 59, 70
Williams, Susan, 108
Williamson, Fred, 82
Willie Dynamite, 101
Wilson, Dooley, 41
Wilson, William Julius, 6, 154, 161
Wirth, Louis, 155
Witcher, Theodore, 211
Within Our Gates, 49, 50–52, 53, 143. *See
    also* race films
Wizard of Oz, The, 129
Woodard, Alfre, 212
Woodberry, Bill, 107, 108
Wooing and the Wedding of a Coon, The, 45
World War I, 12, 14, 30, 31, 39, 42, 47, 52,
    56

World War II, 30, 31–32, 38, 39, 41, 42, 43,
46, 70, 77, 79, 81, 119, 121, 149
Wright, Jeffrey, 221
Wright, Richard, 87, 200

Yakim, Boaz, 181
Yancy, Emily, 89
"Yo! MTV Raps," 123

youth culture: *Do The Right Thing*, 136–37;
Los Angeles, 150–52

Zane, Billy, 185
Zebrahead, 181
zoot suit, 99
Zoot Suit Riots, 41